Phily Baumann

Psychology and Deterrence

Perspectives on Security
Richard Ned Lebow
CONSULTING EDITOR

Psychology and Deterrence

■

Robert Jervis
Richard Ned Lebow
Janice Gross Stein

with contributions by
Patrick M. Morgan and Jack L. Snyder

THE JOHNS HOPKINS UNIVERSITY PRESS
Baltimore and London

The Johns Hopkins University Press, 701 West 40th Street, Baltimore, Maryland 21211
The Johns Hopkins Press Ltd, London

The paper in this book is acid-free and meets the guidelines for
permanence and durability of the Committee on Production Guidelines
for Book Longevity of the Council on Library Resources

Library of Congress Cataloging in Publication Data
Jervis, Robert, 1940–
    Psychology and deterrence.

    (Perspectives in security)
    Bibliography: p.
    Includes index.
    1. Deterrence (Strategy)—Psychological aspects—Addresses, essays, lectures.
I. Lebow, Richard Ned.   II. Stein, Janice Gross.   III. Title. IV. Series.
U162.6.J47 1985   355'.0217'019   85-8060
ISBN 0-8018-3277-2 (alk. paper)

■
CONTENTS

■
PREFACE AND
ACKNOWLEDGMENTS

■ The idea for this book was conceived at the 1982 annual meeting of the International Political Psychology Association, held in Washington, D.C. At the invitation of Ralph White, Robert Jervis organized and chaired a panel on psychology and deterrence. Papers were presented by Henning Behrens, Richard Ned Lebow, Patrick Morgan, Jack Snyder, and Janice Gross Stein. George Quester and Silvan Tompkins served as discussants.

As sometimes happens, the panelists found themselves in agreement with respect to a number of key questions, among them the need to evaluate the psychological underpinnings of deterrence and to do this by marshaling evidence from empirical case studies. The panelists also discovered that their papers were to a great extent complementary. These realizations led to the decision to revise or even to rewrite the papers with a view to publishing them as a book.

Psychology and Deterrence, the result of this collective effort, represents an attempt to use history to shed light upon the most fundamental assumptions of deterrence theory and to test their validity in a broad variety of geographical, cultural, and temporal circumstances. This is not the first time historical case studies have been employed to study deterrence; Alexander George and Richard Smoke, Glenn Snyder and Paul Diesing, Richard Ned Lebow, and Janice Gross Stein have all carried out research of this kind. We make every effort to build upon their findings.

What distinguishes our effort from its predecessors is the common attempt by the several co-authors and contributors to draw on propositions and concepts from major areas of psychology in order to understand how deterrence works—or fails to work—in practice. We have chosen this approach because deterrence is fundamentally a psychological theory. It is based on a series of "hidden" assumptions about the relationship between power and aggression, threat and response, and the ability of leaders to influence the calculations and behavior of their would-be adversaries. Until recently, these assumptions had to be accepted or rejected as matters of faith as there was little evidence that could be mustered in support of or opposition to them. This is no longer true. A growing corpus of empirical research, to which the case studies in this volume make a significant contribution, permits us to evaluate the psychological underpinnings of deterrence and to conceptualize about them in a more sophisticated manner. Needless to say, insights of this kind have important policy implications.

Chapter 1, by Robert Jervis, discusses the need to treat the theory and practice of deterrence not as a deductive model based on the assumption that people are highly rational, but inductively, by looking at historical cases in some detail and by applying perspectives of cognitive psychology. The cognitive approach is valuable, Jervis argues, because the ways in which states actually behave present many puzzles for deterrence theory, some of which can be explained by taking into account the process by which statesmen respond to information and reach decisions. In the next chapter, Jervis applies some of the ideas and findings of psychology to a problem that classical deterrence theory puts to one side: just how decision makers decide that others are a threat to their vital interests and need to be deterred. He finds that a number of important biases are at work in this process and lead to systematic perceptual errors.

The next two chapters, by Janice Gross Stein, explore Egypt's decisions to use force from 1969 to 1973 and Israel's attempts to dissuade Egypt from doing so. They draw on recent psychological research to demonstrate how both challengers and defenders behave in ways that contradict some of the most important assumptions of deterrence theory. Stein argues that the explanation for much of this behavior can be found in policy makers' proclivity to distort reality in order to make it consonant with their personal, institutional, and political needs. She demonstrates how such a process influenced Egyptian and Israeli behavior and was responsible for serious misjudgments in both countries.

The following chapter, Richard Ned Lebow's analysis of the origins of the Falklands-Malvinas War, attributes it to two serious and mutually reinforcing misjudgments. These were the belief in

London that Argentina would not invade the contested islands and the expectation in Buenos Aires that Britain would accommodate itself to their military "liberation." He makes the case that both misjudgments can be explained by reference to many of the same kinds of cognitive and motivational biases that Stein found to have been important in Egyptian and Israeli policy making in 1973.

Chapter 6, by Patrick M. Morgan, represents an imaginative effort to explain the well-documented U.S. fixation with demonstrating resolve in terms of psychological principles. Morgan argues that it derives from what he calls the "paradox of credibility." Leaders of nuclear powers are uncertain as to how they would respond to a major challenge by another nuclear power because of the suicidal nature of nuclear war. As a result, they become more disposed to uphold lesser commitments because these are the only ones in defense of which they can safely fight. By doing so, they seek a reputation for resolve in the hope that it will discourage challenges of more important commitments. A concern for reputation, Morgan argues, may be less a rational extension of the art of commitment than it is an effort by policy makers to hide their insecurity over what to do if their most vital interests are challenged.

Jack L. Snyder's contribution explores another aspect of the deterrence dilemma: the ways in which deterrence policies can intensify adversarial feelings of insecurity and thereby elicit the very behavior they seek to prevent. Snyder attempts to explain the outbreak of World War I in terms of such a cycle of action and reaction. In doing so, he employs the concept of the security dilemma and describes three different kinds of security dilemmas that he believes were operative in the years before 1914. Snyder also discusses some of the policy implications of the 1914 experience for contemporary international relations.

This theme is further explored in Richard Ned Lebow's subsequent essay on ways out of the deterrence deadlock. His premise is that deterrence fails to address what may be the most common cause of aggression; this is the perceived need to pursue a confrontational foreign policy because of weakness at home or abroad. He proposes a policy of "reassurance" to address this problem and offers it as an alternative or parallel strategy of conflict management. The chapter also explores some of the implications of reassurance for Soviet-U.S. relations.

The conclusion, also the work of Lebow, pulls together the findings of the individual chapters in the form of a critique of deterrence both as a theory of international relations and as a strategy of conflict management. It attempts to explain much of the observed variance from the predictions of deterrence theory in terms of various psychological processes. In doing so, it demonstrates the utility of psychological insights for the study of international relations.

The authors would like to acknowledge the financial and intellectual support received from various quarters. The revising and rewriting process was substantially assisted by grants from the Rockefeller Foundation and the German Marshall Fund to Richard Ned Lebow, then at the Bologna Center of the Johns Hopkins University. This permitted two of the three principal authors to meet at Bellagio, Italy, to discuss at length the main themes of the book and the collective significance of the individual contributions. Further discussions among the authors, a final conference, and the timely completion of the project were made possible by a grant by the Ford Foundation to the Research Institute on International Change of Columbia University. We are also indebted to Henry Y. K. Tom, senior social sciences editor at the Johns Hopkins University Press, whose interest in our project from the very beginning encouraged us to proceed with the book.

Two of the chapters have already appeared in the form of articles, and are used with the kind permission of the editors of the journals concerned: Chapter 5, "Miscalculation in the South Atlantic: The Origins of the Falklands War," was published in *The Journal of Strategic Studies* (1983); Chapter 8, "The Deterrence Deadlock: Is There a Way Out?" was published in *Political Psychology* (1983).

The two-year collaboration among the co-authors and contributors was profitable for all of us above and beyond the product it resulted in. We established much closer personal and intellectual relationships from which we, Empire Airlines, and various telephone companies continue to benefit.

Ned Lebow

Psychology and Deterrence

1

■

INTRODUCTION: APPROACH AND ASSUMPTIONS

Robert Jervis

■ Deterrence posits a psychological relationship, so it is strange that most analyses of it have ignored decision makers' emotions, perceptions, and calculations and have instead relied on deductive logic based on the premise that people are highly rational. Deterrence theory began and prospered not out of the analysis of particular cases but as an abstract analysis of the behavior to be expected when two sides are able to threaten each other. Indeed, until recently we did not even have many case studies of deterrence attempts and deterrence failures. This is particularly striking because, once one looks in detail at cases of international conflict, it becomes apparent that the participants almost never have a good understanding of each other's perspectives, goals or specific actions. Signals that seem clear to the sender are missed or misinterpreted by the receiver; actions meant to convey one impression often leave quite a different one; attempts to deter often enrage, and attempts to show calm strength may appear as weakness.

The essays in this book seek to capture these rich confusions, develop a psychological perspective on deterrence, and broaden the usual focus of research. Instead of looking at Soviet-U.S. interactions, they look either at pre–World War II cases or at conflicts that involve neither superpower. This greatly enlarges the stock of material we can mine.

I would like to thank Richard Betts, Alexander George, Richard Ned Lebow, Edward Kolodziej, Jack L. Snyder, Janice Gross Stein, and Ralph White for comments and suggestions.

Of course, we cannot be sure that generalizations derived from these cases can be applied to superpower relations today, because the ultimate threat now involves not losing a war but destroying both sides' civilizations. The development of nuclear weapons has caused a true revolution in strategy. Deterrence by punishment is now more important than deterrence by denial; the ability to deny the adversary a military advantage is no longer crucial.[1] But the cases we have studied and the superpower bargaining of today remain linked by the obvious point that states try to persuade others that starting a war is foolish. Nuclear weapons have altered what is threatened, but the use of threat remains. As we will show, the effects of threats often differ from those posited by deterrence theory and expected by statesmen because people process information and reach decisions in different ways. That is what we are interested in here, and we suspect that, because our findings are rooted in human psychology, they will apply to cases of nuclear deterrence.

In looking at the cases, we will examine the decisions and policies of the state challenging the status quo as well as those of the defender. Many questions are best addressed by focusing on both sides. Fruitful here is the framework of a mediated stimulus-response model in which one first looks at one state's behavior and the impact it expects its actions to have on its adversary and then examines how the policy is perceived by the other side, how it responds, and how it expects its response to be interpreted. Attention is then shifted back to the first state to see how the response is interpreted and how the cycle continues. Of course, streams of policy are never as neat as this, and the historical research required is difficult, but the few attempts in this vein have been extremely interesting.[2]

The essays in this volume by Lebow, Snyder, and Stein employ this form of analysis and reveal patterns that would not be seen through the examination of either side alone. Looking at both sides is also valuable in facilitating comparisons that can test alternative explanations of national behavior. To the extent that two states in a conflict find themselves in roughly the same situation, one can probe for differences caused by different personalities and different domestic systems. Or one can examine the differences created by being on "different sides of the hill." Challenging the status quo is usually more difficult than sustaining it because, in most cases, the status quo power has a greater stake in preventing change than the challenger has in bringing it about, but detailed comparisons between the two tasks have not been common. One obvious question that unfortunately remains unanswered is whether the psychological problems and decision-making processes of policy makers challenging the status quo differ from those of statesmen supporting it. Another is whether there are differences in kind between the policies likely to influence a potential challenger and those likely to influence a status quo power. For example, is the optimum mixture of rewards and punishments different in the two situations?

To the extent that we cannot supply good comparative studies, it is appropriate that we rectify the previous imbalance of attention between studies of the two sides. Because of the interest in U.S. foreign policy and the accessibility of U.S. decision makers, we know more about deterring than challenging. The chapters here, by contrast, focus more on those states that are seeking to alter the status quo.

Focusing on challenges is particularly useful in showing that even a careful and well-crafted policy that is supported by credible threats may fail to maintain the status quo. George and Smoke have shown that challengers may be able to design around deterrent threats, confront defenders with *faits accomplis,* or embark on expansionism, if they believe the risks of so doing will remain in their control.[3] In other cases, states defy clear and credible threats because they are driven by the belief—or often by the feeling—that the alternatives to confrontation are intolerably bleak. Under these conditions, states can decide to challenge the status quo even though the chances of success are slight.[4] Indeed, if it is believed that war is inevitable and that striking first is preferable to receiving the first blow, deterrence, which involves not only the threat of war if the other side takes prohibited actions but also the promise of peace if it does not, becomes irrelevant.[5]

Furthermore, defenders rarely understand these pressures. Instead they usually believe that, if their threats are appropriate and credible, the other will be deterred. Defenders usually think that war is more likely to arise out of an expansionist's perception of some appealing opportunity, and they overlook the dynamics described in the preceding paragraph. The pessimism, the fear, the sense of being driven into a corner are hard for outsiders to grasp. To the extent that the adversary feels pressure to challenge the status quo because it believes that the defender will soon be strong enough to dominate it, empathy is made even less likely because statesmen have difficulty seeing that others can believe them to be a menace. The deterioration in the challenger's environment will rarely be clearly seen by the defender, in part because both sides are likely to be calculated conservatively. Thus neither the Entente powers in 1914 nor the United States in 1941 believed that they would soon be able to dominate their adversaries or realize that the latter had this perception. Thus neither statesmen nor scholars had paid sufficient attention to the circumstances that can lead to challenges to the status quo, with the result that decision makers often fail to grasp the nature of the problem they are facing.

The chapters in this book will examine cases in light of psychological factors that affect the way people perceive and calculate. First of all, we have to understand cognitive or unmotivated psychological biases. Biases are ways of treating information that diverge from standard definitions of rationality. (Of course, these standards are not always clear or beyond dispute.) The processes we are concerned with under the heading *unmotivated biases* are the products of the complexity of the environment and the inherent limitations of our cognitive capabilities. They conserve cognitive resources and allow people to avoid being overwhelmed by complexity and ambiguity, but the cost is a variety of systematic errors and misperceptions. Time and cognitive resources permitting, we would try to avoid committing these errors if they were pointed out to us. Although most of the evidence for the existence of these biases comes from Western experience, they do not seem to be cultural; it is difficult to relate them to the peculiarities of our environment or society.[6] Instead, as far as we can tell, they are the product of the way our brains are "hard wired" to process information.

While these biases and their implication for deterrence have not been fully explored, they have received more attention from political scientists and, in recent years, from psychologists than have motivated biases, which are a second focus of this volume. As the term implies, motivated biases arise from the emotions generated by conflicts that personal needs and severe situational dilemmas pose. These biases serve important psychological functions,[7] primarily minimizing the discomfort that would be created by a full appreciation of the negative attributes of objects the person values, such as his or her country or favored policy. These errors, then, would not be corrected if they were pointed out to the person, because they provide a shield against painful perceptions. The individual will pay a high price in the future as reality inescapably shapes and defeats the policy, but in the interim he or she avoids intolerable psychological stress and conflict.[8]

Although the word *deterrence* has its etymological roots in the Latin term for "terror," most political scientists—myself included—have been remarkably slow to explore the implications of strong emotions on beliefs and calculations. Although psychologists have done some work in this area, it has not been grounded in a careful analysis of the nature of the international politics and has not closely examined particular cases.[9] Early critics of deterrence argued that fear would lead not to compliance but to rage, increased conflict, and miscalculation.[10] But these analyses downplayed the importance of political conflicts and ignored the operation of unmotivated biases. More frequently, affect has simply been ignored or treated as an "add-on" rather than as integral to the decision process.[11] Eventually, of course, we want to develop a theory that integrates motivated and unmotivated biases. Indeed, separating the two can be extremely difficult, and there is reason to suspect that many processes of thought are fed by both sources.[12] At this point, however, we cannot provide an integrated theory and instead seek the lesser goal of at least dealing with both cognition and affect.

The Rationality Postulate and Deterrence Theory

We should recognize the costs of trying to understand deterrence by examining the way statesmen process information, calculate, and make decisions. The older, rational models had the enormous advantages of rigor and parsimony. Although the study of decision making yields important generalizations that not only explain a number of cases but can form the basis for further propositions, it still involves details and analysis of idiosyncrasies. It can be argued that it would be more productive to ignore this dimension and push a purely rational deterrence theory as far as we can in order to see what propositions can be produced. The fact that people are not completely rational does not automatically vitiate this approach. As Milton Friedman and Kenneth Waltz, to cite only two, have persuasively argued, theorizing based upon assumptions that people are rational is not defeated by empirical studies showing that they engage in mental operations that violate this assumption.[13] Instead, the theory stands or fails on its ability to produce propositions that are significant, testable, and valid. Just as neoclassical economic theories have proved powerful and productive, so standard deterrence theory has not only greatly increased our understanding of conflict behavior but continues to yield new insights.

Before indicating why we feel that alternative approaches should be explored, we should note that, even if a particular argument must either accept or reject the postulate of rationality, this is not true of the work of the entire discipline, or even of the work carried out on different occasions by a particular scholar. Multiple approaches can be explored, leaving for later the question of which were blind alleys. Even if it were possible to set a unified research agenda for the field, it probably would be a mistake to do so. Picking "sunrise scholarship" is even harder than picking "sunrise industries," and the field as a whole can hedge its bets if different groups of scholars pursue different approaches.

Three considerations, however, lead the authors of these chapters not to rely on the rationality postulate but rather to look at deterrence from the perspective of how statesmen actually make decisions, and to seek insights from psychology and try to develop theories that more closely follow the way nations behave. First, many events present unexplained puzzles for standard deterrence theory. In most circumstances, states are more cautious than the theory implies. Thus they often fail to take advantage of military "windows of opportunity" to coerce or attack their adversaries.[14] They usually avoid pushing the other side as hard as they can or approaching the brink of war as closely as deterrence theory would lead one to expect. On the other hand, they sometimes lash out and challenge their adversary's commitments when they have no reasonable grounds for believing these efforts will succeed.[15] Similarly, in some circumstances states are blind to threats that call for deterrence policies, and on other, probably more frequent occasions, they exaggerate the dangers they are facing and downgrade their own strength. In either case, deterrence will be hindered in ways that standard theories cannot explain.

Still other puzzles are presented when the military strategies espoused are not matched to the environment but rather create problems for the state that could have been avoided. Thus Jack Snyder shows that states may adopt offensive strategies in situations in which defense would actually prove stronger.[16] The result is to fuel unnecessary arms competitions, increase the danger of spirals of fear that can lead to preemption, and decrease rather than increase the state's security.

Of course, in an uncertain world the utility of the rationality postulate is not undermined by the profusion of cases in which the policy turns out to have been ill designed. Given the information available and the dilemmas posed by the external environment, policies will often fail. But in many cases there is more to it than this—the beliefs and policies are so removed from what a careful and disinterested analysis of the situation reveals that the failure is hard to fit into the framework generated by rationality. Thus puzzles for deterrence theory arise when errors are the rule rather

than the exception, when statesmen frequently see their environment in bizarre ways, continue to follow policies in the face of
mounting evidence that they are failing, or ignore obvious and
attractive alternatives.

Indeed, as Betts has argued, almost by definition many deterrence failures are likely to represent exceptions to most generalizations.[17] Statesmen are aware of many of the conditions under
which deterrence usually holds. If they are taken by surprise, the
reason is less likely to be their ignorance than the lack of fit between
the attacker's behavior and the statesmen's expectations generated
by their experience and beliefs about international politics. The very
fact that policy makers think their deterrence would succeed sometimes makes them complacent, thus permitting attackers to take
advantage of them. This means that while theorists might be able to
dismiss the significance of a few exceptions, statesmen must be alert
to them. Furthermore, scholars who are concerned with explaining
deterrence failures are also unable to put these exceptions aside.

Finally, some puzzles are interactive in nature. That is, the full
extent to which they are incompatible with most versions of deterrence theory is revealed only when one looks at the way each state's
behavior is linked to that of others. One such puzzle starts out from
the obvious point, which itself is a troublesome one for deterrence
theory, that leaders within a country often disagree about policies to
be followed to deter the adversary. (Indeed they may disagree about
whether deterrence is needed, a point to which I will turn in the next
chapter.) Many of these conflicting policies can be reconciled with
the logic of deterrence, but this only serves to underline the vague-
ness of the theory on crucial points and to stress that it cannot tell us
ahead of time what policy the state will adopt. This leads to further
problems for deterrence theory because it implicitly assumes that
statesmen can predict—presumably by using the theory—how
others will respond to their policies. But if the outcome of the
internal debate is not explicable in terms of the deterrence theory,
then states find it hard to adopt policies it suggests, because the
success of these policies depends in part on how others will behave.

Another interactive puzzle is that, on the one hand, complex and
sophisticated strategies of coercion usually fail because they make
excessive demands on the state's ability to understand its environment and to coordinate its policy instruments, but, on the other
hand, statesmen are slow to realize this and so many attempt policies
of this type. Such complex policies are consistent with standard
deterrence theory, and so the fact that states adopt them is partial
confirmation of the theory. But the failure of these policies, and the

refusal of decision makers to see that they are too complicated to work, cannot easily be explained by it. A nice example is provided by the U.S. attempt to make force support diplomacy in Vietnam.[18] The U.S. policy of combining negotiations with pressure—sometimes in the forms of explicit threats, more often in the form of bombing (which both inflicted pain and carried the implicit threat to inflict more if the North continued to be recalcitrant)—looks like a textbook case of coercion. But the policy failed, not only because the North was willing to absorb a startling amount of punishment,[19] but also because U.S. statesmen could neither understand the North's framework of beliefs nor coordinate the complicated series of U.S. actions that the policy called for. The latter problem meant that the careful "orchestration" of threats and promises was so mistimed in its implementation that each part of the policy defeated rather than reinforced the other. And the former problem meant that even if the coordination had been better, the effect on the North might not have been the intended one. Although current theories of coercion can, then, explain why the policy was adopted, they cannot tell us why it failed or why the decision makers were so slow to see the problems.

The Need to Examine Decision Making

Even in the absence of these puzzles, a second reason for looking at how decision makers act in deterrence situations is that such investigations are needed to supply some of the information that standard deterrence theory must assume as given. The theory says very little about such matters as how and when states decide that their vital interests are at stake, when deterrence needs to be invoked, and when a conflict can safely be avoided by a discreet retreat. Indeed, it assumes the existence of a situation of high conflict in which one or both sides are using threats. This is perfectly legitimate—a theory has to start from somewhere, and deterrence is not a theory of a state's entire foreign policy.[20] But it means that deterrence theory must beg a lot of questions, perhaps the most important ones. I will return to the topic of threat perception in the next chapter, but here I want to note that determining whether one state is a menace is often extremely difficult for later scholars, let alone for contemporary statesmen. The essential question for British foreign policy before World War I and World War II, to take just two examples, was whether Germany could be conciliated or could be contained only by threats. Chamberlain was wrong when he gave the former answer, and it can be argued that his pre-decessors were wrong when they reached the latter conclusion. The pre–1914 policy was appropriate for the situation of the 1930s; appeasement might have worked before 1914. In both cases, the crucial factor in understanding the policy's adoption is the British assessment of Germany; the crucial factor in understanding the policy's effect is the accuracy of this judgment. Similarly, much of the strategic debate in the United States turns on competing views of Soviet intentions. Deterrence theory cannot tell us which view will prevail or which is correct. To answer these questions we must examine decision making on each side.

The importance and difficulty of determining the other side's intentions raise a prescriptive dilemma, since the policy appropriate for dealing with a state with one kind of intentions may be harmful in dealing with one that seeks different goals. Two implications follow. First, statesmen should usually combine threats with re-assurances, although doing so in a way that would deter without increasing unnecessary conflict is extremely difficult.[21] Second, statesmen should devote a great deal of time and resources to trying to determine what the other's intentions are. That this is rarely done cannot be fully explained by the difficulty of the task, forbidding as it is. Rather, in most cases decision makers act on two premises: first, that the other state does not need to be reassured because it can easily tell that the decision maker's own state is not a menace; and second, that the inferences drawn by the decision maker about the other's intentions are almost certainly correct. In fact, these prem-ises are often incorrect, and only an analysis of decision making can explain why statesmen so frequently adopt them.

Deterrence theory also assumes that states are—and should be—terribly concerned about their reputations for living up to their commitments. At first glance, this seems both to follow from the basic argument of the theory and to be imposed on decision makers by the nature of the situation that they are in. If a state defaults on one commitment, other states will be less likely to believe it in the future. The credibility of one threat is linked to that of others, and states therefore must be willing to pay high costs for minor stakes if they are to deter others from challenging their vital interests. In-deed, in most treatments, credibility is closely related to the concept of commitments, with the argument that most threats and promises will be believed if and only if they are part of a broader framework supported by and, in turn, supporting other positions. There is certainly some validity to this structural argument, but it is not completely compelling. The world may not be as interconnected as it implies; statesmen may not draw such wide-ranging inferences from the way others behave in minor disputes. To the extent that states judge the probability that their adversaries will stand firm by the relative importance to the two sides of the specific issue in contention, then the states' reputations for living up to their commitments are not crucial. Logic alone cannot tell us whether statesmen do this, and some of the little available evidence indicates that they do not.[22] Indeed the pattern may vary with situational, national, and personal differences.

Once we know whether decision makers see the world as tightly interconnected, we can tell how deterrence theory will be applied, but the theory cannot tell us about the circumstances under which this belief will flourish. Morgan points out that the costs of nuclear war are so high that reputation should be relatively unimportant in the decision to go to, or over, the brink.[23] (Note again that, even if this argument is correct, it does not demonstrate that statesmen accept this reasoning. It is possible that decision makers would pay more attention to reputation than a careful analysis of the situation indicates that they should.)[24] Furthermore, he argues, the preoccupation with reputation cannot be explained by general logic of deterrence but is in part a peculiarly U.S. fetish that has to be accounted for both by the situation the United States is in and by its cultural and political traditions.

The Russians seem to be less concerned with their reputations and more willing to retreat when the pressure on them is too great. They did not seem inhibited from backing down in the Cuban missile crisis[25] and, contrary to the expectations of many observers, did not cancel Nixon's trip to Moscow in the spring of 1972 when the United States bombed North Vietnam and mined its harbors. Soviet leaders do seem to think that it is vital, however, to maintain their position in any country over which they have gained dominance.

Rational, deductive theories have been highly productive in economics even though there are many puzzles and many variables must be treated as exogenous. On a third point, however, deterrence differs from economics. The latter deals with phenomena that are characterized by large numbers—of people, of transactions, and often of firms. The laws being sought are statistical; they apply only on the average, and individual deviations do not matter.[26] This greatly eases the problem posed by the assumption of rationality, since only actors on the margin need be highly rational to produce the predicted outcomes. This is not the case in international politics, especially in situations that involve deterrence. When we talk about wars, both those that occur and those that have been avoided, we care about specific cases. To an extent, then, political scientists will share some of the concerns and methods of their colleagues in history. Without giving up the search for generalizations, we also want to know whether certain cases fit the general pattern or not. This is a question that rarely arises in economics.

We care about specific cases for three related reasons. First, wars kill large numbers of people. It is hard, then, not to be as concerned about why a particular war occurred as we are about whether it is an exception or a typical case. Second, wars can determine the course of later events. Who wins and who loses, who is destroyed and who comes out with resources intact, who decides that the gains are worth fighting for again and who feels that the burdens are too great—all have a great impact on the future of international politics. As long as we cannot predict wars and their outcomes by general theories, we must recognize the significance of particular conflicts. Since wars that have the most impact often .kill the most people, these two concerns reinforce each other. The ways in which deterrence strategies were or were not tried in the eras preceding the world wars and the reasons why Germany initiated these conflicts have interest beyond the extent to which they are instances of more general phenomena. And third, we are concerned lest contemporary deterrence fail in a way that produces nuclear war. Here again we must pay attention not only to the rules but also to the exceptions. Presumably we should concentrate on the most likely ways in which a nuclear war could break out, but we also want to open our eyes to less probable dangers.

None of this is to deny the fruitfulness of theories of deterrence that assume rationality and try to deduce state behavior from the external environment. We could not begin the investigations reported here without the baseline of expectations generated by these theories. But they will rarely suffice for a full understanding and, in many areas, are misleading. Melding them with a study of how statesmen perceive others, process incoming information, and reach decisions can give us a richer and more accurate understanding of deterrence.

Indeed, if we can build generalizations about the motivated and unmotivated biases that create deviations from rationality, we can probably use them to replace the rationality postulate in deterrence theories while preserving the deductive structure of the theories and so retaining the benefits of power and parsimony. In other words, the close examination of the psychological factors at work in a number of cases may provide us with sufficient understanding of how people think to make it unnecessary for us to look as carefully at all the other cases. Rather, we will be able to assert, at least on a probabilistic basis, what is likely to have happened and how the outcome is to be explained.

The essays in this volume cannot develop a full-blown theory along the lines we have indicated. Our knowledge of specific cases is still limited, and our understanding of psychology and decision making still falls far short of requirements. What we can do is to show how our knowledge of psychology can illuminate a number of the troubling omissions or puzzles in deterrence theory.

2

■

PERCEIVING AND COPING WITH THREAT

Robert Jervis

■ Deterrence theory takes the perception of threat for granted and goes on to prescribe and explain the policies that are and should be adopted. As was noted in the previous chapter, this is a legitimate approach—any theory has to start from somewhere. But it leaves us with the question of the circumstances under which states see others as menaces to their security,[1] a question that psychological theories can help answer. At the start a methodological problem should be noted: in order to determine what leads states to perceive others as threats one needs to examine cases in which this perception is absent as well as cases in which it is present. When one looks at only the latter—which is common in this area, as in many others in social science—the factors one locates may be necessary conditions but may not separate the circumstances that lead to the feeling of menace from those that do not. Although I will make the appropriate controlled comparisons when possible, I will often lapse into this error as well.

The most obvious way for states to judge whether others are a threat would be by monitoring their capabilities. Using worst case analysis, they could assume that others were preparing to do as much harm to them as possible. Indeed, some versions of balance of power theory imply that statesmen should and do draw inferences

I would like to thank Richard Betts, Alexander George, Richard Ned Lebow, Edward Kolodziej, Jack L. Snyder, Janice Stein, and Ralph White for comments and suggestions.

in this way. But this does not seem to be the case. Although capabilities are rarely ignored, they do not determine the image that is formed. On the one hand, the United States could easily destroy Britain, France, and West Germany, yet those countries do not fear a U.S. attack; Britain and France could inflict grave damage on the United States, but the United States wants to see those countries increase rather than decrease their arms. On the other hand, in the mid and late 1940s the United States came to see the Soviet Union as hostile even while realizing that it was weak. Indeed, it was even weaker than Americans thought; and, to a significant extent, perceptions of Soviet strength seem to have been more the product than the cause of perceptions of Soviet hostility.[2]

Judging others' intentions is notoriously difficult. Any number of methods of inference can be used, all of them fallible. Statesmen can concentrate on what they believe is the other's objective situation if they believe that the external environment is the most important source of its behavior; they can look to its past behavior if they think national character or stable domestic attributes are crucial; they can study the goals, beliefs, and personalities of their opposite numbers if they think idiosyncratic characteristics matter. Of course, all three kinds of variables may and probably do influence foreign policy, but statesmen are no more able than scholars to construct useful hypotheses based on an excessive number of factors. Unfortunately, however, at present we know too little about decision makers' implicit views about the level of analysis problem to make this a useful vantage point for our investigation.[3]

Attribution and Threat Perception: How, Not What[4]

Although we cannot be sure what else statesmen do, they often use the recent behavior of others as important sources of information. They take the pattern they think they observe and project it forward into the future. When high costs are incurred, observers will assume that major objectives must be being sought; even if the costs are low, when the immediate stakes seem still smaller, more far-reaching goals will be imputed. Small incidents, then, will have large implications if they are taken as indicating that the other will harm the state later.

A related form of reasoning has been located by Raymond Cohen. He argues that a major cause of the perception of threat is the belief that the other has broken a rule of the game of international politics.[5] Although it is difficult to determine the existence of such rules a priori, I think it is true that statesmen are often more worried about how the other acts than about what it does. That is, the actual gains the other makes—or the losses it inflicts on the state—are often less troublesome than the methods by which they were pursued. A state is likely to be seen as a threat if it displays a willingness to ignore accepted procedure, a disregard of what are usually considered the legitimate rights of others, and an exceptionally high propensity to accept risks in order to improve its position. It is interesting to note, for example, that the principal grounds on which President Kennedy protested the Russians' putting missiles into Cuba were not that this had a direct impact on military balance, but rather that the kind of behavior it represented was a menace. He stressed that the deployment contradicted "the repeated assurances of Soviet spokesmen," was "secret, swift, and extraordinary," and constituted "deliberate deception."

What is at work here is the quite rational way decision makers go about attributing causes to the behavior of others. They analyze it in a form something like an equation, assuming that what the other expects to gain from an action must be at least equal to the expected costs and risks. By examining the other's behavior, statesmen can then develop a picture of the value the other places on various objectives. The assumption that the other side is consistent, if not rational, means that high threat is likely to be inferred when the other's reaction seems disproportionate to the objective—if the other will be unpleasant when the stakes are fairly minor, the reasoning goes, it will be more unruly when disregard for established procedures can bring it greater immediate advantages. This is the significance of the unease over the possibility that the Soviet Union is using chemical and/or biological warfare in Afghanistan and Southeast Asia. If one concentrated on the actual changes in the distribution of power, what would matter would be the growth of Soviet influence in these areas, not the particular weapon being employed. In this approach the limited size of the gain in Soviet power would dampen the perception of threat. But in fact it magnifies fears, as statesmen believe that the USSR's willingness to break a treaty in order to make a marginal advance shows how little she values international understandings. It is then hard for the West to rely on anything other than the threat of direct and immediate responses to temper Russian pursuit of narrow self-interest. Had the situation confronting the Soviet Union been more desperate or the expected gains greater, then the expectations for the future would have been less disturbing.

Nice examples of this attribution process are provided by Sir Eyre Crowe's long memorandum of January 1907.[6] Although famous among political scientists as an analysis of the need for Britain to follow a balance of power policy, it is really a fascinating and detailed—if biased—analysis of German behavior. Crowe pointed out that Germany had not reciprocated British concessions even in areas that were not of primary importance to her. It would have been understandable if Germany had refused to make concessions on issues that were vital to her—on such questions great powers are expected to do whatever they must. But when the objects pursued are of lesser importance, a failure to pay proper heed to the interests and sensitivities of others is much more troublesome. The lack of proportion between the immediate object that Germany gained and the costs that she incurred and imposed was most readily explained by seeing Germany as a bully, unwilling to accommodate others even when this could be done at a reasonable price. Perhaps Germany did not understand the normal rules of international politics; perhaps she thought that refusing to reciprocate concessions would establish her dominance over others. In either case, this pattern of behavior was alarming and could be coped with only by firmness.

In much the same way, it is extremely worrisome to find another state spending great sums of money for a project that can be justified only if war occurs. (Of course, this indicates only that the other state expects war, believes that high spending can prevent it, or is unusually sensitive to even slight dangers. It does not necessarily mean that it is aggressive, although that is the more frequent inference.) Thus the British ambassador to Russia in 1905 explained to the foreign minister why Britain was so disturbed by Russian activities in Central Asia. "There, a system of railways of purely strategic importance had been built by the Russian Government at the cost of great sacrifices and had been brought down to the frontier of Afghanistan, which the Russian Government had repeatedly declared to be outside their sphere of influence, and to the very gates of Herat."[7] If the railroad net had been cheap, or if there had been significant commercial advantages to be gained by building it, then the British could have attributed the Russian behavior to nonthreatening motives.

Similar attributions underlay the British analysis of why the German program of naval building before World War I was so threatening: in the words of Winston Churchill, "a German fleet is a luxury, not a national necessity, and is not therefore a fleet with a specific object."[8] The British argued—and believed—that since Germany lacked important colonies and its adversaries on the continent were not sea powers, there were no good security reasons for the fleet, and it therefore had to be aimed at threatening Britain. If the fleet had been useful for some other mission, this conclusion would not have been so compelling.

The same effect operates even more strongly when the state takes an action that observers believe is against its own economic interest. In 1945–46, for example, "Soviet ideologists believed Moscow would be doing the Americans a favor by accepting economic assistance" and thereby staving off a postwar depression.[9] It followed that these people believed that for the United States to refuse aid would be to inflict significant costs on itself. Only a strongly felt desire to harm the Soviet Union could then account for this behavior. Had the Russians realized that the Americans saw assistance as a net cost, not a net benefit, the logical inference would have been that the United States was unwilling to make sacrifices to assist the Soviet Union, not that it sought to go out of its way to harm her. (Ironically, U.S. decision makers wanted the Soviet Union to believe that they would respond with firmness to Soviet demands, and so the mistaken attribution may have been one that the Americans desired.)

By the same chain of reasoning, the intent to harm will be attributed to an actor when observers believe that he could have reached his ostensible goal without hindering someone else. Thus in 1766 one American pamphleteer wrote about the Stamp Act, "If the real and the only motive of the minister was to raise money from the colonies, that method should have undoubtedly been adopted which was least grievous to the people." Choice of a measure that would trigger strong resistance, therefore, "has induced some to imagine that the minister designed by this act to force the colonies into a rebellion, and from thence to take occasion to treat them with severity, and, by military power, to reduce them to servitude."[10] The belief that there were easier ways to have raised money leads to the inference that the British had some wider purpose in mind.

The same analysis of alternative courses of action that the other could have taken will be employed when another state rejects proposals that the statesman believes will reach the ends that the other claims to seek. For example, in 1946 many U.S. decision makers argued that strong evidence for Soviet agressiveness was provided by the Soviet rejection of a four-power treaty guaranteeing the disarmament of Germany. As Secretary of State Byrnes put it to Molotov, "Such a treaty as had been proposed and also the similar treaty suggested for Japan . . . would effectively take care of the question of [Russian] security." The obvious inference was that, as Senator Vandenberg put it in his diary, "if and when Molotov finally refuses this offer, he will confess that he wants *expansion* and not 'security.' "[11] The refusal to take the alternative measures that, it was believed, would reach the goal the Russians said they sought showed that they had other concerns. Similarly, at the Potsdam Conference Truman was very disturbed when the Russians refused to entertain his proposal to neutralize the major waterways in Eastern and Central Europe. This, Truman wrote in his memoirs, "showed how [Stalin's] mind worked and what he was after. . . . What Stalin wanted was control of the Black Sea straits and the Danube. The Russians were planning world conquest."[12] The Russian rejection of the Baruch Plan led to similar inferences because the Americans also thought that the proposal would meet legitimate Soviet security needs. In retrospect, it seems obvious that the plan would have left the Soviet Union highly vulnerable, and so later observers do not think the rejection shed any light on Soviet intentions. But the U.S. inference processes were not illogical; they were merely based on mistaken premises.

Unmotivated Biases Affecting Threat Perception

As they seek to judge whether others are a threat, statesmen are subject to both motivated (that is, affect-driven) and unmotivated (that is, purely cognitive) biases.[13] But a theory that shows how these are combined, is still beyond our grasp. Indeed, even the unmotivated biases can be presented only as a list of factors, albeit ones that are consistent with one another and often produce reinforcing effects. These biases arise because the problem of dealing with complex and ambiguous information leads people to adopt short-cuts to rationality that simplify perceptions in order to make more manageable the task of making sense out of environments. The resulting biases systematically affect deterrence and threat perception. By understanding them we can grasp some common patterns and some common errors that, in principle, could be corrected.

Impact of Cognitive Predispositions

The most important unmotivated bias which influences several aspects of deterrence, is that people's thinking is heavily theory-driven. Our perceptions are strongly colored by our beliefs about how the world works and what patterns it is likely to present us with.[14] The decision maker who thinks that the other side is probably hostile will see ambiguous information as confirming this image, whereas the same information about a country thought to be friendly would be taken more benignly. On a more abstract level statesmen probably vary in their predisposition to perceive threat; some believe the world is generally one of high conflict, and others think common interests are more likely to prevail.[15] Whatever the sources of these outlooks—an important topic about which we know little—they strongly affect threat perception.

Beliefs and predispositions exist on many levels, and when they reinforce each other their influence is especially potent. Much of the explanation of the reason most people were so slow to see the Iranian revolution lies in such reinforcing beliefs. Not only were the Shah and his regime perceived as strong, but also the specific image was supported by the general belief—based on good historical evidence—that leaders who control large and effective internal security forces are not overthrown by popular protest. These preconceptions were reinforced by several others that were more peculiarly American: the menace to pro-Western governments comes from the left; modernization enjoys the support of the strongest political elements of society, and those who oppose it cannot be serious contenders for power; religious motives and religious movements are peripheral to politics. Although motivated errors probably played a role in the later stages of revolution, given these cognitive predispositions a recognition of the situation was bound to be delayed until the evidence was overwhelming. (Indeed it appears that those people in and out of the government who were relatively quick to see that the Shah was in trouble differed from the majority of analysts not in their desires or in their more careful examination of particular bits of evidence, but in their long-standing rejection of one or more of the predispositions.)

U.S. and Israeli perceptions during and before the 1973 war similarly bring out the power of interrelated preconceptions. An Arab attack seemed terribly implausible for the sensible reason that it could not succeed. Egypt and Syria were weaker than Israel and lacked the air power that was believed essential to fight a war. The errors—which were widely held and are still easily understandable—were several. First, Arab military strength was badly misjudged. While the gap between the two sides was great, it was not as enormous as had been believed. The predisposition was so deeply ingrained that the image of the Arabs as weak and incompetent was not shattered on October 6, at least not in the United States. Throughout the first week of the war the United States kept expecting Israel to go over to the offensive and establish its dominance. Reports of heavy Israeli losses were discounted; rumors that Israel had crossed the Suez Canal were accepted; desperate moves such as the attack on Port Said were taken as showing that Israel was in control.[16] The result was to render insensible U.S. diplomacy during the first week as it slighted the problem of resupply and engaged in elaborate maneuvers to stall the cease-fire moves in the expectation that Israel would soon be winning the war.

A second and a third error show the way in which preconceptions can limit imagination and empathy in ways that distort appreciation of threats: outsiders understood neither the way Egypt would fight nor its goals. They were right to see that a successful attack could not be launched in the face of Israel's ability to control the air over the battlefield, but they thought that the only way to contest this dominance would be through a strengthened air force. The alternative route to this goal of deploying a dense network of anti-aircraft missiles had never been used before and was not given much thought by observers. In parallel with the possibility of "designing around" deterrent threats analyzed by George and Smoke, the challenger need not accept a temporarily adverse military balance as final. As Stein points out, the Egyptian generals at first agreed with the outsiders' assessment that Egypt lacked military options. Sadat fired them and brought in replacements who would keep looking for ways to attack.[17] Observers could not know this: neither were they likely to be strongly enough motivated to spend months analyzing various military plans to see whether any of them might work. The Egyptian leaders had no choice but to carry out such investigations.

The third error lay in a predisposition that seemed so obviously true that few people gave it much thought. Even if observers had realized how Sadat saw the military balance, they might not have been alarmed. Success at the start of the war would inevitably be followed by defeat thereafter, leaving Israel in an even better military position. In addition to underestimating the strength of the need Sadat felt to challenge the status quo—a frequent kind of misjudgment—observers misunderstood his goal. For them, victory was conceived of in a military sense. But, for Sadat, losing battles was not necessarily incompatible with gaining his political objectives. As Kissinger put it, "what literally no one understood was the mind of the man: Sadat aimed not for territorial gain but for a crisis that would alter the attitudes into which the parties were then frozen—and thereby open the way for negotiations." Egypt could not advance reasonable diplomatic proposals while she was humiliated, a condition only a bold military move could correct. But "our definition of rationality did not take seriously the notion of starting an unwinnable war to restore self-respect."[18] Since the observers' basic concepts and understanding of the situation were so different from Sadat's, they could not perceive the threat he was posing.

Instead, they were preoccupied with a different kind of threat. The Israeli government, and many U.S. analysts, thought that the prime danger was of a spiral of fear and misunderstanding that would lead to preemption.[19] Egypt would therefore strike to salvage whatever military advantage she could. Thus, as late as a day before Egypt attacked, Israel thought that the source of the tension was the Arabs' expectation that they were about to be attacked, and the last-minute efforts of Israel and the United States were to reassure the Arabs that this was not the case.

These predispositions had several consequences. Most obviously, neither the United States nor Israel made concerted efforts to deter an Arab attack since they thought such efforts not only were unnecessary but also might bring on the conflict they wanted to avoid. Second, because the Israelis and Americans believed that if war came it would be preemptive, not premeditated, almost all evidence for the latter kind of war was seen as indications of the former. Short of the most unambiguous warnings, defenders of the status quo could not tell that they were focusing on the wrong kind of threat. Their incorrect images, then, played into the hands of those who wanted to launch a surprise attack.[20] Third, this case is an exception to an important generalization. An acute consciousness of the extent to which the state inadvertently threatens others is not common. States are rarely willing to restrain military preparations that would benefit them if war broke out in order to reduce the chance that the other side will attack out of the fear of being struck. The security dilemma is persuasive in international politics, but statesmen usually underestimate rather than overestimate its impact. Fourth, while the short-run result of the misperceptions was a costly war, over the following several years the outcome was favorable to both Israel and Egypt. Without the shock of a war that Israel did not dominate, that country probably could not have brought herself to trade territory for a treaty; without a partial military victory, Egypt could not have regained the self-respect needed to allow her to accept Israel. Accurate perceptions of threat and successful deterrence probably would have been a barrier to more cooperative relations.

It is much easier to demonstrate the effects of cognitive predispositions than it is to explain their origins. Yet if the likelihood that statesmen will perceive various kinds of threats is strongly influenced by what they expect to see, it is particularly important not to accept this variable as a given but to seek its determinants. It is possible that personality is important, in the sense of either ego-dynamics or belief systems. The former phenomenon would call for a psychoanalytic investigation, the latter for the use of a construct like the operational code.[21] I cannot develop either of the approaches here but instead want to point to one sort of un-motivated bias that will affect most people's predispositions—the impact of international history. People are strongly influenced by events that are recent, that they or their country experienced first-hand, and events that occurred when they were first coming to political awareness.[22] The preceding war usually fits at least two of these categories. Furthermore, the lessons people learn are usually oversimplified and overgeneralized—they expect the future to re-semble the past. So if a state recently fought an agressor, it will be prone to see states it later encounters as threats. States with years of experience in a less hostile environment will be much less alarmed by ambiguous stimuli. If decision makers conclude that the previous war was unnecessary—that the other side could have been concili-ated—they will be predisposed to see later conflicts as similarly amenable to conciliation. Many statesmen saw World War I as avoidable, and this fed appeasement. In turn, the obvious lesson of the 1930s was that aggressors could not be appeased and so post–World War II decision makers were predisposed to see ambiguous actions as indicating hostile intentions.

The unmotivated bias produced by lessons from the preceding war supplies much of the explanation for the unusual Israeli pre-dispositions in 1973. In retrospect, many Israeli decision makers concluded that the 1967 war could have been avoided.[23] Nasser was not, as they had not unreasonably concluded at the time, about to strike. So after 1967 they were doubly alert to the dangers of preemption: first, because they had acted from this motive, and second, because their actions had been based on what they thought was an overreaction to their adversaries' moves.

Representativeness and Availability

Predispositions constitute the most important unmotivated in-fluence on perceptions, but two other unmotivated biases affect both predispositions and perceptions. One is what psychologists call availability: a person's inferences are influenced by the ease with which various patterns come to mind. For example, if we are asked whether there are more words that start with a given letter than words in which that letter appears in the third position, we are likely to answer the former (even if this is not correct) because it is easier to generate examples of words starting with a letter than to think of ones in which it appears third. Similarly, we overestimate the frequency of dramatic causes of death because they tend to stick in our minds and we confuse ease of recall with frequency.[24] When, as is often the case, the speed with which phenomena come to mind correlates with their frequency, availability supports accurate perception. But this short cut to rationality often leads us astray. As we have just seen, if a person has been strongly affected by a recent event, it will be readily available as a model for later happenings. But the experience will not have increased the likelihood that the model will be appropriate.

What is highly available to a decision maker is his own plans and intentions. He will see the behavior of others in light of what he is thinking of doing himself and will use his own procedures and approaches to interpret what they are doing. Thus before World War II the British Air Ministry based its estimates of the size of the German air force on the assumption that "the best criteria for judging Germany's rate of expansion were those which governed the rate at which the RAF [Royal Air Force] could itself form efficient units."[25] Similarly, when trying to determine how their adversaries might use a new weapon, states usually start by asking how they themselves would use it. For example, because the RAF stressed strategic bombardment, the British were predisposed to believe that Germany planned to attack their cities. Thus availability influenced the kind of threat the other was seen as posing.

The propensity to perceive threats and the kind of threat likely to be seen are also influenced by the bias of representativeness. Representativeness means determining whether object or event A belongs to category B by the degree to which A resembles B. This seems like common sense until it is remembered that unless the resemblance is believed to be completely compelling, one also has to consider the inherent likelihood that the phenomenon being examined is an instance of what it resembles. In other words, to give the best judgment representativeness must be combined with a priori probabilities or base rate statistics (the probability one would give that A is a B before one received any specific information about A). The exact way the two interact is given by Bayesian statistics, but what is important here is that, under certain conditions, people are insensitive to base rate data and concentrate almost exclusively on representativeness. This process—and the meanings of the terms— is illustrated by an experiment in which people are told that there is a bowl containing thumbnail descriptions of 100 people, 70 of them lawyers and 30 engineers. One description, taken at random, is read, and people are asked to estimate what they think the person's profession is. "Jack is a 45-year-old man. He is married and has four children. He is generally conservative, careful, and ambitious. He shows no interest in political and social issues and spends most of his free time on his many hobbies which include home carpentry, sailing and mathematical puzzles."[26]

Most people say Jack is an engineer, because the sketch fits the stereotype of someone in this profession; they ignore the fact that the a priori probability or base rate is a 70 percent chance that he is a lawyer. Their behavior would be fully rational only if they think the short description is completely diagnostic—that is, if they believe that everyone who fits the description is an engineer. But even if we leave aside the brevity of the information provided, few people think that there is a complete match between personality and profession. They must know that the information is less than a perfect guide, but they still rely on it and pay little attention to the base rate, as is shown by experiments in which the base rate data are altered but the inferences drawn are largely unaffected.

When statesmen ignore the base rates, as they will usually do if these data are not linked to their beliefs about how other states are likely to behave,[27] they will be excessively prone to perceive others as having intentions that are quite rare. They will seize on dramatic bits of behavior that indicate such intentions without paying heed to the inherent likelihoods. As in the experiment discussed above, this would be rational if it were believed that the behavior were completely diagnostic—that is, if the behavior were unambiguous and were highly correlated with the intention. But this is often not the case. Thus states can be unreasonable and belligerent in one case or even a series of cases without being set on a highly aggressive course. Base rates, then, need to be considered. Hitlers are very rare, but when a state acts in a way that resembles this model,[28] statesmen are likely to infer that the state is very aggressive. They will not modify the judgment that stems from resemblance by a consideration of the base rates. The result will be that an excessive number of states will be seen as highly aggressive.

Motivated Biases Affecting Threat Perception

Motivated biases also influence threat perception. The inferences statesmen draw often serve functions other than reality appraisal. Some shortcuts and errors can be explained not by the workings of our cognitive processes, which are trying to make sense out of a complex and ambiguous world, but by affect and the subconscious need to see the world in certain ways. Two such biases are particularly relevant to threat perception. First, the needs of decision makers and their states can strongly influence whether others are seen as threats, the kind of threats they are seen as presenting, and the best way of dealing with the threats.[29] For example, variations in British perception of Russian hostility in the period preceding the Crimean War cannot be explained by variations in Russian behavior. Nor can unmotivated biases account for the shifts, many of which were quite rapid. Rather, the imperatives of British domestic politics were crucial: perceptions changed in ways that reflected the needs of British leaders in their internal conflicts.[30] Ernest May provides a similar explanation for the perceptions and positions held by U.S. decision makers during the deliberations that led to the Monroe Doctrine. Each person's beliefs were those that were most helpful in the domestic maneuverings to succeed Monroe as president.[31] It is important to note that, when motivated biases are at work, one cannot predict the person's perceptions from his general belief system. Indeed, the inability of earlier views to account for current ones is evidence for the operation of strong pressures, since predispositions are usually very powerful. Of course, unambiguous information can also produce perceptions that are at variance with predispositions. But when this is the driving force, all people exposed to the same information develop the same beliefs, irrespective of their interest and needs.

When the motivated biases play a dominant role, many of the beliefs that seem to provide the reasons for the choice of policy are actually rationalizations. The policy comes first, often for reasons that are politically illegitimate or psychologically painful to recognize, and the justification follows, reversing the normal order in which beliefs about other states precede and lead to the foreign policy. Thus Richard Cottam found that the images of Egypt held by British decision makers over the period 1876–1956 changed in a way that followed and supported the needs of policy determined on other grounds.[32] When European tensions were low and the domestic pressures on Britain to grant Egypt more freedom were considerable, Egyptian society and leaders were seen as quite strong and benevolent, thus making the desired policy seem possible. When the European scene was tense and it was important for Britain to keep tight control over her valuable colony, the Egyptians were believed to be immature and irresponsible, and any devolution was thus precluded. Of course, the policy still rests on some images and beliefs, and it is important to try to see what they are and how they are established, but the perception of threat from the target state is an effect, not a cause.

Motivated errors can lead decision makers to underestimate or overestimate threats. The latter can produce self-deterrence, as occurred in Britain in the late 1930s.[33] Although most British leaders underestimated German hostility, they overestimated German air power, and especially German intention and ability to attack British cities. The appeasers were motivated to hold this view because it reinforced their argument that war had to be avoided; the anti-appeasers found it congenial because it fit with the belief that Hitler was planning for a war with Britain. Of course errors like this can occur at random. But the lack of evidence that Germany had the necessary air capability and the sloppy analysis that was accepted uncritically indicate—although they do not prove—that the error was at least in part a motivated one.

Under other circumstances, states will be motivated to perceive a threat as smaller or less troublesome than it actually is. When statesmen become committed to a given policy, they will feel strong psychological pressures to perceive that the threats they face can be overcome.[34] Thus I doubt if it is an accident that people who believe that costly domestic needs require immediate attention and that total government spending cannot be increased are likely to esti-mate foreign threats as lower than those who do not share these beliefs. The same phenomenon can have even more dramatic mani-festations, as is shown by the Japanese reaction to the dilemma they faced in 1941. Committed to gaining control over China and faced by the U.S. oil embargo, they saw no alternative to seizing the Dutch East Indies, which in turn required a war with Britain and the United States. If this were not to be thought suicidal, the threat of the war had to be seen as manageable. Thus Japanese leaders came to believe that the United States would fight a limited war and make peace on the basis of Japanese control over East Asia. But U.S. public opinion and worldview indicated that she would not do so, and, even more tellingly, the Japanese undertook no careful inves-tigation into the likely U.S. reaction.[35] Thus it seems likely that the error was motivated.

Not only the perception of threat but also the way to meet it can be affected by motivated biases. Thus, Snyder shows, the great powers' adoption of offensive military strategies before World War I cannot be explained by the evidence available to them compounded by unmotivated distortions.[36] One must also consider the interests of the military organizations that predisposed them to believe in the efficacy of the offensive. The military ethos generally supports attacking rather than leaving the initiative to others, perhaps because, without special spurs to action, the horror of having to attack prepared positions would lead generals to be too passive. More specific motivations were also at work, especially in the French case, where offensive tactics and the belief that Germany could not make a sweeping attack through Belgium served the important function of reducing the role of reserves. This reduction was needed to preserve the traditional role and power of the regular French army, which was then under strong domestic pressure. The result was that the powers adopted military postures that magnified the security dilemma, made it impossible for the states to deter their adversaries without simultaneously provoking them, and cost them dearly in the actual fighting.

When motivated biases are at work, it is particularly hard for others to predict the state's behavior. The state is acting irrationally, often following internal imperatives whose strength, if not nature, is shielded from outsiders. Observers who look at the external situation, the state's interests, and even its previous behavior will, then, be led to incorrect conclusions. Furthermore, motivated biases usually lead to the belief that others will allow the state's policy to succeed. It is particularly difficult for the adversary to empathize with this perception because it knows that it will not cooperate, that it will use its full force to prevail. The predictable result of Pearl Harbor was, after all, the destruction of the Japanese empire, and so people who followed out the lines of rational calculation would not have expected the attack. This is one reason why moves that gain their success through surprise often succeed in the short run but then lead to disaster. They gain surprise because they are implausible; they are implausible because there are good reasons for not carrying them out. Over a longer period, the larger considerations that pointed to the unwisdom of the act make themselves felt, as they did by the end of World War II. Similarly, Janice Stein's first chapter shows how badly flawed was the Egyptian reasoning preceding the War of Attrition.[37] So it is not surprising either that the Israelis failed to foresee the campaign or that the Egyptian policy eventually failed.

Biases after Threats Have Been Perceived

The same kinds of biases, both motivated and unmotivated, affect deterrence policies in their later stages, after the threat has been perceived. Limitations of space require brevity, and so I will focus on deterrence theory's implication that states should and do develop complex bargaining strategies that are "fine tuned" to the environment.

Statesmen often believe that they can design and implement a policy that exerts just the right amount of pressure on the other side—enough to restrain but not to lead the other to believe that an all-out conflict is inevitable. If the policy is slightly altered in one direction or the other, the argument goes, it will fail. In fact, such precision is usually beyond our grasp. As the chapters of this book show, the impediments to the proper evaluation of the environment often defeat such attempts and, when decision makers are aware of these problems, limit the extent to which they are employed.

The hold of predisposition is probably the most important characteristic that makes it doubtful that deterrence can be supported by detailed strategy carefully matched to the changing nuances of the situation. As was noted earlier, a person's interpretation of specific bits of information is strongly influenced by that individual's general beliefs about the way the world works and what other states are likely to do. If these beliefs are correct, the person is likely to be able to do quite a good job of predicting the behavior of others, interpreting their messages, and designing actions that will make the desired impressions on them. But the images states have of each other are frequently inaccurate. Even when the general outlines are correct, crucial details are usually inexact in ways that can defeat policies. Before World War II U.S. policy makers realized that Japan was very hostile but were wrong in many details of their beliefs. The underestimation of Japanese military capability—in particular to stretch the range of the Zero and to develop a torpedo that would run in shallow water—contributed to the surprise of December 7. The failure to understand Japanese economic problems led the United States to ignore one possible path of conciliation. Most importantly, the inability to grasp the strength of the Japanese motivation to expand led U.S. statesmen to downgrade the danger that Japan would strike if cornered.

Furthermore, a state needs not only to develop an accurate image of the other but also to grasp the other's worldview and view of the state, since these images influence the other's behavior in general and its reactions to the state in particular. A nice example is provided by the U.S. attempt to increase slowly the pressure on Spain in the dispute over Cuba in 1898. A culminating move in this policy was the quasi ultimatum that McKinley included in his annual message to Congress. The policy failed, and one reason was that the communication did not register. In the Spanish archives Ernest May found the translation of the message that had circulated to the cabinet. "It has innumerable marginal marks and underlinings, but none around McKinley's warning of "other and further action" in the "near future." The Spanish government was not yet concerned with anything McKinley said or did, except as it seemed likely to affect rebel morale [in Cuba]. Since the message contained passages discouraging recognition and praising the offer of autonomy, the Foreign Minister advised the Spanish ambassador in Paris that the cabinet found it 'very satisfactory.' "[38]

The U.S. strategy was not foolish or irrational. The message seems clear enough to later scholars, at least American ones. But because it was designed with the U.S. frame of reference in mind rather than the Spanish, it was not read as it was written. The concept of availability is relevant here. Because the Americans did not understand the Spanish beliefs and concerns and instead were guided by their own, the inferences that were easily available to the Spanish were obscure to the Americans and vice versa. It would have been very hard for the U.S. diplomats to see the world through Spanish eyes, but without their doing so all but the most blunt and direct messages were likely to be missed or misinterpreted.

It is particularly difficult and particularly important for the state to determine how the other sees it. This task is difficult because the relevant evidence is not easy to obtain, a state's beliefs about itself are so powerful that it is hard to imagine others having a different view, and a state's self-image carries a heavy load of affect. But if the state does not understand how the other sees it, it is not likely to be able to predict how the other will interpret the actions it plans to take. Since one of the purposes of these actions is to influence the other, the failure to grasp the other's image of the state will often make it impossible for the state to design effective deterrence policies. This is especially true if these policies depend on conveying precise and subtle messages.

U.S. policy in 1941 is again relevant. For the United States to have developed an appropriate deterrence policy, decision makers would have had to realize that the Japanese were ready to go to war in the belief that the United States would be willing to keep the conflict limited. I think it is fair to say that this idea never crossed the minds of the U.S. leaders. The discrepancy with the U.S. self-image was so great that a considerable feat of imagination would have been required to come up with it. And had it occurred to the Americans, it probably would have been rejected out of hand.[39] Motivated as well as unmotivated processes are involved here. To think that others might hold this view opens the possibility that it has some validity. To have abandoned our friends and commitments would have been dishonorable, and to think that others would expect this implies that our traditions and past behavior were not without ambiguity. But without understanding the Japanese image of the United States, U.S. decision makers could not see what they needed to threaten and what message they needed to convey.

Carrying out a complex policy and adjusting your moves to those of your adversary assumes the ability to judge how he is responding. But here the problem discussed in the previous paragraphs becomes compounded. Because statesmen believe that they understand the other side's view of the world, they usually assume that their messages have been received and interpreted as intended. If the other ignores a signal, statesmen often conclude that it has been rejected when in fact it may not have been received. U.S. leaders interpreted in this way the Spanish nonresponse to its threat described earlier. When there is a response, but not the desired one, the state is likely to draw conclusions based on the assumption that the adversary acted in full understanding of what the state had sought. When this assumption is wrong, the information derived from the other's behavior is likely to mislead the state further rather than correct its initial misapprehensions.

Indeed, this problem, along with others created by the strong influence of preexisting beliefs, would be much smaller if sustained interaction validated correct images and altered incorrect ones. States could then probe their environments; subtle signals that did not find their targets would yield information that would provide the foundations upon which complex bargaining strategies could be erected. But Snyder and Diesing's examination of crises indicates that this pattern is the exception.[40] More frequently errors are not corrected; one cannot build a theory on the assumption that feedback will reduce rather than magnify false beliefs.

Deterrence requires both understanding the other side's view of the state and predicting its view of the state's policy. Unfortunately, often each side will have a different view, with the result that the actual impact of the policy greatly differs from the expected one. Most commonly, the state is likely to view its policy as the legitimate, and indeed obvious, defense of its vital interests, while its adversary will see an attempt to alter the established patterns.

Such discrepancies almost surely arose from the U.S. attempts to deter a Soviet invasion of Poland in late 1980. The United States saw this as a legitimate attempt to maintain limited freedom in Poland and restrict the use of force to change the status quo. But it is likely that Soviet perceptions differed: the Russians had reason to see a change in the pattern of U.S. acceptance of the Soviet sphere of influence in Eastern Europe. Although the United States had always objected to such Soviet control, from the early 1950s it never made serious efforts to challenge it. Indeed, one argument for the Helsinki Agreements was that they decreased Soviet paranoia by providing reassurances that the United States would not seek to undermine its sphere. Such efforts are especially important because of their links to the policy of deterring Soviet expansion: if the United States is to convince the Soviets that it will punish any attempt at forcible growth, it must also convince them that sanctions will not be applied if the USSR is restrained. For the United States to do otherwise is to run the risk that the Russians will think that Western hostility is rooted not in the fear that the USSR is an expansionist power but in the desire to encroach on established Soviet positions.

Motivated biases further distort information to the detriment of policies that require precise understanding of the environment. Values often conflict with one another; the world is rarely so benignly arranged that the policy that is best on one value dimension is also best on others. Yet decision makers tend to avoid seeing such value trade-offs. The policy they favor is seen as furthering multiple independent values.[41] Two points are relevant here. First, deterrence theory requires the statesmen to balance the risks of confrontation with the costs and risks of concessions. In fact, one often finds this done only implicitly, without analysis or careful thought. People who advocate standing firm often deny that their policy is more risky than that of making concessions. Instead, they argue that retreating, while avoiding the immediate danger, only increases it in the longer run. In a similar manner, those who favor conciliation see the cost of retreating as relatively minor. To put this another way, those who favor standing firm usually evaluate the risks of doing so as lower and the costs of retreating as higher than do those who advocate conciliation. Logically, differing on only one dimension would be sufficient to determine the person's choice. That there are differences on both dimensions implies that something more than logic is at work.[42]

The effect is that the careful calibration of risks and the balancing of expected gains and losses are thrown off. Although decision makers believe they are paying attention to several important values, in fact their actions seem to be driven by only one or two. The statesman reaches his decision largely on the basis of the value that is most salient to him and then brings his evaluations of the other value dimensions into line with this. Inertia is thereby increased because the person underestimates the problems with his favored policy. Thus a state that has embarked on a policy of either confrontation or conciliation will maintain it in the face of a great deal of evidence that it is failing. The case of the appeasers in Britain is well known. Here the danger of getting into a disastrous war with Germany were uppermost in the minds of Chamberlain and his colleagues and led them to underestimate the risk of encouraging aggression. Similarly, once a state is committed to a belligerent policy, it will downgrade the risks involved and come to believe, in the face of massive evidence to the contrary, that the other side will not dare to go to war.[43] Here the advantages of an unyielding policy and the disadvantages of conciliation determine the policy. But in neither kind of case are the relevant values carefully balanced against one another. Because the world is not as benign as these perceptions, values are sacrificed. But this is not done as explicitly as deterrence theory implies, and the choice is not sensitive to new information about the environment.

A related effect is for deterrence to fail because states become overextended. By refusing to see that some commitments must be withdrawn in order to allow others to be protected, states take on too many burdens and too many enemies. Germany before World War I and Great Britain in the interwar period are examples. Although both states were in difficult situations, the former because of geography and the latter because of its heritage as the leading world power, they might have avoided disastrous wars by conciliating any one of their adversaries. In these cases, domestic considerations made such choices difficult, but the psychological inhibitions against fully recognizing the problem removed some of the urgency that should have energized the search for a way to balance resources and commitments.

It seems likely that both motivated and unmotivated processes are at work in the tendency to avoid value trade-offs. What probably happens is that one value dominates the choice of the policy and that perceptions of other value dimensions are brought into line with the initial preference in order to minimize psychological distress. We can see this by returning to the British example in the previous paragraph. In part because of the horrors of World War I, the appeasers felt they had to do everything in their power to reduce the chance of war. Furthermore, the model of an avoidable war was highly salient to them. The resulting imperatives drove the policy of appeasement and colored the estimates of the policy's dangers and costs. Similarly, when the disadvantages of conciliation are seen as overwhelming, the belief that firmness can succeed follows the adoption of a belligerent policy. In both kinds of cases the decision makers avoid the psychological pain of dwelling on the costs of their policies. Chamberlain did not have to acknowledge to himself that he was purchasing the value of avoiding an inadvertent war by increasing the chance of German aggression; in 1962 Nehru did not have to realize that he was gaining territory on the frontier and domestic support at the cost of risking a war with China.

Conclusion

Parsimony and a coherent theory are still beyond our grasp. But we hope this book shows that examining how people think opens the way to a richer and more accurate understanding of how deterrence works, of when it is thought to be necessary, and of when and why it fails. The need for people to simplify the enormous amount of information they receive and the psychological pressures that result in motivated distortions mean that there will be serious discrepancies between the perceived and the actual environment. The problem is multilateral and interactive. That is, we are not dealing with one state that is perceiving a passive environment, but with many states that are perceiving and reacting to one another. To interpret what others are doing, judge how others are perceiving them, and predict how others will interpret their behavior, states have to understand the beliefs and images that others hold, which may be very different from those held by the state. As these processes continue over time, furthermore, errors are likely to be compounded, not corrected. The difficulty in determining the other side's intentions underscores the need to try to develop policies that can both deter and reassure, that can communicate that the state will resist encroachments on its vital interests but has no desire to challenge the vital interests of the other. Snyder's discussion of the "imperialist's dilemma" reminds us that such a policy would not be a cure-all.[44] But it is a feasible one when conflicts of interest are significant but not overwhelming and when mutual security is mutually acceptable. Mixing promises and threats, rewards and punishments, is necessary, but combining them so that they reinforce rather than defeat each other is particularly difficult. A first step is to grasp the other side's values, beliefs, and perceptions and to understand the motivated and unmotivated biases that influence information processing and decision making.

3

■

CALCULATION, MISCALCULATION, AND CONVENTIONAL DETERRENCE I: THE VIEW FROM CAIRO

Janice Gross Stein

■ The attempt to prevent war through the threat of force is by now an all too familiar strategy in contemporary international life. Formal theories that prescribe deterrence as strategy reason deductively, speak to the motivation of both the challenger and the defender in an adversarial relationship, and treat both as rational. Paradoxically, however, although formal theories are well articulated, the axiomatic logic parsimonious, and the prescriptive thrust evident, the workings of deterrence continue to remain elusive.

This chapter and the next seek to illuminate how deterrence works, to contribute to an explanatory theory of deterrence that is empirically rather than deductively derived. To do so, I look empirically at the calculations of the two protagonists in a deterrent relationship, the challenger and the defender, and attend in the first instance to the practice rather than the theory. In this chapter I begin with an examination of the calculations of Egypt's leaders from 1969 to 1973, five years in which they considered a use of force five times. I pay careful attention not only to those instances where

I wish to thank Alexander George, Robert Jervis, Ned Lebow, Patrick Morgan, George Quester, and Jack Snyder for their detailed and extraordinarily helpful comments on an earlier draft of this chapter.

they chose to attack—where deterrence failed—but also to the cases where they refrained from a use of force—where deterrence held. In the next chapter I proceed to look at the estimates of Israel's leaders during much of the same period when they sought to deter military attack. Inevitably, though, I weave back and forth to some extent as I explore the dynamics of an interdependent relationship; these two chapters can best be conceived as the two sides of the same deterrence equation. They are animated by a common intellectual agenda: first, to explore the divergences between the expectations of formal theories of deterrence and the reality of its practice in an interdependent relationship over time; and second, to determine whether there were systematic perceptual biases in decisions about the use of force by the challenger or the defender—or both—and whether these biases were sufficiently important to defeat deterrence.

I begin with an examination of the calculations of Egypt, in this relationship the challenger contemplating a resort to force. Formal theories of deterrence speak clearly to this set of calculations. Elaborated largely through deductive reasoning, they build on the central proposition that, when a challenger considers that the likely benefits of military action will outweigh its probable costs, deterrence is likely to fail. If, on the other hand, leaders estimate that the probable costs of a use of force are greater than its putative benefits, deterrence succeeds. Crucial to these estimates of a challenger is the credibility of a defender's commitment, either to punish or to deny. Credibility in turn, formal theories hold, is generally a function of a challenger's estimate of a defender's capability and resolve. At its core, then, the concept of deterrence assumes that a rational challenger weighs all elements of the deterrence equation equally and pays attention to probability, cost, and benefit in choosing whether or not to use force. The deterrence argument, *au fond*, is one of motivation.

Precisely because it is a theory of motivation, deterrence cannot rest on axiomatic logic alone but must deal with the metaphysics and the psychopolitics of a challenger's calculations. Consequently, it is very much the abstract formalism and parsimonious logic of deterrence that has generated so much criticism among experts. Many consider deterrence ahistorical because, in the articulation of a set of logical maxims, it ignores important differences among challengers over time. It is also apolitical in its inadequate treatment of the political context of decisions and the political environment that shapes and alters the valuation of interests. It is remiss, behavioral scientists tell us, in its failure to treat fundamental cognitive processes, processes that compromise the capacity for the kind of rational calculation required by formal theories of deterrence. Cognizant of these difficulties, scholars turned from formal theory to empirical investigation of the workings of deterrence.[1]

The central building block of theories of deterrence is the subjective estimates challengers make of the likely costs and benefits of the consequences of military action. To assess these estimates of probability and value, one needs to know first how leaders identify their interests and perceive the issues and how they evaluate their military capabilities and the military balance. To examine their decisional calculus, one needs to know as well whether leaders consider alternatives to a use of force. And, to understand their choice, one must establish the weight they give to different elements of the deterrence equation: How do they weigh the interests at stake, the military balance, the importance of the available bargaining space, the alternatives to force, and their calculations of expected gain and loss?

Three sets of questions guide the examination of these factors. First, do leaders consider each of these factors? These elements may be part of their conceptual schema, or they may be omitted entirely from the analysis. If leaders do consider these factors, do they, as the rationality postulate expects, accord equal attention to all the critical components? Or, as much of psychological theory expects, are leaders selective in their attention? Are they systematically biased in what they include and what they ignore? Second, are there differences in the pattern of perception when leaders choose to use force and when they refrain from military action? This is not a trivial question if one holds that psychological processes are a necessary component in an explanation of deterrence failure. Finally, wherever hindsight permits, I propose to assess the accuracy of leaders' subjective judgments. Do senior leaders seriously miscalculate, and if they do, what is the impact of miscalculation on the outcome of deterrence? Does miscalculation defeat deterrence? If leaders had assessed interest, capabilities, or bargaining space more accurately, if they had been less biased in making critical decisions, would they likely have refrained from a resort to force?

Before an empirical investigation of the practice of deterrence can properly proceed, at least two conditions must hold. First, a challenger must actively consider a use of force, and second, a defender must actively try to prevent that use of force through a threat of military retaliation. If defenders are not trying to deter or challengers are not considering force, then deterrence is, of course, irrelevant. If these two conditions do obtain, however, not only the failures but also the successes of deterrence can be identified and analyzed.[2] From 1969 to 1973 Egypt's leaders seriously contemplated the use of force at least five times, and Israel threatened retaliation to deter military action. The context of the deterrence relationship set the framework for the strategic choices Egypt confronted.

The war of 1967 was one of miscalculation, an unplanned war that was unintended by any of the belligerents. It began with tension on Israel's border with Syria, escalated to an Egyptian blockade of the Straits of Tiran, and ended with Israel's occupation of the Sinai Peninsula, the Golan Heights, and the West Bank of the Jordan. The changed map at the core of the Middle East reshaped the strategic equation of the Arab-Israeli conflict and the memories, perceptions, and calculations of the major belligerents. Israel became the quintessential conservative power with an overwhelming interest in deterring military attack, while the Arab states were even less willing to accept the status quo after 1967 than they had been before.

At the end of the war, the intelligence services of the United States, the Soviet Union, Egypt, and Israel all agreed that Egypt's military capability was inferior to that of Israel: Egypt could not recapture the Sinai Peninsula in a general war. In formal terms, the stage was set for the success of conventional deterrence. Yet Egypt's leaders repeatedly considered a challenge to deterrence and at times did choose to use force. In early 1969 President Nasser abrogated the cease-fire and in March launched a war of attrition across the Suez Canal. Israel's deterrent strategy had failed. In 1971, not quite a year after Nasser's death, Anwar el-Sadat proclaimed a "year of decision" and planned an air strike against Israel's military installations in the Sinai preparatory to a landing of paratroopers. This time, Egypt's leaders chose not to attack as planned. Again in 1972 the president ordered the Egyptian general staff to prepare to attack across the canal but cancelled the attack in mid-November after dismissing his senior military commanders for refusing to follow his orders. For the fourth time, in early 1973, Egyptian military officers planned a surprise attack for limited military objectives in coordination with Syria. And again, in May, the attack was postponed. In the summer of 1973 Egypt and Syria jointly planned an attack across the cease-fire lines, and on 6 October the two armies launched a coordinated military attack. Five times, then, Egypt planned military action, but only twice did Egyptian armed forces actually attack. Israel's deterrent strategy may have succeeded three times but it failed, and failed badly, twice. Why?

The major obstacle to a valid answer to this question lies in the paucity of reliable evidence on the perceptions of Egypt's leaders and the processes they used to make their choices. This problem plagues the historian as well as the social scientist, and, other than waiting the usual thirty years for the opening of archives, there is no obvious and satisfactory solution. In Cairo, moreover, there are special problems with the classification and referencing of government documents. On the other hand, in Egypt fewer players were involved in making these decisions. Power was concentrated heavily in a few very senior officials and, except for a short period in 1970–71, particularly in the presidency. The president and senior army officers have written autobiographies and memoirs, generating a great deal of heat and some light.[3] Civilian advisers have also written extensively. Mohamed Heikal, an influential adviser to both President Nasser and President Sadat until 1974, regularly used the editorial page of the semiofficial *Al-Ahram* to dissect government attitudes and policies. In their accounts of important debates and decisions, at times there are discrepancies between the president and his senior military commanders or civilian advisers. When these discrepancies do occur, I work with the president's reconstruction of the decision since, for all but the short interval from September 1970 to May 1971, the power and authority of the president to determine policy was unquestioned. In addition to the writings of senior military and civilian leaders, the semiofficial Institute for Strategic Studies at *Al-Ahram* in Cairo has an excellent collection of legislative debates and speeches given by government leaders. Finally, some of the senior leaders have been interviewed, and although these interviews are often illuminating, they are not especially valid since the "remembered probabilities of once-future things" differ quite markedly from the estimates leaders are likely to have made at the time.[4] With careful attention to the validity of different kinds of evidence, I drew on these sources to reconstruct the calculation of Egypt's leaders about the use of force.

Deterrence: A Challenger's Perspective

Estimates of Interests

The first important component in the calculations of leaders contemplating a challenge to deterrence is their evaluation of the interests at stake, an evaluation that logically should shape their assessment of the cost and benefit of military action. One of the weaknesses of formal prescriptive theories of deterrence is their inadequate attention to the interests at stake, especially those that are "intrinsic" rather than "strategic."[5] Intrinsic interest refers to the tangibles at issue and their worth, while strategic interest includes the bargaining reputation, the resolve, the credibility, and the prestige of a participant in an ongoing conflict. Deductive statements of the logic of deterrence can treat the interconnectedness among interests and the importance of reputation in an ongoing conflict, but they cannot speak to the initial evaluation challengers make of the interests at issue. One must look beyond the formal assumption of rationality to the psychological dynamics that may influence leaders' estimates of their interests.

I begin by looking at a challenger's comparative assessment of the interests at stake. Although formal theories of deterrence do not address these estimates directly, by implication one would expect first that leaders do compare interests.[6] If they then consider their opponent's interests to be more heavily engaged than their own, they will estimate the defender's resolve to be high and the commitment to retaliate credible and, other things being equal, will forego military challenge.[7] In an examination of crisis bargaining, however, Snyder and Diesing uncover very few instances of explicit estimation of the intensity of an opponent's interests. Rather, leaders appear to assess their own resolve by considering the worth of their interests but infer an opponent's likely resolve from its past behavior. In his study of Argentinian decision making before the occupation of the Falkland Islands, Lebow finds as well that leaders in Buenos Aires paid little attention to the underlying interests of Britain.[8] Their evidence is consistent with psychological explanations that suggest that leaders are likely to pay attention to their own interests, interests that are psychologically salient, rather than to those of their opponent. A challenger's assumption of a favorable asymmetry of interest may be faulty in part because interests are rarely compared explicitly. Insofar as leaders do evaluate the interests of their adversary—and the estimates of these interests by the opposing leadership—they are likely to underestimate their worth in comparison to the value they attach to their own interests at stake in the conflict. Whether the bias is motivated—a challenger may seek to justify a use of force—or unmotivated, evaluations by leaders of the interests at issue will bear little resemblance to the expectations of formal theory.

When one looks at the calculations of Egypt's leaders from 1969 to 1973, one finds a poor fit between the expectations of deductive theories and Egyptian estimates. First, Egypt's leaders engaged in almost no comparison of interests; indeed, in only one case did they discuss asymmetries in the interests at issue. As Egypt was about to launch the War of Attrition, Heikal noted that the importance attached by Egypt to return of the conquered territories was greater than Israel's readiness to defend the status quo.[9] In the other four cases, although the credibility of Israel's commitment was not at issue, there is no Egyptian estimate of Israel's interests: the interests of their adversary were not psychologically salient. Certainly Egypt's leaders did not develop finely tuned calculations of relative interest to estimate Israel's likely response to a use of force. Perhaps they did not do so because they were considering direct military attack on the forces of their adversary and, consequently, had little doubt about Israel's response.[10] Indeed, it appears that Israel's leaders succeeded, after the War of Attrition ended in 1970, in persuading Egypt's senior officers that a renewal of limited warfare would be met with a much broader military response.[11] This is not usual: Lebow finds, for example, that challengers frequently resort to force, anticipating that defenders will acquiesce rather than retaliate.[12] Although Egyptian leaders were not plagued by uncertainty and consequently had little incentive to examine Israel's interests, the almost complete inattention to the likely estimates of Israel's leaders is nevertheless striking: the estimate of a favorable asymmetry was an implicit premise in the calculations of Egypt's political and military leaders. Equally to the point, however, misperception did not confound deterrence: Egypt read Israel's threat to retaliate and did so accurately and independently of any explicit assessment of Israel's intrinsic or strategic interests.

What we do find is consistent emphasis by Egypt's leaders on the centrality of their own interests. They used almost apocalyptic language to describe the interests at stake: in November 1972 President Sadat defined the issue as "to be or not to be," and Heikal explained that the conflict with Israel was the "crisis of our life."[13] Egypt's leaders paid more attention to their strategic interests, however, than to the worth of the specific interests at issue. Although they made frequent reference to the liberation of the Sinai and to the rights of the Palestinians, they placed these issues within a broader context. In 1969 General el-Shazli explained that Egypt would initiate military action "to symbolize our refusal to remain defeated," and in 1973 President Sadat argued that Egypt would refuse to acquiesce in a *fait accompli*. There is little specific reference to the worth of the intrinsic interests at issue.

What does this examination of Egyptian assessments of their own interests and those of Israel suggest? First, a strong emphasis on strategic interests dominated Egyptian thinking throughout. The limited attention that Egyptian leaders paid to Israel's interests, either intrinsic or strategic, suggests that Egyptian leaders operated with an implicit premise that required no discussion.

Second, and equally interesting, although I could find almost no discussion of the relative interests involved, this gap in perception did not translate into a flawed estimate of Israel's commitment to retaliate. This particular misperception had no impact on the success or failure of deterrence; it was irrelevant. Paradoxically, however, in the one case where Egypt's leaders did consider asymmetries of interest, in 1969, they seriously underestimated Israel's interest and consequently miscalculated the scope of its response. They did not anticipate that, in response to unacceptable levels of casualities, Israel would escalate both its objectives and the scope of its military retaliation. Heikal based his estimate directly on an assessment of Israel's intrinsic interest: because Israel had no interest in the west bank of the canal, its forces would not cross in retaliation against Egyptian artillery fire. Moreover, he insisted, Israel was less committed to defending the status quo than was Egypt to recapturing the occupied territories. This analysis seriously underestimated Israel's strategic interest and did not consider the consequences of a prolonged and costly military stalemate for Israel's deterrent reputation. It seems likely that the bias in the estimate was motivated— Heikal underestimated the probability of an undesirable consequence. Whether motivated or unmotivated, this miscalculation was critical in defeating deterrence. It was not inattention to an adversary's estimate of its interests but underestimation of these estimates that led to a flawed calculation of the acceptable limits of risk and an inappropriate military challenge.

Finally, although Egyptian leaders placed great emphasis on the importance of the interests at stake, in only two of the five cases did they challenge deterrence and resort to force. Because Egyptian leaders consistently valued their interests highly, their estimates varied too little to explain the difference between deterrence failure and success; consequently, perceptions of interest provide a very weak explanation of the outcome of deterrence. My evidence suggests that, at most, a high valuation of strategic interest may be a necessary but insufficient condition of deterrence failure. And, more surprisingly, it seems that a low valuation by a challenger of its interest is not a prerequisite to the success of deterrence.

Estimates of Military Capabilities

A second component in a challenger's calculation, a component that is at the heart of the deterrence argument, is a leader's estimate of the military balance. Formal theories of deterrence begin with the premise that interests are strong and leaders are powerfully motivated to attack, and then they consider a challenger's assessment of the balance of military capabilities as the critical component. Deterrence succeeds when leaders calculate that the likely costs of military action will outweigh its expected benefits. Central to these calculations are their estimates of military capabilities.

Working with a common assumption of rationality, students of deterrence have looked at different dimensions of military capabilities. The costs of military action generally refer to the estimated capacity of a defender to inflict military punishment or to deny military success on the battlefield. Not only assessments of the general balance but also estimates of changing trends in the balance may shape a decision on whether or not to resort to force. If leaders consider trends to be adverse, quite rationally they may feel a growing sense of urgency to act. Japanese leaders made very much this kind of calculation before choosing to strike at Pearl Harbor in 1941.

Analysts of military history have suggested that more important than the quantitative balance of power is the estimated impact of technology and force postures on strategy and the capacity for offense. If leaders consider that military technology or force postures favor the offense, they are likely to challenge.[14] Evaluation by officers of the mobility of their forces may also be important in their estimates of offensive capability, but mobility can favor the defense as well. More to the point is a challenger's evaluation of the prospects of its military strategy. When leaders think they can launch a successful blitzkrieg that promises rapid military victory, again quite rationally they are likely to resort to force. When they see no alternative but a long, costly war of attrition, or a limited strategy that may degenerate into stalemate, they are likely to be deterred. Finally, in their empirical examination of the practice of deterrence, George and Smoke suggest that challengers will try to devise options that can finesse a defender's military superiority. They will attempt to choose a type of action at a level of violence that will make it difficult for a defender to use its most potent military resources.[15] Leaders may examine any or all of these dimensions of military capability, and when they do so, theories of deterrence suggest, they carefully calculate the expected costs and benefits of military action and make the rational choice.

Psychological explanations do not expect leaders to engage in careful, "objective" consideration of military capabilities. On the contrary, a variety of biases may intrude to color the estimates they make of their own and their adversary's military options. Analysts of national security suggest that leaders often tend to underestimate their own capabilities and overestimate those of their adversary. Biased estimates of this kind are especially common when military action does not seem imminent. The error may be motivated—challengers may try to increase defense spending and mobilize public support—or unmotivated—biases of anchoring and availability may lead senior officials to overgeneralize from their past military performance or that of their adversary.[16] When leaders are considering immediate military action, they may underestimate the strength of an adversary and exaggerate their own. Highly motivated to challenge, they may well deny unpleasant value trade-offs. Estimates of military capability and usable force, the crucial estimates in a deterrence equation, are subject to the same set of biases that generally affect judgment and inference.

A careful inspection of the Egyptian evaluation of these military factors—their own capabilities as well as those of their opponent, their capacity for offense, usable military options, the likely battlefields results—challenges the central postulate of the deterrence argument. First, there is strong evidence of miscalculation in the estimates of Egyptian leaders. Even more damaging, if the bias in the estimates is discounted and the Egyptian analyses of military capabilities are taken as givens, the theory of deterrence fits poorly with the practice.

In March 1969 there is at least a partial fit between Egyptian estimates and the expectations of deterrence theory. Before they initiated the War of Attrition, Egyptian leaders considered that their forces enjoyed local superiority in the projected theater of battle. Muhammed Fawzi, the minister of war, estimated that although Egypt was inferior to Israel in its capacity for offense, it did have defensive superiority in manpower, armor, and artillery along the canal, and Heikal, writing in *Al-Ahram*, concurred that although Israel had superiority in the air, Egypt had the advantage on the ground in the canal zone. President Nasser argued even more strongly that Israel could not attack across the canal: it would confront a "sea of Arabs" and a massive Egyptian deployment along the line.[17] At least along the canal front, both civilian and military leaders estimated that the military balance was favorable.

This estimate was central in Egyptian consideration of alternative military options. Closely related to this evaluation of local, defensive superiority in weaponry was an emphasis on quantitative superiority in manpower and a far greater capacity to absorb punishment. Heikal argued that, because of the depth of Egyptian territory and its unlimited population, a strategy of attrition was uniquely suited to Egyptian capabilities: just as "lightning war" suited Israel, so protracted war suited Egypt. Even if Egypt sustained 50,000 casualties, it could absorb these losses, but if it inflicted 10,000 casualties, Israel would be forced to terminate the fighting. Drawing on these estimates, Egypt's military planners designed a four-part challenge to Israel's deterrent strategy: six to eight weeks of massive artillery bombardment, followed by hit-and-run commando attacks, then larger action across the canal to disrupt Israel's supply lines, and finally a large-scale canal crossing.[18] As George and Smoke suggest challengers may do, Egyptian leaders "designed around" deterrence. They attempted to develop a military strategy to minimize Israel's advantages, to exploit the available constraints on the use by Israel of the full range of its military capabilities, to impose ground rules on the level and pattern of violence that would favor their assets and diminish their liabilities. In so doing, Egypt's leaders anticipated neither a rapid battlefield victory nor offensive military action. On the contrary, they quite deliberately eschewed a blitzkrieg strategy and chose a limited strategy of attrition warfare. Estimates of offensive superiority and rapid military success were not preconditions to this military challenge.

Were these estimates accurate? With the benefit of hindsight, it is apparent that almost every one of the critical estimates and attendant corollaries were flawed. Egypt enjoyed local superiority in fire power along the canal only so long as Israel refrained from committing its air force, but it was highly unlikely, indeed almost illogical, that Israel would refrain in the face of protracted war and high casualties. Indeed, within six months, Egypt's anti-aircraft defenses had been destroyed and Cairo's forces on the ground were exposed to punishing fire. It was not that Egyptian leaders failed to consider the risk of an escalation by Israel, an escalation that they knew would be damaging if it occurred. In the first place, they considered the risk and then dismissed it, despite their choice of a military strategy that would provoke the very contingency they sought to avoid. In the second place, Egyptian leaders miscalculated the relationship between military objectives and strategy: were Egypt's forces to cross the canal, the war would not remain limited, yet all Egyptian planning was based on a static limited war that would constrain Israel's options. Although military leaders had eliminated the option of a general war with Israel, the four-phase strategy they designed led precisely to such a war. Finally, Egyptian leaders grossly underestimated Israel's capacity for endurance and overestimated Egyptian capability to inflict casualties. Indeed, it is difficult to understand precisely how Egyptian leaders expected to inflict casualties of

10,000; at the height of the war, Israel's casualties reached 150 per month—and provoked the escalation to air power. Yet Egyptian planners spoke of massive casualties within six to eight weeks. An error of such magnitude in an estimate is one of kind rather than degree.

The Egyptian analysis in 1969 was shot through with miscalculation that was critical to the defeat of Israel's deterrent strategy. In assessing the balance of capabilities and Israel's likely response, Egyptian leaders overestimated their own capacity to determine events and underestimated that of their adversary. In planning a strategy of local and limited war that would nevertheless culminate in a canal crossing, they denied unpleasant inconsistencies central to the analysis. In anticipating massive casualties among Israel's forces, casualties that would nevertheless provide only a limited military response, Egyptian analysts tolerated logical contradiction in their expectations that can be explained only by some dynamic of wishful thinking. These errors were not the product of constrained information processing: Egyptian leaders were not confronted with a steady stream of new evidence. Nor did they grow out of biased estimation of probabilities: the usual heuristics of anchoring, availability, and retrievability were not relevant since Egyptian planners confronted a strategic dilemma with no precedent in their national experience. The biased estimates stemmed rather from processes of inconsistency management in response to an extraordinarily difficult and painful value conflict: Egypt could neither accept the status quo nor sustain a general military challenge. In seeking to escape this dilemma, Egyptian leaders embarked on a poorly conceived and miscalculated course of military action rather than acknowledge the value conflict and make the difficult trade-offs. In 1969 Israel's deterrent strategy failed not because it was badly designed but because Egyptian calculations were so flawed that they defeated deterrence. What Israel's leaders did not do, however, was recognize the costs to Egypt of a perpetuation of the status quo, costs that were so heavy that they were likely to promote motivated errors like wishful thinking and denial in an effort to escape an intolerable dilemma.

Much had changed by 1971. The available referent to Egyptian planners was now the War of Attrition, and they believed Israel's repeated threat to retaliate with a general attack should Egypt attempt to renew limited military action. Israel's deterrent strategy and Egypt's experience ruled out the option of attrition warfare. Yet no other military option seemed feasible, much less attractive. Despite the strong air defense capability provided by Soviet personnel who manned an extensive and well-integrated anti-aircraft system, Egyptian military leaders argued strongly that Egypt was still incapable of a general attack across the canal. The general staff emphasized the lack of bridge-building equipment and aircraft that could strike at bases deep within Israeli-held territory. Again and again, senior Egyptian officers demanded improved offensive capability in the air as well as the equipment to strike at Israel's population centers to deter renewed strategic bombing of Egypt's civilians.[19] In 1971, after seriously considering a challenge, President Sadat was deterred.

Deterrence held again one year later. Following the expulsion of Soviet military advisers from Egypt in July 1972, Egyptian officers were even more pessimistic in their evaluation of the military balance. Senior commanders strongly opposed President Sadat's directive to prepare to attack in mid-November 1972. At an acrimonious meeting of the Armed Forces Supreme Council on 24 October, the commander of the Third Army, General Wasel, the commander in chief, General Sadeq, and the vice minister of war, General Abdel Qader Hassan, all opposed military action, arguing that even a limited ground operation without adequate offensive capability in the air could turn into a disastrous defeat. General el-Shazli, commander of the Red Sea District and a member of the general staff, acknowledged that Egypt's air force had limited capability to provide cover and ground support for offensive operations and that the army was deficient in its ground transport capability. He suggested nevertheless that Egypt did have the capability to mount a limited operation across the canal. The commander of the Third Army insisted, however, that both offensive and defensive capability were inadequate even for a limited operation. The commander of the central district, General Ali Abdel Khabir, was even more alarmist in his insistence that Egyptian capabilities were decreasing rather than increasing in comparison to those of Israel; the trend was adverse.[20] Two days later, President Sadat dismissed the principal dissenters and confirmed as chief of staff General el-Shazli, the leading proponent of attack for limited military objectives. General Ahmed Ismail Ali became the new minister of war.

By May 1973 the pessimistic evaluation of the military balance had changed significantly, not only in response to accelerated arms deliveries from the Soviet Union, which had resumed in early 1973, but also, and equally importantly because of the reorientation of Egypt's military strategy. The general staff was now planning a canal crossing and a ground offensive that would not exceed the range of a dense anti-aircraft system. Consequently, the absence of offensive capability in the air became considerably less important. Nevertheless, Egyptian commanders and even the president were uncertain of Egyptian capability to mount a successful attack, even if the campaign were limited. They worried about their capacity to move troops quickly across the canal and to storm the formidable defensive fortifications Israel had built along the east bank. Egyptian officers wanted additional time to absorb new deliveries of Soviet equipment and to coordinate planning with the Syrian armed forces. Egyptian military and civilian leaders decided to delay the planned military action. At the end of August, after Soviet delivery of the long-promised SCUD missile, which could strike at Israel's population centers, the receipt of large numbers of antitank and anti-aircraft missiles, and intensified joint planning with Syria, Sadat estimated that Egypt, though still inferior to Israel, had nevertheless reached the zenith of its capacity. Egypt was unlikely to achieve military parity with Israel in the foreseeable future, nor was it likely to receive further significant military aid. The president concluded that this would be Egypt's best chance for several years to come.

This overview of Egyptian military calculations from 1971 to 1973 suggests at least two conclusions, both of which again challenge conventional wisdom about conventional deterrence. First, an estimate of inferior military capability was only a temporary deterrent to a use of force. When Egyptian military leaders first began serious consideration of a military option, their negative assessments of the military balance dissuaded them from a use of force. As expected, they emphasized their inferior offensive capability. A determined president, however, replaced these military leaders and challenged their successors to develop a military strategy to compensate for strategic weakness. Egypt's generals did just that. A new set of senior officers planned force deployments, adapted military technology, and built deception into their strategy to confound the advantage of their opponent. By multiplying military advantage through surprise, Egyptian officers hoped to meet their limited military objectives even from a position of military inferiority. This reading of Egyptian estimates of the military balance over time underlines the frailty of superior military capabilities as a durable deterrent to a use of force. An unfavorable estimate of the military balance was not an insuperable barrier but an obstacle to be overcome.

Second, more important than the negative assessment of the military balance in the debate about the use of force was the evaluation of trends in relative capabilities. When military officers saw a growing gap in relative capabilities in the autumn of 1972, they opposed the use of force. But when the president considered that Egypt's capabilities had peaked and that decline was likely in the future, he urged his generals to attack. A negative assessment of future rather than present capabilities was an essential component in Egyptian calculations. Here Egypt behaved very much as did Japan in 1941.

Were these Egyptian military estimates generally complete and accurate? Unlike their assessment of the interests at stake, Egyptian leaders paid attention to all the obvious elements of military capability: the balance of capabilities, trends in that balance, and the capacity for offense and defense as a function of technology. Quite legitimately, they did not evaluate the likelihood of rapid military success since their estimate of the military balance precluded strategies of blitzkrieg and quick decisive victory. In 1971 and 1972, moreover, their analysis was generally correct: Egypt did not have the offensive capability to mount a general attack.

By the spring of 1973, however, after Egyptian strategy had been reformulated and the ground forces equipped with Soviet antitank as well as anti-aircraft missiles and other military supplies, the general staff underestimated their army's capability to cross the canal and hold a limited amount of territory. The estimate was quite different in Israel. In April of that year, Israel's military intelligence estimated that Egyptian forces had the capability to cross the canal, but that they would not do so because of their continuing emphasis on their inadequate capability in the air.[21] The paradox is striking: Egypt could but thought it couldn't, while Israel thought Egypt could but wouldn't because Egypt thought it couldn't. It is not difficult to trace the origin of the Egyptian miscalculation. Both in 1967 and more recently during the War of Attrition, Egyptian ground forces had suffered badly at the hands of Israel's air force. These available and salient analogies explain both the inordinate emphasis by the Egyptian general staff on offensive aerial capability and their underestimation of their ground forces. In the spring of 1973, Egyptian miscalculation reinforced rather than defeated Israel's strategy of deterrence. By October 1973 this miscalculation had been partially corrected, and deterrence failed.

Egyptian evaluations of the military balance were the central component in determining the timing of their challenge to deterrence. Their estimates of military capabilities, however, did not have quite the impact one would expect from a reading of formal, prescriptive theory. First, in all five cases, military leaders dismissed completely the feasibility of an offensive strategy and rapid military success, but nevertheless challenged deterrence twice. And in only one of these challenges did they consider the military balance favorable; an estimate of inferior military capability did not preclude a use of force. Second, over time even unfavorable estimates served as a spur rather than as a barrier to Egyptian officers, who designed a strategy to compensate for acknowledged military weakness. Third, leaders weighed their estimates of the trends in the military balance heavily in deciding whether or not to use force. Finally, misperception of military capabilities occurred at least twice, but its impact varied. In 1969 miscalculation defeated deterrence, but in May 1973 it reinforced deterrence.

Estimates of the Bargaining Space

A third component in the calculus of leaders is their evaluation of the alternatives to a use of force. Formal theories of deterrence pay no explicit attention to diplomatic options; they concentrate exclusively on the likely costs and benefits of the single option of military action. More recently, empirical investigations of the workings of deterrence have suggested that a challenger may abstain from a use of force if its leaders see a plausible diplomatic alternative to military action. If, on the other hand, leaders consider that no option but military action can bring about the minimum change they require, and if this judgment is reinforced by a sense of urgency, then deterrence failure becomes likely.[22] I explicitly move beyond consideration of the single option of military action to assess both the impact and the accuracy of leaders' evaluation of bargaining space.

In examining the perceptions of Egypt's leaders, one notices a very modest relationship between a pessimistic estimate of bargaining space, a low expectation of a favorable diplomatic outcome, and a use of force. In the first of the five cases, there was no relationship, a priori, between the estimated bargaining space and a challenge to deterrence: in 1969 President Nasser excluded diplomatic negotiations as a policy option. When the four-power talks began at the United Nations that year, he urged the Soviet Union to make no concessions and insisted that what had been lost by force could be regained only by force.[23] It is not surprising, given Nasser's rejection of diplomacy, that he moved to a strategy of military attrition. This was no longer so after Sadat assumed the presidency in 1970. In February 1971, in a speech to the People's Assembly, Egypt's president departed from past practice and offered to sign a peace agreement with Israel in return for a full withdrawal to the borders of 4 June 1967.[24] Sadat explicitly rejected the normalization of relations but expressed interest in a diplomatic resolution of the conflict. Shortly before, Israel's minister of defense had proposed an interim agreement along the canal, a proposal received with some interest by President Sadat. For the next several months, the U.S. secretary of state worked on the details of a partial agreement. Although the two sides were unable to agree on terms, throughout most of 1971 Egypt's leaders did see some alternative to force and actively pursued diplomatic options even while they prepared for military action.[25]

They were considerably less optimistic by the end of 1972. Diplomatic negotiations were stalemated, and, in a speech to the Arab Socialist Union that December, President Sadat argued that there was no alternative to a use of force if Israel were to be dislodged from the occupied territories.[26] At the same time, however, Sadat engaged in private diplomacy with the United States in an effort to get the United States to exert pressure on Israel to alter its bargaining posture, and that autumn secret negotiations through a "back channel" began between Henry Kissinger, then national security adviser to President Nixon, and Hafez Ismail, his counterpart in Cairo.[27] At least in these two cases—when Egypt did not resort to force—its leaders could see some prospect, no matter how dim, of diplomatic progress. Scope for bargaining, though not large and constantly diminishing, nevertheless did exist.

Even this residual hope of diplomatic progress had disappeared by 1973. In his May Day speech President Sadat acknowledged that negotiations with the United States had failed to produce results and again concluded that Egypt would not receive help from any quarter unless it took military action to break the deadlock.[28] Six months later Egypt challenged Israel's deterrent strategy.

An evaluation of even modest diplomatic prospects does appear to have made some contribution to the success of deterrence, at least for Egypt between 1969 and 1973. Egyptian leaders did not resort to force when they entertained some hope of diplomatic progress but did so when they considered negotiations fruitless. This is not to suggest that these assessments were sufficient in and of themselves to determine the outcome of deterrence; far from it. Other considerations—the estimates of military trends, for example, and the sense of urgency—were crucially important in determining whether or not to challenge deterrence. Thus, although Egyptian leaders were not optimistic about the prospects of bargaining in the spring of 1973, they did not resort to force then because of their expectation of future military aid that would help to compensate for ongoing military inferiority. However, even in the hostile climate that then prevailed between Egypt and Israel, estimates of the prospects of bargaining did contribute, to some degree, to the success or failure of deterrence.

Because there are no objective boundaries to a bargaining range, it is far more difficult to evaluate the accuracy of estimates of the scope for bargaining than it is to assess their impact. Generally, leaders first set the minimum limits for bargaining and then consider whether or not negotiation promises to reach these thresholds. In Egypt's case, evaluation of the prospects of negotiation within the given limits was generally accurate, but the limits themselves often precluded negotiation. Bargaining was excluded not through miscalculation, however, but because of an unwillingness to meet the minimum criteria of the adversary. By 1969, for example, President Nasser had ruled out recognition of and negotiation with Israel; given these limits, he was of course accurate in his estimate that there was no scope for bargaining. In 1971 President Sadat extended Egypt's limits, and his estimates of very modest prospects seem reasonable. In 1973, after two years of indirect bargaining with an at times not very enthusiastic United States—bargaining that failed to produce tangible results within the limits imposed by both Egypt and Israel—Sadat's pessimistic evaluation was appropriate.[29] Bargaining failed not through miscalculated moves or misread signals but for the far more fundamental reason of mutually exclusive objectives. Consequently, deterrence failed not because leaders misinterpreted the intentions of their adversary but because they preferred military action to diplomatic concession.

Calculation of Likely Costs and Benefits of Alternatives

Egyptian valuations of the interests at stake, their estimates of military capabilities, and their assessments of the alternatives to military action were the crucial components in their final calculations about a use of force. Central to the theory of deterrence is the assumption that leaders make rational choices, that they estimate the probable consequences of a use of force and conclude that the likely costs of military action exceed its expected benefits. Consequently, if challengers do not calculate expected cost and benefit, if they do not choose the option that maximizes expected value, then they cannot be judged rational, and deterrence cannot work as expected.[30] Still working with the postulate of rationality, some scholars have reformulated classical deterrence theory to argue that leaders do not compare expected cost and benefit of action but rather assess the likely losses of action and inaction; they compare the "alternative risks" of action and inaction and choose the least damaging option.[31] Here the minimization of expected loss rather than the maximization of expected gain is the decision rule. The reformulation is not trivial: it directs our attention beyond military action to assessments by leaders of the likely costs of accepting the status quo. But, whether a challenger minimizes loss or maximizes gain, formal statements of deterrence assume some variant of a probability-utility calculus and rational choice as the critical mechanism of decision.

Psychological explanations question this fundamental assumption of rational choice. There is some evidence that leaders at times do approximate relaxed norms of comparative calculation and efficient choice, but most empirical studies of national security decision making document considerable deviation from the formal requirements of a probability-utility calculus. Leaders often weigh only one option at a time and have considerable difficulty identifying the relevant consequences of options, much less calculating their likely cost and benefit.[32] Cognitive psychologists who have examined risk taking in controlled environments find that people tend to pay far more attention to payoffs than they do to probabilities.[33] If this proposition were to hold in international politics as well, leaders would not, contrary to the expectations of the rationality postulate, weight all parts of the deterrence equation equally. When calculations are obvious because interests and consequences are prominent, these deviations from rational norms may have little impact on the outcome of deterrence. If, however, consequences are numerous and interests varied, the more finely tuned calculations that are required may prove too demanding of a challenger and defeat deterrence.

To assess the rationality of Egyptian decision making and its impact on deterrence,[34] one looks to the number of policy options leaders considered and to their identification of the consequences of these options. Did Egypt's leaders list the obvious consequences, examine their likely cost and benefit, and compare policy alternatives? If they even roughly approximated these procedures, then they met the minimum requirements of procedural rationality. If, however, they deviated significantly from these norms, were their miscalculations of sufficient magnitude to defeat deterrence?

It is immediately apparent that Egyptian leaders deviated grossly from norms of rational procedure in making their decisions about the use of force. The significance of these deviations, however, is not clear: biases in the process of choice persisted both when deterrence succeeded and when it failed. Leaders were most adept at structuring the problem and identifying policy options, but their processes of estimation and evaluation bear little resemblance to the archetype of rational choice required by formal theories of deterrence.

In 1969, for example, Egypt's leaders put four options on the table: a direct frontal attack across the canal; an aerial strike; a strategy of attrition; and continued inaction. A problem structure of four options is a good approximation to rational norms, but leaders estimated the consequence of these options far less thoroughly. Some of the consequences were obvious. Military officers were unequivocal in their estimate that a direct attack would lead to defeat; they considered that such an attack required a two-to-one force ratio in favor of the challenger, and Egypt simply did not have that advantage. Similarly, a first strike in the air would fail: Israel's air force was always on full alert; Egypt's fighters and bombers did not have sufficient range to strike deep at Israel's bases; its interceptor aircraft, the MIG-21, was slow and vulnerable; and Israel had a capable air defense. The third option, continued inaction, would lead to an unacceptable perpetuation of the status quo.[35] By a process of elimination, the only remaining option was a strategy of attrition.

Ironically, however, Egyptian leaders were least thorough in costing this option. As we saw, they miscalculated Israel's response, anticipated a canal crossing within eight weeks, and spoke only in very general terms of casualties and damage to economic and civilian installations in the canal zone, losses they judged acceptable. In discussing these consequences, Egyptian leaders offered almost no quasi-probabilistic estimates; only once, when considering a direct military attack, did officers estimate that at best a canal crossing stood a 50 percent chance of success. It can be argued, perhaps, that a strategy of attrition, unlike the alternative policy options, did not require as finely tuned calculations; leaders could monitor the program and its costs and continually reassess whether it was worth continuing. Egyptian leaders did consider the likely consequences of attrition, however, but spoke in the language of certainty. Theirs was not an attitude of trial and error. Because their judgments were categorical, they could not, by definition, have approximated a probability-utility calculus in making their choice. In 1969 Egypt's decision to challenge deterrence was the product of a highly simplified and biased process of estimation, a process that ignored probabilities and emphasized loss.

It is not surprising that a biased process of choice should precede deterrence failure, but very much the same kind of decision making occurred when deterrence succeeded. Under President Sadat, military and civilian leaders emphasized the losses of the options they considered and again resorted to categorical judgments of certainty rather than estimates of likelihood. In 1971 and 1972 military officers debated the merits of the three alternatives of general attack, an attack for limited objectives, and inaction; by the spring of 1973 they had eliminated a general attack as an option. Both when they chose war and when they refrained from action, Egyptian leaders paid a great deal of attention to the losses that would accrue from inaction as well as action.

As early as 1971, after learning from his minister of finance that the treasury was virtually bankrupt, the president concluded that Egypt's economy could not recover as long as Egypt took no military action. Sadat was also pessimistic about the political and diplomatic consequences of inaction; his argument that time was running out as Egypt came face-to-face with "lasting facts" reflected his sense of urgency. And as I have pointed out, the general staff also considered that the losses of action would be grave. Moreover, so resonant were the memories of 1967 and 1969–70 that Heikal argued that war should not be initiated until victory was "certain."[36] In 1971 leaders dealt in certainties, not in probabilities. They were certain and negative about the consequences of both action and inaction. Theirs was a painful choice.

One year later the dilemma had become even more acute. The president warned that if the stalemate were not broken, there would be serious domestic disturbances. He worried also that postponement of action month after month would consolidate the cease-fire: "the world will forget our problem."[37] On the other hand, Sadat too was unwilling to risk war if defeat were even possible. "We cannot go to war unless victory is guaranteed. The country cannot take another defeat."[38] On this point his generals were pessimistic: while most spoke of the unfavorable certainties, some did worry about the uncertainties. General Ismail, at that time the head of the National Intelligence Service, warned that a renewal of attrition would invite a 'certain" and sharper response from Israel, while General Hassan, the vice-minister of war, considered the uncertainties so great that even limited military action could develop into a full-scale offensive very quickly. The commander in chief, General Mohammad Sadeq, in turn firmly opposed a large-scale attack that might lead to "disaster."[39] Again, leaders made no reference whatsoever to benefits from either action or inaction. They thought in terms of loss and compared the costs of action to those of inaction.

In the spring of 1973 President Sadat spoke again of the "explosive" consequences of continued inaction, the intolerable impact on domestic morale, and the alarming deterioration of Egypt's position in the Arab world.[40] He still anticipated substantial losses, however, from military action. Inadequate opportunity for coordination with Syria, deficiencies in deliveries of Soviet equipment, military readiness in Israel—all these factors dimmed the prospects of a use of force. The president also expressed reluctance to disrupt the Nixon-Brezhnev summit, a consequence that would follow inevitably from an Egyptian attack.[41]

By the end of the summer, however, President Sadat identified fewer losses from a use of force. The summit was over, extensive consultation had taken place between Egyptian and Syrian officers, and the president anticipated that military aid from the Soviet Union had peaked. Sadat subsequently recalled the Soviet estimate that an attack across the canal would probably entail the loss of 40 percent of Egyptian aircraft and a high level of military casualties, losses he did not consider insupportable.[42] He was graphic, however, in his evaluation of the losses of inaction: Egypt was the "laughing stock" of the Arab world, and its economy had "fallen below zero."[43] The choice was much easier than it had been six months earlier.

Evidence drawn from this look at Egyptian decision making shows, then, that contrary to the expectation of formal theories of deterrence, Egypt's leaders did not compare the likely gains and losses of military action. Rather, they concentrated heavily on projected loss and estimated the costs that would flow from a use of force and from inaction. Their estimates were rough and qualitative rather than precise. In formal language, civilian and military leaders saw no "good" choice, and so they considered "alternative risks" and concentrated on minimizing their losses. In considering these losses, however, they paid strikingly little attention to probabilities but focused almost exclusively on payoffs; this pattern is consistent with the expectations of cognitive psychologists and violates the norms of rational choice.[44]

If this pattern of decision making were to prove more generally valid, concepts of deterrence would have to accommodate a substantially revised mechanism of decision. This is so because prescriptive theories of deterrence assume rational choice on the part of a challenger in generating policy recommendations for the defender. The impact of a revised mechanism of decision on the design of deterrence strategies, however, is not obvious. Both when deterrence succeeded and when it failed, Egyptian leaders were remarkably consistent in their processes of choice: in all five cases, we find an overwhelming emphasis on loss but very little attention to the probabilities of these losses. Consequently, this particular pattern of ovesimplification and partial calculation cannot be associated with deterrence failure or success.

Calculation and Miscalculation: Their Impact on Deterrence

In an effort to develop an empirically based explanation of the outcome of deterrence, I began this inquiry by asking three sets of questions. First, what factors do leaders consider and what do they omit when they contemplate a challenge to deterrence? Do they, as deductive theories expect, weigh all parts of the deterrence equation equally, or are leaders systematically biased in what they include and what they ignore? Second, are there differences in the pattern of perception when deterrence succeeds and when it fails? And finally, do characteristic kinds of miscalculations have predictable kinds of consequences for the outcome of deterrence? To address these questions, and to compare the expectations of formal theory with evidence of how a challenger considers a use of force and chooses among available options, I examined Egyptian calculations at five points in time over five years.

What can be concluded from this examination of Egyptian thinking? First, caution must be the watchword here. This is only a partial analysis of Egyptian calculations. Second, the five cases are not truly independent of one another; on the contrary, what leaders thought and did at one point very likely influenced what they thought and did in subsequent consideration of the use of force. Finally, it is inappropriate to generalize to other cases in different historical contexts. Yet Egypt's response to Israel's deterrent strategy is in many ways an interesting and relevant case. First, deterrence here was conventional rather than nuclear. Conventional deterrence generally has received less attention over the last three decades, but it is terribly important. We need only look at the incidence of war during these last thirty years, wars that often threatened to embroil the nuclear powers, to appreciate its relevance. In the post–World War II period as well, conventional deterrence has been most frequently studied from the perspective of the defender, which, moreover, was trying to deter attack on smaller allies rather than on its own territory;[45] undoubtedly this is at least partly a function of the ready access to U.S. evidence. The case under scrutiny here is different in both respects: Israel was trying to deter an attack against its own forces rather than against an ally and, secondly, I look at the success and failure of deterrence from the perspective of the challenger. Finally, because there is good evidence that Egyptian leaders considered and rejected a use of force at least three times, deterrence success and failure can be compared, a comparison essential to the development of valid explanations of deterrence.

The overriding conclusion that emerges from this investigation is the limited usefulness of formal theories built around the concept of rationality in explaining the success or failure of deterrence. Its shortcomings are of three kinds. First, it did not identify some of the relevant dimensions of leaders' calculations. Formal statements of deterrence, for example, do not direct our attention to a challenger's estimate of the alternatives to force, yet this was an important component in Egyptian thinking. More troubling, when leaders did consider those factors identified by formal theory, their processes of evaluation and choice did not conform to the norms of rationality. Evaluation of their adversary's interests, for example, was generally unimportant in Egyptian estimates of Israel's likely response to a use of force. At least in this relationship, when the challenger considered a direct military attack against the defender, finely tuned calculations of relative interest were conspicuous by their absence. Nor did Egypt's leaders make their decisions about the use of force through some variant of a probability-utility calculus. In violation of the norms of rationality, they paid overwhelming attention to loss and virtually ignored probabilities; they did not weigh all components of the deterrence equation equally. Finally, and perhaps most damaging to a formal prescriptive theory of deterrence, the challenger did not always behave as expected even when its leaders considered the relevant factors and made the appropriate calculations. Although Egyptian officials evaluated multiple dimensions of capabilities and acknowledged their general military inferiority, they chose to challenge deterrence in 1973. To explain the workings of deterrence, one must look beyond formal deductive theories that purport to predict the outcome of deterrence and examine the perceptions of policy makers who are considering a possible resort to force.

This analysis of Egyptian calculations suggests that two perceptual parameters and two variables may help to explain the outcome of deterrence. First, Egyptian leaders valued their strategic interests highly when they chose to use force, but they did so also in the three cases when they were deterred. Consequently, an estimate of strong interest appears to be a necessary but far from sufficient component of deterrence failure. It is worth noting as well that Egypt's leaders paid more attention to their strategic interests than to the worth of the specific interests at stake. They talked less of the Sinai than of their reputation—and their humiliation. Second, Egyptian leaders paid overwhelming attention to loss when considering a use of force. What was unusual was not the focus on the losses of action but the heavy emphasis on those of inaction, both when deterrence succeeded and when it failed. And, far from becoming resigned to an unpleasant reality, over time Egyptian leaders were increasingly persuaded by their negative assessments of the economic, political, and diplomatic consequences of the status quo. Like an assessment of strong strategic interest, this emphasis by a challenger on the losses of inaction appears to be a necessary but insufficient condition of these deterrence failures.

What did vary were estimates of military capabilities and alternatives to force. When deterrence held, leaders did see some prospect of bargaining, but when they chose to use force, they had no hope of diplomatic progress. Egyptian leaders also resorted to force when they considered that they had local defensive superiority in the battle zone or that trends in the balance would further erode their capability. They made this decision despite their adverse estimate of the general military balance. Two points are relevant here. First, an estimate of inferior military capability was only a temporary deterrent to a use of force. Examination of a sequence of cases over time shows that such an estimate spurred military planners to design a strategy to compensate for weakness; given the ingenuity of the military mind and the flexibility of modern multipurpose conventional technology, development of such a strategy was only a matter of time. Second, an explanation of deterrence that ignores leaders' estimates of the bargaining range is seriously incomplete.

Finally, the evidence shows that the impact of misperception on the failure of deterrence is mixed. Certainly, misperception was rife throughout these five cases. Egyptian leaders ignored the interest of their adversary in all but one instance, and then they underestimated Israel's interests, but this gap in perception generally had little consequence for their estimates of the defender's response. Far more relevant were errors in the estimation of both their own and their adversary's military capabilities. Capability estimates at times were exaggerated or undervalued; very likely, the errors were both motivated and unmotivated. The impact on deterrence of over- and underestimation is, of course, quite different: when capabilities were exaggerated, miscalculation was central to deterrence failure, but when Egyptian leaders underestimated their military prowess, their misperception contributed to the success of deterrence. As has been noted, Egypt's leaders did not even roughly approximate the rational processes of choice anticipated by theories of deterrence. Yet here again the impact of biased estimation and decision did not appear to be terribly significant. Leaders were not more rational in the performance of essential decisional tasks when deterrence succeeded than they were when it failed.

Generally, the highly abstract formulations characteristic of so much of the writing on deterrence were of little help in pinpointing the critical expectations of Egyptian leaders as they considered a use of force. The practice often bore little resemblance to formal prescriptive theory. If there is to be a better fit between theory and practice, we must relax some of the norms of rationality and encompass the substance of leaders' expectations and their processes of decision making both when deterrence succeeds and when it fails. The agenda for research is clear.

4

■

CALCULATION, MISCALCULATION, AND CONVENTIONAL DETERRENCE II: THE VIEW FROM JERUSALEM

Janice Gross Stein

■ As a necessary complement to the analysis of Egyptian calculations in the last chapter, I turn now to an empirical examination of the other half of the deterrence equation, the calculations of Israel's leaders from 1971 to 1973. I do so to assess the impact of a defender's perceptions—and misperceptions—both on deterrence and on defensive preparedness. I begin with an assessment of the estimates by Israel's leaders of the capabilities and intentions of Egypt under President Sadat. How sensitive were Israel's leaders to the four critical dimensions of Egyptian calculations—their assessment of their intrinsic and strategic interests, their estimates of military capabilities, their evaluation of the alternatives to force, and, most important, their emphasis on loss? Did Israel's leaders anticipate a challenge to deterrence? Were there important motivated or unmotivated biases that skewed crucial judgments? Did Israel's leaders consider the possibility that deterrence was buckling before it visibly collapsed? Did they make obvious and important errors that could have been avoided, were they blinded by their own preconceptions, or were their judgments reasonable under the circumstances, the best that could be expected given the kind of evidence they had in an uncertain environment?

Second, I look at the definition of policy options by Israel's leaders and their processes of choice. Did they identify the obvious policy alternatives available to a leadership attempting to deter? Were they aware of the most important trade-offs among alternative policies, or did they treat their preferred option as the best possible on all dimensions, as the dominant strategy? What were the critical determinants of their choice? Here, too, I try to identify and assess the impact of both motivated and unmotivated bias on the decisions leaders made. In so doing, I evaluate the impact of misperception as one of several contributing factors to the failure to anticipate the collapse of deterrence in October 1973. These first two set of questions both address the scope of misperception and its impact on strategy.

Third, I struggle with the policy implications of misperception. Since misperception is deeply rooted and yet only one among multiple causes of deterrence failure, the remedies are far from obvious. Nevertheless, I ask how leaders can better hedge against the consequences of flawed estimates and partial calculations. Finally, I ask not only if the failure of deterrence could have been predicted but—the far more difficult question—of whether it could have been avoided. Could Israel's leaders have deterred an attack at all in 1973, even if they had not been captive to their conceptual schema? To address this issue, one must situate the strategic debate in its broader political context. An attempt to consider, if not answer, this broader question meshes evidence drawn from the calculations of both the challenger and the defender and examines the interactive sequences of perception and action to assess whether alternative and/or complementary strategies might conceivably have avoided war.

Just as formal theories of deterrence treat a challenger's intentions axiomatically, so they reason deductively to prescribe a defender's course of action. In so doing, they assume that leaders can accurately evaluate an adversary's intentions and military capabilities and that they can predict the impact of their statements and actions on the perceptions of a challenger. These are both highly problematic assumptions. Although it is unlikely in practice that a defender will choose among policy alternatives without considering the capabilities and intentions of a challenger, it is the kind of consideration that is at issue. Evidence of pervasive bias in these judgments is cumulating in empirical studies of the practice of deterrence.[1]

Misperception by a defender can have profound consequences at almost every stage in the design and implementation of a deterrent strategy. At a minimum, a defender's estimate of its adversaries' capabilities and intentions influences the formulation of basic commitments and their scope and specificity, as well as the modalities of signaling and communication.[2] The focus in this chapter, however, is not only on the impact of misperception on the development of deterrence as strategy and policy, but also on the effect of a defender's miscalculations on the outcome of deterrence. We look particularly at two kinds of misperceptions—miscalculation of both a challenger's intentions and its capabilities—and at two quite different kinds of consequences.

First, if a defender overestimates the hostility of a challenger's intentions, if its leaders anticipate a military challenge even though its adversary is not preparing to resort to force, their defensive action may provoke the very challenge they are trying to avoid. This is especially so when offensive preparations are indistinguishable from defensive measures, when the "security dilemma" is acute, as it so often is in the contemporary international system.[3] On the other hand, underestimation by a defender may seriously impair its capacity to respond should an adversary choose to challenge deterrence. If leaders underestimate the capabilities or misjudge the intentions of a challenger, if they are overconfident in the effectiveness of deterrence, they may well be surprised, caught unawares, and unprepared. They may fail to reinforce deterrence before a challenger is fully committed to military action, thus forfeiting the opportunity to avoid war. They may also delay the military action necessary to defend against attack.

In designing their deterrent strategies, leaders run different kinds of risks from different kinds of miscalculations. Overestimation can culminate in miscalculated escalation by an adversary and underestimation in surprise and defensive unpreparedness.[4] In our century, it is conceivable that the Kaiser and the Czar were entrapped by the first error in 1914 and Neville Chamberlain by the second in 1938–39.[5] And to compound the difficulty, these two kinds of errors are not independent of each other: as leaders try to avoid one, they become more vulnerable to the other.[6] In estimating Egyptian intentions and capabilities, Israel's leaders confronted precisely this dilemma.

Deterrence, Defense, and Miscalculated Escalation: Prevailing Strategic Assumptions

In the autumn of 1970 Israel's leaders reviewed the basics of their strategy toward Egypt and other Arab states. Deterrence had failed, and failed badly, twice within three years. In 1967 President Nasser had challenged deterrence by blockading the Straits of Tiran and, in so doing, propelled both sides into a war that neither had planned. In 1969 Egypt designed around Israel's military superiority and launched a long, punishing war of attrition that ended in military stalemate eighteen months later. These two challenges to Israel's deterrent strategy provoked a major debate among senior military officers about appropriate lines of defense but, equally important, a new concern among civilian as well as military leaders with unintended war and a heightened emphasis on deterrence.

Egypt and Israel read the results of the War of Attrition quite differently. Paradoxically, both sides claimed victory even though both had suffered serious losses. Although Egypt had failed to compel even a partial withdrawal by Israel from the territory it had occupied during the war in 1967, its leaders insisted that they had won a significant victory because they had neutralized Israel's air superiority over the canal zone. And with only one or two exceptions, Israel's civilian and military leaders insisted that they had prevailed: they had shown themselves capable of withstanding significant military pressure in a long war and had resisted Egyptian as well as international pressure to withdraw from the Sinai without compensating political concessions.[7]

The protracted and costly war had apparently settled little, and the lines of the conflict were, if anything, more clearly drawn. Egypt remained actively revisionist, frustrated and dissatisfied with the status quo. Some of Israel's leaders were well aware of the strong incentive to yet another challenge. The minister of defense, for example, spoke openly of the intense motivation in Egypt, Jordan, and Syria to attack to recapture lost territory.[8] Recognition of the incentive to challenge led to a renewed emphasis on military superiority as the basis of deterrence. And, following the War of Attrition, both the minister of defense and the chief of staff declared repeatedly that they would treat a limited military challenge as a prelude to a general war. Israel's leaders knew precisely what they wanted to deter, and consequently there was little ambiguity in the specification of the scope of deterrence and the accompanying commitment. Signals were clearly sent and clearly read: as we have seen, Egypt's leaders received and believed the signals.[9] After 1970 the principal and almost exclusive focus of Israel's deterrent strategy became a general attack. Egypt and Israel were agreed on the likely scope of a future military challenge.

Simplicity in the evaluation of the focus of deterrence was replicated—with much less reason—in Israel's examination of the calculus of its opponents and the likely conditions of deterrence failure. Military intelligence worked largely with one hypothesis, which was developed after the War of Attrition and strengthened by Egypt's expulsion of Soviet advisers in July 1972. This hypothesis or "conception" argued first that Egypt would not attack until the Egyptian air force could strike at Israel in depth and at Israel's airfields in particular, and second, that Syria would attack only in conjunction with Egypt.[10] This assessment of Egyptian thinking assumed rational cost-benefit calculation, as deterrence always does, and relied on evidence of Egyptian military thinking. Members of Egypt's general command had argued through a large part of 1972 that until the Egyptian air force acquired advanced medium-range bombers that could strike at Israel's airfields, a general attack was impossible. This Egyptian evaluation was known to Israel's intelligence and became the basis of its estimate: Egyptian evaluation of their capabilities emphasized net cost and constrained their intent to attack. Air superiority was and is a basic principle of Israel's strategic planning, and military intelligence was receptive to an evaluation by Egypt that stressed the deterrent effectiveness of Israel's air force: such an evaluation was consonant with Israel's expectations. An Egyptian attack, therefore, was considered unlikely before 1975, the earliest date by which Egypt could acquire and absorb the required aerial capability.

This analysis of the conditions necessary for challenge was plausible and convincing. It was not, however, sufficient. Heavy concentration on a single condition—improved aerial capability—and a single option—general attack across the Sinai—was a considerable oversimplification of Egyptian calculations and options. And in part because the argument was oversimplified, it would provide few indicators for civilian or military leaders to monitor and, simultaneously, prove extremely difficult to invalidate. Since the argument relied on Israel's estimates of Egyptian evaluation of their relative capabilities, the principal indicator of the probability of attack would be a change in Egypt's evaluation of its relative aerial capability. Such a change, logically, could occur only if there were a significant increase in Egypt's capabilities. A major change in Egypt's aerial capability, however, would not be a sufficiently sensitive indicator to be useful for estimation and decision. Because it measures aggregate changes in capabilities—which Egyptian leaders must perceive—it is more useful for long-term predictions than for short-term estimation. Military intelligence did use changes in aerial capability to forecast an Arab attack by 1975,[11] but this indicator could be of little use in estimating probable Egyptian action in the interim.

Consistent with their analysis of a change in capabilities as an indirect indicator of attack, Israel's leaders rejected statements of intention as indications of likely Egyptian action. In an interview given in April 1973, Elihu Ze'ira, the director of military intelligence, explained that intentions of Arab leaders frequently exceeded their capabilities; were these statements of intention to be treated as valid indicators, "the rhetoric could lead to frightening miscalculations."[12] Such concern was not misplaced, for threats of impending war had been voiced repeatedly since 1971. Foreign Minister Eban shared this analysis; commenting on the frequent threats by President Sadat to attack, Eban offered an explanation of bluff and suggested that Egypt's president was attempting to escalate pressure for diplomatic concession.[13] By the spring of 1973, political and military leaders alike rejected statements of intention as relevant evidence in estimating the likelihood of attack. The prevailing concept of deterrence concentrated on a change in Egypt's evaluation of its relative aerial capabilities and offered no guidelines for the interpretation and assessment of any other evidence.

This strong emphasis on one contingency and a single indicator was not fully accepted by all military and intelligence analysts until May 1973. Uncomfortable at times with a prediction based on a single factor, civilian and military leaders searched for tactical indicators unrelated to strategic assumptions. As early as 1969, long before the current analysis was established, Moshe Dayan, the minister of defense, suggested and rejected the use of one tactical indicator: concentration of troops along the cease-fire lines.[14] Concentration of troops had been a reliable and valid indicator before 1967, but since 1969 Egypt's army had been stationed regularly along the front line. Moreover, since January 1973 both Egyptian and Syrian assault forces had been deployed in position, missile and gun batteries were on continuous alert, and supply echelons were at the forward line. As forces were already concentrated, deployment could not indicate attack.

If deployment of Egypt's army could not serve as a tactical indication of attack, redeployment for offensive action might. At least three times before October 1973, however, Egyptian troops were redeployed and reinforced, but Egypt did not attack. In July 1971 the president of Egypt, Anwar el-Sadat, proclaimed a "year of decision," and in December Egyptian reserves and civilian vehicles were mobilized, field forces engaged in maneuvers, general formations of armor advanced toward the canal, bridging equipment was brought forward, and civil defense procedures were activated.

Egypt's president, addressing the troops, was explicit in his intention. "The time for battle has come. . . . The next time we shall meet in Sinai."[15] Military intelligence in Israel did not consider an attack very likely; the chief of staff at the time, General Bar-Lev, accepted the estimate and did no more than put the army on alert, reinforce selected units at the front line, and delay his scheduled retirement for a short time. For a citizen army that relied on mobilization of its civilian reserves, the response was modest. Egypt did not attack.

Again at the end of 1972, a second large Egyptian mobilization took place, differing only in detail from the preparations of the previous year. Field forces maneuvered, soldiers were recalled from leave, and construction of ramps and fortifications along the canal was accelerated. Civil defense units were not mobilized, however, nor did ground forces advance to the canal with bridging and crossing equipment. Moreover, earlier that year, in July, President Sadat had expelled Soviet military personnel. In so doing, in the estimation of Israel's senior military officers, he had further constrained Egypt's military option. Military and civilian leaders continued to receive a stream of information detailing the skepticism of the Egyptian general staff about its capability to wage war. Particularly important was the Egyptian estimate of its inadequate capability to strike at Israel's airfields and to deter strikes by Israel's aircraft against its civilian population. Nevertheless, a report was received from a "highly reliable source" that an attack was imminent. After reviewing the conflicting evidence, military intelligence estimated the probability of an attack as "low."[16] In a restrained response, the chief of staff, now General David Elazar, alerted the army and postponed plans to shorten conscript service. Again, Egypt did not attack.

By the spring and early summer of 1973, some of Israel's most senior officers, although not military intelligence, were alarmed. Again, Egyptian military preparations were extensive, and the secret transfer of sixteen Mirage fighters from Libya to Egypt was known to intelligence officers.[17] In an interview on 9 April, President Sadat spoke of his satisfaction with the pace of arms shipments from the Soviet Union and warned once more of the coming battle.[18] And during the third week of April, Israel again received a report from a "reliable source" that set a definite date for the impending attack.[19]

General Ze'ira, then head of military intelligence, reviewed the evidence on 13 April and again for meetings of the general staff on 16 April, 9 May, 14 May, and 21 May. Intelligence continued to receive a flow of documents reiterating the emphasis within the

Egyptian military on adequate capability in the air as a precondition to attack. These reports, which did not reach military intelligence directly but came through another intelligence channel, were circulated to senior civilian as well as military leaders. Drawing on this evidence, General Ze'ira concluded that no fundamental change in Egypt's evaluation of its own capabilities had occurred; deterrence still held. He suggested rather that by increasing tension, President Sadat was trying to improve the Arab bargaining position in the private talks soon to take place between Egypt and the United States and at the Nixon-Brezhnev summit scheduled for June. Sadat's strategy was one of coercive diplomacy, and consequently, alarm in Israel would invite U.S. pressure and accomplish Egyptian purposes.[20] Questioned subsequently at a closed meeting of the Foreign Affairs and Defense Committee of Israel's parliament, Ze'ira explained that although Sadat found it difficult to tolerate the status quo, all other available alternatives were worse.[21]

The head of the *Mossad*, the Central Intelligence Collection Agency, was skeptical of the analysis provided by military intelligence and, at one of the general staff meetings, challenged the assumptions on which the estimate was based. General Zamir suggested that Sadat's preconditions for war had been met: an invading Egyptian army could operate on the east bank of the Suez Canal under the protection of its missile umbrella, and the dense anti-aircraft system could defend Egypt's heartland against strategic bombing.[22]

The chief of staff was also concerned. Alluding to the fruitless exchange between Hafez Ismail and Henry Kissinger and to Egyptian frustration over the continuing deadlock, Elazar suggested that Egypt might be tempted to launch a military attack to force negotiations. Although the risks of a use of force were greater than its prospects, Sadat might chance military action rather than suffer the consequences of continued stalemate. Alternatively, it was possible, as military intelligence suggested, that Egypt was seeking to manipulate military tensions for political purposes; Sadat would go to the brink and then retreat. By military logic, Egypt should be deterred, but, the chief of staff concluded, he was not persuaded that Egypt would not attack.[23] A careful reading of the testimony of Elazar before the parliamentary committee on foreign affairs and defense demonstrated the difficulty the chief of staff encountered in interpreting evidence that could not discriminate between alternative interpretations of Sadat's intentions.

The minister of defense shared the concerns of his chief of staff but was also chary of needlessly alarming the United States and, consequently, inviting unwelcome pressure. Accordingly, pre-cautionary measures, falling far short of full-scale preparations to defend, were put into effect: the date of previously scheduled military exercises was advanced, the army was put on extended alert, major improvements to infrastructure and defense were undertaken, and a very small number of reservists—largely technicians—were mobilized.[24]

For the third time, Egypt did not attack. And when Egypt did not attack, confidence in the validity of redeployment as a tactical indicator decreased, while confidence in the validity of the strategic assumption increased. Indeed, it was only after this third large redeployment by Egypt failed to culminate in attack that the concept developed by military intelligence was accepted by the chief of staff and the minister of defense. Their skepticism of redeployment as a useful tactical indicator was founded not only in its repeated trial and failure but also in its inability to discriminate among multiple interpretations. It could indicate either preparation to attack or brinkmanship—which would support arguments of effective deter-rence and bluff.

When the same indicator is consistent with competing interpre-tations, with arguments of successful and failing deterrence, it is problematic as a guide to the interpretation of evidence and the estimation of likely actions. Nevertheless, all other tactical indicators had been eliminated, and the strategic argument offered by military intelligence had not been proven wrong even if it could not be proven right. In an uncertain environment, civilian and military leaders reluctantly accepted a concept of successful deterrence. Drawing on this concept, they would concentrate on the con-tingency of a large-scale attack and would approach their task with a single prediction and a related indicator that varied too slowly to be of much use. Yet other indicators were unconnected to a set of logical arguments and, moreover, were of questionable validity. By the summer of 1973 Israel's leaders were intellectually impover-ished: conceptual examination of deterrence was incomplete and tactical indicators insufficiently valid to assist in the difficult task of estimation.[25]

Just as the changed strategic climate affected the concept of deterrence, so it affected those of defense and miscalculated escala-tion. Here the war of 1967 was particularly relevant. Looking back on the three weeks preceding Israel's preemptive strike in 1967, some of the senior military officers argued that war grew out of miscalculation. Israel's large-scale military mobilization in response to Egypt's expulsion of the United Nations Emergency Force, though defensive in nature, was indistinguishable from preparation for offense. At best, Israel had misjudged Egypt's strategy: President Nasser had deliberately provoked a preemptive strike and so forced Israel to initiate the war it had wished to prevent. At worst, Egypt's president had misinterpreted Israel's defensive intentions as offensive.[26] Egypt's difficulty in distinguishing offensive from defensive intent flowed, in part, from Israel's reliance on a citizen army as the basis of defense. Standing forces are inadequate to defend, and reserves must be mobilized, but as units are called up in large numbers, the army acquires the capacity for attack as well as defense. And as it does so, an adversary is encouraged to strike first. Indeed, it was this line of reasoning that led Israel to preempt in 1967.

This concept of miscalculated escalation directly affected evaluation of an option of mobilization. Leaders considered that there were costs other than economic and consequences other than those of deterrence and defense to the call-up of reserve forces. The emphasis on miscalculation, moreover, was consistent with a status quo power; leaders who wished to preserve the status quo would be more reluctant to risk unintended escalation and consequent destabilization. The policy implications were obvious: no mobilization or preemption until and unless leaders estimated a high probability of deterrence failure. A concept of miscalculated escalation demands strong indication of an impending attack before any defensive response is appropriate. And leaders were restricted to a single indicator of deterrence failure. Until and unless Israel had evidence that Egypt had altered its assessment of relative capabilities in the air, or abandoned improvement in its offensive aerial capability as a requirement of attack, a defensive response could be premature and dangerous. Strategic concepts did not consider a range of responses that might differ in their escalatory potential yet be appropriate to different degrees of warning. Again, the argument was oversimplified: a single and restrictive criterion of warning, linked to a high probability requirement, reduced the attractiveness of all defensive options.

If mobilization was considered more dangerous than it had been before 1967, it was also deemed less necessary in the changed strategic conditions after 1967. Military leaders had adapted the concept of defense to extended frontiers, which decreased the danger to civilian centers and made mobilization less urgent. Plans assumed that tank battalions of the regular forces on the front, together with the air force, could contain an attack until the arrival of reserve forces.[27] General Yariv, the director of military intelligence until 1972, was explicit on this point.[28] In May 1973, respond-ing to a request by the minister of defense, the general staff prepared a series of contingency defense plans. In the south, regu-lar forces would reinforce front-line troops (Operation Dovecote), while the defense of the north required a limited mobilization of reserve units (Operation Chalk). If time were available, the full deployment of all reserve forces would be completed before an attack began (Operation Rock).[29] Strategic concepts and planning dealt, however, only with the two contingencies of complete warning or no warning at all.

A related though less important factor was recognition by civilian and military leaders of the economic and social costs of repeated cycles of mobilization. If Israel were to respond to every Egyptian mobilization with a countermobilization, it would have had to do so some twenty times since January 1973. Frequent mobilization, Min-ister of Defense Dayan explained, would disrupt the fabric of life in a country dependent on a citizen army.[30] The regular army and strategic depth were treated as substitutes for the frequent mobiliza-tion that would be necessary if Israel were to respond in a reciprocal fashion to Egyptian and Syrian military activity.

Concepts of defense and miscalculation interacted to reduce the likelihood that mobilization would be chosen as an appropriate response, especially if the warning were ambiguous. In their changed strategic environment, Israel's leaders were confident of military victory under almost any contingency of attack; strategic depth made early mobilization less necessary, and miscalculation made early mobilization more dangerous. These constraints would apply principally, however, to the mobilization of large numbers of reserves. A partial call-up would be much less likely to lead to unintended escalation; a selective reinforcement of front-line forces with armor and artillery was simply not a credible prelude to a general attack. Strategic concepts did not consider the probable impact of different levels of mobilization on deterrence, defense, and escalation; they did not systematically relate response to warn-ing and challenge. Again, strategic arguments were insufficiently articulated and differentiated.

This examination of the concepts of deterrence, defense, and miscalculated escalation, developed by both political and military leaders, has pointed to important areas of weakness in strategic thinking. Specifically, an undifferentiated concept of deterrence compounded the difficulties already inherent in estimation and warning. Similarly, a concept of defense that linked response only to unambiguous warning, while unusually sensitive to the danger of unintended war, was of little use in clarifying responses appropriate to varying likelihoods of deterrence failure and to the trade-offs among them.

These strategic concepts were not trivial. On the contrary, they served as collective systems of thought, as organized systems of belief that leaders used to organize and interpret information. Widely shared among civilian and military leaders, they were critically important in setting the parameters for the diagnosis of a problem, the interpretation of evidence, and the formulation of policy options. Insofar as they were widely shared, strategic beliefs would have a major impact on the estimation of their adversaries' intentions and on the choices that followed. This set of interrelated and mutually reinforcing concepts would prove to be a principal source of unmotivated error as Israel's leaders once again considered the possible failure of deterrence in the autumn of 1973.

Estimation and Decision: Warning and Mobilization

After a battle in the air between Syria and Israel on 13 September 1973, in which Damascus lost thirteen planes, Syria reinforced its armor and artillery, not an unusual response to such a major incident. Ten days later, however, Syria had not yet launched its expected reprisal but had intensified its military activity along the cease-fire lines. Egypt had begun its annual army maneuvers, this year with full divisional participation. Responding to the dense deployment of Syrian armor, artillery, and missiles, the minister of defense decided to bring Israel's armored force up to strength in conformity with standing plans. It was almost a routine decision: Israel anticipated some military response by Syria to the loss of its planes.

On 30 September the director of military intelligence, General Ze'ira, met with his staff to consider the growing troop concentrations. The evidence was not at all easy to interpret. Although the Egyptian army was deployed in battle formation, it had been so deployed several times before. These maneuvers were larger in size, but they had been increasing every year for several years, and this time civil defense organizations in Egypt were not activated, as they had been on previous occasions. However, in the early hours of the morning of 1 October, a report arrived alleging that that day, or at the latest on 6 October, Egypt and Syria would launch a full-scale attack.[31] After a long discussion that lasted into the early hours of the morning, military intelligence concluded that an attack was unlikely.

At a regular general staff meeting the next morning, General Ze'ira reported the results of the extended evaluation. Egypt had begun a large-scale multibranch exercise that would end on 8 October. The high level of alert was routine in an army on such large maneuvers. Alternatively, it was possible that Egypt mistakenly anticipated military action by Israel—Israel recently had conducted large paratrooper exercises in Sinai. The alert also might be designed to deter military action against Syria: Egypt viewed the air battle with Syria as a premeditated attack by Israel and was attempting to prevent any further military action. The alert could be defensive, deterrent, or the result of miscalculation.

Syria, too, was reinforcing its lines following the hijacking by Palestinians of a train carrying Soviet Jews to Vienna. Israel's analysts considered that Syria could be preparing a reprisal for the loss of its own planes or that it now anticipated (mistakenly) a reprisal by Israel for the hijacking and was taking appropriate defensive action. In a regress of expectations, military intelligence considered that Egypt and Syria, for quite different reasons, might miscalculate Israel's intentions. The director of military intelligence concluded that the probability of attack was low.

Military activity on the two fronts continued, and three days later, Minister of Defense Dayan asked for an informal meeting with the prime minister and her close advisers. The head of intelligence research reported some unusual deployment of artillery, but, on the other hand, there had been no activation of civil defense; critical indicators were inconsistent. He told those assembled that both armies were so deployed "that they were able at any moment to launch an attack."[32] Nevertheless, he concluded, although the capability to attack was present, "the possibility of an Egyptian-Syrian war does not seem likely to me, since there has been no change in their assessment of the state of forces in Sinai so that they could go to war."[33] To estimate likely Egyptian action, military intelligence relied on the single indicator derived from its strategic assumption: Egypt's evaluation of its relative military capabilities. More important than evidence of capability to attack was documentary evidence of perceptions by the Egyptian military of its inadequate capability. Additional explanations of routine activity and miscalculated fear of an attack by Israel were consistent with this estimate of Egypt's evaluation of its inadequate capabilities and could explain the scope of Egyptian military activity.

The prime minister asked whether additional troops were needed to strengthen front-line forces. Chief of Staff Elazar responded that if additional troops were transferred to the north, force levels in the south would be affected. Some mobilization of reserves, therefore, would be required, and if Syrian deployment along the lines persisted as it had in the past, the mobilization could be protracted. Alternatively, front-line forces could be strengthened by additional equipment. Elazar's rapid evaluation and elimination of partial mobilization as an option is not surprising. If the standing army could block an attack, which in any event was considered unlikely, mobilization of additional forces made little sense.

Dayan was considerably less sanguine, about both Syria's intentions and its capabilities. Most important, the forward deployment of anti-aircraft missiles could not be explained by the prevailing analysis; it was not consistent with a miscalculated Syrian estimate of an impending reprisal by Israel and suggested preparation for offense. In a then inconsistent use of the concept of miscalculation, however, the minister of defense concluded with the statement that he hesitated to issue orders "which would mobilize Syria to attack."[34] Dayan appeared to argue that defensive action by Israel could spark preemptive action by Syria—but such an argument is not consistent with his increased estimate of the probability of a Syrian attack. The implications of the two arguments were directly contradictory: the former called for caution, while the latter required strengthening of deterrence and defense. Although he used both, Dayan did not consider the contradiction inherent in his simultaneous use of the concepts of miscalculated escalation and defense.

Although the chief of staff shared the intelligence assessment that Egypt and Syria were technically capable of attack with little advance warning, he nevertheless concurred with the estimate that a coordinated attack was unlikely. He concluded, however, by reiterating his expectation that he would be given adequate warning of an attack. Indeed, most war-gaming had been premised on a warning period of two to six days, and he considered a warning of only twenty-four hours catastrophic. Yet this assumption of certain warning was logically inconsistent with Elazar's assessment that Egypt and Syria could attack with very little notice. The chief of staff paid no attention to this contradiction between these two critical expectations. Simply as a precaution, General Elazar authorized a transfer of additional armor and artillery to the more vulnerable northern border.

Late in the evening of 4 October, photographs from a special air reconnaissance mission revealed considerable strengthening of Egyptian forces along the canal and the forward movement of bridging equipment toward three different sectors of the front.[35] The director of military intelligence received other disquieting information that same evening: units of the Soviet fleet stationed near Alexandria and Port Said had begun to move out, and Antanov-22 aircraft had arrived in Cairo and Damascus to withdraw the families of Soviet advisers. Military intelligence considered at least three explanations of the withdrawal. First, the Soviet Union knew of an impending attack and, anticipating the military consequences of a counterattack by Israel, was withdrawing its personnel. Such an interpretation was alarming in its implications. Alternatively, if Soviet-Syrian relations had deteriorated badly, as some speculated, Syria might have requested all Soviet advisers to leave, but this would not explain why Soviet personnel were being withdrawn simultaneously from Egypt.[36] Third, it was possible that the Soviet Union had accepted Syrian allegations, broadcast repeatedly in the preceding several days, that Israel was about to attack.[37] Again, however, if this were so, Moscow would have asked Washington to warn Israel against attack, and no such warning had been received. Uncommitted yet to any explanation, the director of military intelligence considered the withdrawal so disquieting that he immediately informed the chief of staff. Within moments Elazar decided to alert the air force and mobilize its support personnel.

Throughout that night and the following morning, senior intelligence, military, and civilian leaders debated the significance of the Soviet withdrawal. General Ze'ira preferred the first of the three interpretations, even though it was inconsistent with his estimate that Egypt and Syria would not attack, that they were deterred. The other two explanations, as he pointed out, were inconsistent with the evidence. Yet, General Ze'ira did not pursue his reasoning to its logical conclusion. Rather, in a series of briefings to military and civilian leaders the next morning, he presented all three interpretations, two with their attendant qualifications, but accepted none, explaining that he did not know why Soviet personnel were being withdrawn and was awaiting further information. Here a critical opportunity to revise the estimate of a low probability of attack was missed.[38]

General Ze'ira also reported that the pace of military activity on both borders had quickened. In what appeared to be an offensive deployment, Syria had moved two squadrons of Sukhoi bombers to front-line air bases, and Egypt had sent additional tanks and artillery forward. After reviewing all the evidence, the director of military intelligence estimated that the probability of attack was still low. Nevertheless, his confidence in the success of deterrence began to waver, and he concluded by informing his colleagues that he anticipated confirmation of Egyptian intent from a "reliable" source within a few hours.[39] The chief of staff added that he, too, expected additional evidence if Egypt and Syria intended to attack. Because of the growing uncertainty, however, Elazar recommended a full-scale alert at the highest level.

The minister of defense concurred with the recommendation. Dayan considered the evacuation of Soviet personnel significant but again expressed his concern that any movement of Israel's forces could spark preemptive action by massed Arab armies. He urged that the United States be contacted to prevent any misunderstanding of Israel's intentions and that Washington be asked to persuade Moscow to restrain Egypt.[40] Dayan worked simultaneously with the hypotheses of failing deterrence and miscalculation, with the contradictory expectations of premeditated and preemptive attack. To resolve the contradiction between the two in the face of ambiguous evidence that could not validate either, he added that, even if Israel mobilized and preempted, it could not prevent an attack by massed Arab armies:[41] he discounted the value of mobilization to diminish the value conflict.

This was a critical series of meetings. If an option of mobilization were to have been seriously considered, it should have been debated that morning. Neither in the larger nor in the smaller meetings, however, did mobilization of reserves receive any consideration.[42] That it did not can be explained not only by the use of a single oversimplified concept, as the Agranat Commission, set up after the war to examine the causes of the intelligence failure, held, but, more important, both by the way military and political leaders and intelligence analysts used several interrelated concepts and by the inherent difficulty of the problem they were analyzing.

First, as the chief of staff subsequently made clear, mobilization was excluded unless and until there was "an evaluation that hostilities [were] about to break out."[43] Such an evaluation depended, largely, on a single concept, a single indicator, and a single source of information. But even if concepts had not been oversimplified and underdifferentiated, unambiguous warning would not have been likely. Such warning is almost always difficult because the evidence is frequently open to several plausible and conflicting interpretations. The Agranat Commission, for example, charged that the chief of staff had evaluated improperly the improvements to the descents to the canal in the three days immediately preceding the attack. Elazar responded, quite properly, that this kind of work had been done tens of times by Egyptian forces during 1972–73.[44] Unequivocal warning was unlikely, in large part because the evidence was ambiguous and intentions were difficult to estimate. The error lay in the specification of unambiguous warning as a necessary prelude to serious consideration of mobilization. That it was considered necessary can be explained largely by the reference, by civilian as well as military leaders, to the concept of miscalculated escalation. The chief of staff, for example, made explicit its causal connection to a refusal to mobilize. "In most cases, there were definite warnings of an attack, but we didn't mobilize because we feared this would cause escalation and war."[45] His concern was shared even more strongly by the minister of defense. Because leaders feared miscalculated escalation, unambiguous warning became the prerequisite to any deterrent or defensive action, and different levels of response were not calibrated to different kinds of warning. Warning and response became an either-or matter.

Finally, an estimate that defensive capability was adequate—even if deterrence failed—made mobilization less important. The Agranat Commission noted this confident evaluation of the capacity of the standing army to absorb and contain an Arab attack until reserves could reach the front.[46] Indeed, General Ze'ira relied on these assurances of adequate defensive capability to increase his margin for error, General Elazar relied on the assurances by military intelligence of adequate warning, and civilian leaders relied on both when they dismissed the need for further defensive action. Given estimates of low probability and limited loss from an attack, mobilization became unnecessary. Choice flowed ineluctably from the set of interrelated strategic assumptions.

Early the next morning, at 0340 hours, the director of military intelligence received a telephone call informing him that Egypt and Syria would attack that day at sunset. Meir and Dayan were informed immediately and arranged to meet later that morning. Warning had finally come. But when it did come, it was not unambiguous and not all decision makers were certain.

First, the message suggested that an attack still was not certain: President Sadat might postpone or cancel the offensive if he were informed in time that Israel now anticipated an attack. This ability to reverse course is a strategic asset for any challenger and compounds the problem of estimation for the defender.[47] Second, the reported timing of the attack was puzzling. Senior officers considered that the late hour would provide insufficient time for opening air strikes and, consequently, questioned the validity of the information.[48] And finally, it was not the first time this kind of warning had come from this source; the prime minister, the chief of staff, the minister of defense all attested to repeated warnings in the past.[49] The source and content of the message created uncertainty in the minds of some, and even the Agranat Commission would describe the report as "ambiguous."[50] The prime minister drastically revised her estimate of the probability of attack—"There was no doubt anymore"—but Ze'ira and Dayan were more reserved: war was very likely but not certain.[51]

At 0500 hours, Elazar informed the assembled general staff of the new intelligence and of his intention to act as if an attack were certain. He told his senior officers that he would propose large-scale mobilization of combat reserves and a preemptive air strike against Syrian airfields and missile emplacements. Dayan objected to the request for large-scale mobilization of reserves as militarily unnecessary and politically risky. Two divisions could adequately meet defensive needs, and, as the Agranat Commission noted, "the Defense Minister wished to delay the mobilization of this additional force so that no friendly country might possibly accuse Israel of causing a conflagration by escalation."[52] Not fully certain that an attack was imminent, and confident of the army's capacity to contain any attack that did occur, the minister of defense gave greatest weight to the international political implications of military action.

Dayan's decision was largely insensitive even to a substantial increase in the probability of attack. The two men could not agree and turned for decision to the prime minister, who acknowledged and resolved the contradiction between escalation and defense. She subsequently recalled the basis of her decision to mobilize large numbers of reserve forces. "I said . . . that I had only one criterion: if there really was a war, then they had to be in the very best position possible."[53] After inquiring what was needed not for adequate but for optimal defensive capability, Meir authorized a large-scale mobilization of forces. To make her decision, she simplified by eliminating all contingencies but the worst and all criteria but the best defense.

While the chief of staff and minister of defense were arguing, theater commanders were making final preparations for the anticipated attack. General Gonen, in charge of the southern front, informed the commander of the Armored Corps in the Sinai that an attack was expected that evening at 1800 hours but ordered the redeployment of tanks—as required by plans—postponed to avoid arousing Egyptian suspicions. At a general staff meeting later that morning, Dayan asked whether the tanks in the south had been ordered toward the front in conformity with Operation Dovecote or whether such deployment would await Egyptian fire and an attempt to construct cross-canal bridges.[54] Unaware of the operational orders issued by theater commanders, the chief of staff replied that three divisions were stationed in the south; one controlled the canal, and the rest were awaiting final information on the detailed Egyptian attack formation.

The chief of staff, General Elazar, had stated explicitly earlier that morning at the general staff meeting that he had no choice but to act as though an attack were certain. Orders and planning should proceed accordingly. Yet it appears that senior officers in Southern Command nevertheless considered miscalculated escalation a consequence not only of mobilization but also of the redeployment of regular forces. This redeployment was the central component of the concept of defense; it was the regular forces that were to block an initial attack and provide cover for mobilization of reserves. Moreover, the delay is understandable only if military commanders were highly uncertain of Egyptian intent. But they were not. Although Dayan and Ze'ira remained skeptical until the very last moment, Elazar had argued earlier that morning that he had no choice, given the accumulating evidence, but to assume that an attack was certain. In making this estimate, he had secured the prime minister's acquiescence and support. And once an attack was treated as though it were certain, miscalculation became irrelevant. Not only that, but it also competed with attempts to strengthen defense and reinforce deterrence. The general staff had been told that if President Sadat considered that Israel was prepared for an attack across the canal, he "might" postpone or cancel the planned offensive; redeployment of armor would provide visible signals of such preparations.

At 1355 hours, 240 Egyptian planes crossed the canal to bomb command posts, airfields, and radar installations, and 1,848 artillery guns opened fire simultaneously along the entire front. In the first ground attack at 1415 hours, Egypt sent 8,000 infantry across the canal, as well as commando and infantry tank-destroyer units to meet Israel's armor. To blunt the thrust of the Egyptian offensive, Israel had 3 tanks and 7 batteries of artillery deployed along a front of 160 kilometers. Two hundred seventy-six tanks were advancing toward the front but were too far behind the lines to assist in containing the initial attack. In the canal strongholds, there were 436 reservists isolated without support. In Tel Aviv, the mobilization of reserves had only just begun four hours earlier.

Misperception, Deterrence, and Defense: An Assessment

This examination of the calculations of the defender in a deterrent relationship generates rather sobering conclusions. Errors abounded with respect to estimates of both the challenger's intentions and its capabilities. The consequences of these errors were not trivial; they had a significant impact on the formulation of strategic policy and the choice among policy alternatives.

If one looks at the series of estimates of Egyptian intentions and capabilities generated by Israel's senior military and civilian leaders, if one tests the accuracy of these perceptions against the evidence now available of Egyptian calculations at the time, the record is not encouraging.[55] The estimates were correct twice—in 1971 and 1972, when deterrence did hold, when President Sadat was deterred by his estimate of Egypt's inferior military capabilities. They were "right" once for the wrong reasons—in the spring of 1973, when President Sadat chose not to attack, but not because of Israel's military superiority; and they were dreadfully wrong in the autumn of 1973, when Egypt and Syria did attack. The evidence of misperception, of underestimation, principally of Egyptian motivation to attack but also secondarily of its capability to attack, is considerable. These errors can be traced in the first instance to the heavy reliance on an oversimplified, single-variable concept of deterrence and to the structure of beliefs, to the interrelatedness of central concepts, that permitted leaders to ignore the inconsistencies in the evidence by moving from one concept to another. More important was the singular emphasis on the military dimensions of deterrence, the apolitical analysis of Egyptian strategy, and the insensitivity to the extraordinarily high Egyptian estimate of the costs of inaction. I examine first the errors in cognitive processes and then the larger political context of deterrence.

Israel's leaders relied heavily on a stream of evidence detailing Egyptian evaluation of its own capabilities. Their perception was fairly accurate from 1971 through 1972, but much less so after Egypt began to receive enormous amounts of military equipment from the Soviet Union in the spring of 1973. Indeed, Israel's military intelligence distinguished between its own evaluation of Egyptian military capability and that of Egyptian leaders themselves. Analysts in military intelligence were more sanguine about Egyptian capability; they insisted repeatedly that Egypt had the capability to attack across the canal even while they were reading detailed descriptions of the doubts of the Egyptian general staff. Nevertheless, even though the misperception of Egyptian capability was less than that of their Egyptian counterparts, Israel's general staff did underestimate the impact of a dense antimissile system on the capacity of its air force to operate over the canal zone and the consequent damage that the Egyptian army could inflict on the standing army in the first forty-eight hours of an attack. Even this allegation of error is questioned by some, however, since the contingency defense plans to meet and contain an Egyptian attack were never put into effect; the accuracy of the original estimate and the consequent validity of the standing defense plans are still debated among Israel's generals.

More to the point than the underestimation of Egyptian capability is the overwhelming weight given to Egyptian perceptions of its relative military capability in the general analysis of Egyptian intentions. Israel's analysts were receptive to evidence of an Egyptian evaluation of its inferior capability, particularly in the air, for two quite different reasons. First, an emphasis on air superiority had been central to Israel's strategic planning for decades. The bias induced by availability would suggest that evidence so consistent with Israel's strategic perceptions would resonate; here the receptivity of Israel's leaders reflected unmotivated error.[56]

Second, and even more important, Israel's leaders paid very little attention to a second critical component in Egyptian calculations—the emphasis on the growing losses of inaction and the consequent urgency to act. Only once or twice did the senior leadership make reference to this dimension of Egyptian perceptions. Yet, as I found, this was a critical variable in the Egyptian decision to challenge deterrence. Although the evidence does not permit conclusive interpretation, it is likely that this was a motivated error: the consequences of focusing on an Egyptian perception of frustration and loss were unpleasant, forcing some consideration of diplomatic alternatives that would change the status quo. This kind of misperception is apparently not uncommon. Lebow finds in his investigation of brinkmanship that defenders frequently underestimated the strength of their adversary's motivation to alter the status quo.[57] Here motivated bias reinforced unmotivated error to sustain a unidimensional perception of Egyptian intentions.

The interrelatedness among the three central strategic concepts—deterrence, defense, and miscalculated escalation—also generated serious unmotivated errors which affected not only the perception of Egyptian intentions but also the consideration of policy options. The contradiction came not between the policy implications of deterrence and defense—here the two were compatible, although they need not necessarily be—but rather between deterrence and defense, on the one hand, and miscalculated escalation on the other.

It should be noted first that the concept of miscalculated escalation was an inaccurate reading, even with the benefit of hindsight, of Egyptian intentions in 1967. Although he did not intend to go to war in May 1967, although he did not plan an attack, President Nasser, provoked in part by his wider Arab constituency, took a series of steps that built toward confrontation. Ultimately, Nasser chose to provoke a first strike by Israel to ensure its diplomatic isolation.[58] There is no evidence to suggest that Nasser was acting in fear, that he was preparing to preempt because he anticipated a first strike by Israel; on the contrary, he awaited a first strike with confidence because he had overestimated Egyptian military capability and its capacity to absorb and then respond to an attack. If there was miscalculation, it derived from Nasser's misperception of Egyptian capabilities, not of Israel's intentions, and from the broader phenomenon of "autonomous risk," from the loss of control as a conflict begins to spiral.[59] This was not the understanding of Israel's leaders in 1973. They mistakenly argued that their premature defensive preparations had been interpreted by Egypt as offensive intent. That Israel's leaders would so misperceive Egyptian intentions, even with the benefit of hindsight, is somewhat surprising; such empathy with an adversary's fears is rare. Perhaps their reading of Egyptian intentions can best be explained as the mirror image of their own reasons for preemptive attack in 1967. Israel's senior military leadership then had feared a premeditated Egyptian attack, and it was precisely this fear that motivated its urgent demand for a preemptive strike. It is conceivable that a cognitive bias of availability now worked to encourage Israel's leaders to transpose their remembered fears to their Egyptian counterparts.

The interconnectedness among these three critical organizing concepts—one, miscalculated escalation, flawed in interpretation, and another, deterrence, flawed in its unidimensional simplicity—had serious consequences both in the misperception of Egyptian intentions and in the consideration of policy options. First, and most directly, evidence of Egyptian behavior inconsistent with successful deterrence could easily fit with a concept of miscalculated escalation. The availability of this second concept permitted leaders to deny rather than confront inconsistency in their estimate of Egyptian intent. Second, and particularly striking, was the establishment of near certainty of attack as a prerequisite for response. This prerequisite flowed directly from the strong emphasis on miscalculation by civilian as well as military leaders. This kind of search for certainty must leave leaders poorly equipped to deal with the ambiguity that is always characteristic of a policy environment where the intentions of another can never be determined with certainty.

Third, the interrelatedness among these three concepts made it easy for leaders to ignore the trade-offs when they considered whether or not to reinforce deterrence. Mobilization was unnecessary because deterrence was succeeding. In any event, it was unnecessary because the standing army could adequately defend until the reserves arrived at the front, and, in addition, it was dangerous because it could spark a preemptive attack when no attack was premeditated. By reference to prevailing concepts, leaders quickly identified a "dominant" strategy. Although this dominance of a preferred option is explained satisfactorily by cognitive predispositions, motivated error may also have played a minor supporting role. The evidence here is far more speculative and open to question, but in October 1973 Israel's leadership was in the midst of an election campaign, eager to demonstrate the benefits of its stewardship of foreign and defense policy, the efficacy of Israel's deterrent strategy. A mobilization of reserves in the middle of an election contest and on the eve of the holiest of Jewish holidays would have alarmed the electorate and reminded them of the ongoing security threat. It is not unreasonable to speculate that Israel's civilian leadership engaged in some wishful thinking when it studiously avoided the trade-offs among alternative policy options.

An important caveat is in order here. Although the explanatory power of cognitive predispositions and biases, supplemented secondarily by motivated error, is strong and persuasive, its weight in a broader explanation of failures in estimation and decision is yet to be established. Obviously important, for example, are the difficulties inherent in the task, the bias to misperception built into the policy environment. Misperception is induced by cognitive dynamics but facilitated by the difficulties of estimating an adversary's intentions in an uncertain and complex international environment. The difficulty in distinguishing offensive from defensive preparation, for example, clearly complicates assessment of an adversary's intentions.

When intentions cannot be inferred from capabilities, as they cannot be when offense is indistinguishable from defense, analysts must look elsewhere for relevant evidence. Israel's analysts acknowledged this difficulty and perforce turned to documentary evidence of Egyptian intentions, documents they considered to be valid. And these documents were accurate, at least in 1971 and 1972. But when the Egyptian evaluation of its military capability began to change, as it did in the spring of 1973, the flow of documentary evidence did not. Egyptian officials have suggested subsequently that Egypt knew that Israel knew of Egyptian military doubts and that, consequently, Egypt continued to provide "disinformation" that emphasized Egyptian skepticism of its own capability long after the change in military strategy made this skepticism less relevant.[60] And, as Whaley argues in his classic study of military deception, there is little defense against disinformation that is consonant with existing preconceptions.[61]

It was impossible, of course, for intelligence officials in Israel to distinguish a priori between disinformation and valid information. Their only recourse was to multiple sources of evidence that, they hoped would produce convergent conclusions. As is clear from the record, military intelligence did draw on several sources of evidence to assess Egyptian intentions, but the thrust of the information was contradictory rather than convergent. From the field, for example, intelligence officers received a warning in December 1972 and several again in May 1973 that an attack was imminent. In each case, these warnings contradicted documentary evidence of Egyptian reluctance to risk war. And at the time, the warnings quickly appeared to be false, although it is now known that President Sadat did seriously consider and then postpone military attack. Ironically, these warnings may well have been "wrong" for the "right" reasons, even as the intelligence estimates were "right" for the "wrong" reasons. Yet the "cry wolf syndrome" operated here: with each successive warning, the prediction of an impending attack became less credible.

The cry wolf syndrome is an occupational hazard in the perception of the intentions of an adversary. Endemic to processes of estimation and warning, its consequences become more difficult to discount over time. To validate the warnings they had received, intelligence officers relied on the accuracy of the forecasts. This, however, was a poor basis for their validation. Built into the process of estimation is an inverse relationship between the inaccuracy of a series of warnings and success over time. To the extent that a warning is judged to be false at one moment, it is more likely that a subsequent warning that is true, coming from the same source, will be treated as false. The general staff in Israel confronted this dilemma writ large: it had no basis for evaluating past estimates by military intelligence that the probability of an attack was low. Just as experts unjustifiably concluded that past warnings from the field were false, with as little basis senior military and civilian leaders concluded that past estimates of military intelligence were true. Despite complex cognitive biases that promote overconfidence and certainty, this kind of judgment is one that both intelligence experts and policy makers must resist making; they must recognize that they cannot determine the validity of a specific warning by its immediate outcome. The estimate of intentions is the most difficult, uncertain, and risky component in the prediction of the outcome of deterrence. To estimate the likelihood of a challenger choosing to use force, a defender has recourse to "hard" evidence of military capability, from which limited inference can be drawn, to "soft" evidence of intentions, from which inferences must be drawn, and to past experience, which is a poor guide to the future.

This analysis of the interactive impact of cognitive and motivated bias with the inherent uncertainties and environmental complexities of deterrence strategies raises two policy questions. The first is the more limited: it operates largely within the framework of deterrence and asks how the prediction of deterrence failure can be improved. The second is far more fundamental. It transcends the assumptions of deterrence by asking whether deterrence failure can be avoided. I now examine each in turn.

There are no easy solutions to the stubborn problem of reducing misperception, of improving the estimation of an adversary's decision calculus. Recognition of both the predisposition to bias, however, and the environmental limits to warning dictates an initial set of recommendations, directed as much to defense planners as to those with primary responsibility for the estimates of an adversary's intentions and capabilities.

First, and most importantly, adequate warning of attack can be devoutly hoped for but never assumed. Rather than plan on certain warning, military officers must build the contingency of error into their defense planning. General Elazar violated precisely this precept in 1973. In discussions with his commanders and senior officers, he reiterated his expectation of a warning of at least forty-eight hours should Egypt move to attack. Given the obstacles to warning—the difficulty in assessing an adversary's intentions, the ambiguity of much of the evidence, the inherent uncertainties—such an expectation is simply not justified. A promise of warning should neither be given by intelligence experts nor be believed by commanding officers. Rather, as Betts concludes from his examination of surprise attacks, leaders must plan for survival despite error.[62] To do so, they must often sacrifice future defensive capability to present defense readiness. That choice is never easy.

Second, defense planners as well as intelligence experts must recognize that warnings cannot be validated, except long after the fact. Consequently, the premises of past warnings that appear inadequate should not be discounted, and the reasoning that generated predictions that do match outcomes should not be inflated. Civilian and military leaders must be as wary of the "cry sheep" as of the "cry wolf syndrome." Given the problematic basis of most politico-military prognoses, arguments must be reevaluated on their merits each time they are made.

Third, military commanders must recognize that intelligence experts deal with ambiguous evidence open to multiple interpretations. They must resist the fallacy of misplaced concreteness. Rather, in discussions with intelligence advisers, they must insist on the presentation of alternative explanations that might plausibly account for the evidence. Those who depend on intelligence estimates can challenge experts to disprove alternative explanations as well as to document and defend the interpretation they offer.[63] Recognition of the inherent uncertainties will encourage healthy skepticism both among those who "consume" and among those who "produce" estimates. Once military and civilian leaders acknowledge uncertainty, they will have to confront the difficult choice between reducing the risk of unintended war by avoiding provocative military action or avoiding surprise by early deployment of defensive forces. That choice is not easy. However, the alternatives are not always mutually exclusive. In Israel's case, for example, partial mobilization would have increased defensive preparedness without creating the capacity to attack. Explicit recognition of these kinds of trade-offs should permit more nuanced policy.

An additional set of recommendations derives directly from my examination of the calculations of Egyptian leaders who considered whether or not to attack. Drawing on the factors they considered important, and matching Israel's estimates to these calculations, I pinpointed the obvious misperceptions. The pattern of misperception suggests categories for inclusion in subsequent estimates and a structure for analysis that may provide a more complete basis for estimating the likelihood of a challenge to deterrence.

Three components in the calculations of Egyptian leaders were particularly important in shaping their decision whether or not to use force. Their assessment that the military balance precluded attack was a strong but temporary deterrent to action. Israel's intelligence analysts gave overwhelming priority to this component of Egyptian calculations. Indeed, drawing on direct evidence of Egyptian thinking, they virtually excluded all other factors from their analysis. Herein lay a major error. The complexity of a decision to go to war suggests that any single factor analysis, no matter how well corroborated by evidence, should be suspect. A calculation of military inferiority, as we have seen, may be at best a temporary deterrent, an obstacle to be overcome, if other factors favor military action. An analysis based exclusively on a challenger's calculation of relative capabilities should become especially suspect as time goes on. It does not provide an adequate basis for assessing the likelihood of deterrence failure.

Leaders can look to at least two other closely related factors to broaden the analytic basis of their assessments. Especially important in the calculations of Egyptian leaders were their estimates of the plausible alternatives to military force and their assessments of the costs of inaction in comparison to those of military attack. Both these calculations emphasize not military factors but rather the political, diplomatic, and economic consequences that color consideration of a military option. Over this period, Egyptian estimates of the domestic and international losses of inaction grew substantially, and as they grew, they reshaped the comparison of the two options of military action or inaction. Closely related was the increasing pessimism in Egyptian estimates of the alternatives to military action. In shaping a decision whether or not to use force, consideration of the prospects and consequences of inaction was as important as evaluation of the consequences of a military option.

A final recommendation is immediately obvious. When intelligence analysts begin to uncover these kinds of estimates—estimates of severe losses of inaction—and repeated expressions of frustration with the available alternatives to a use of force, they should immediately begin to give serious consideration to the possibility of deterrence failure. They should do so, moreover, even if they have solid evidence that opposing leaders consider their capabilities inferior and discount a military option. At the very least, incoming information should be evaluated against the two competing hypotheses of deterrence success and failure to determine which better explains the broadest range of evidence. Such a comparative look at the evidence should reduce reliance on a single factor and generate uncertainty; at a minimum, explicit consideration of the possibility of deterrence failure should do much to alert analysts and policy makers to its probability.

This discussion of technical and procedural improvements to reduce the incidence and consequence of misperception immediately raises the broader and more difficult question, Can deterrence failure be avoided? One answer is immediately apparent: acquisition of additional military capabilities alone will not suffice over time when an adversary is intensely frustrated and highly motivated. Egypt's capacity to design around Israel's superior military capabilities bears eloquent witness to the validity of this proposition.

The obvious alternative is a mix of accommodation and coercion, of reassurance and threat. Snyder and Diesing, in their examination of international crises, conclude, as does Lebow in his study of brinkmanship, that neither coercion nor conciliation alone will work.[64] The policy challenge is to design the appropriate mix. The investigation of Egyptian and Israeli perceptions supports the validity of this general proposition. First, when Egyptian leaders considered that negotiations held some promise of success, no matter how limited, they were reluctant to use force. It is striking that even in a relationship of such intense hostility and suspicion, the challenger nevertheless paid attention to the subtext of diplomacy as well as to the dominant motif of threat and coercion. My analysis suggests, then, that a defender must work not only to inflate its adversary's perception of the likely costs of military action—the principal thrust of prescriptive theories of deterrence—but simultaneously to reduce the perception of the likely costs of inaction. Deterrence is a useful strategy to buy time only if a defender uses the time to address the source of grievance, frustration, and revisionism.

The difficulty, of course, lies not with the general proposition but with its specifics. First, challengers are as likely to misperceive and misinterpret accommodative signals as they are coercive language. If they interpret conciliatory offers as evidence of weakening resolve, as they frequently do, then deterrence failure can become much more likely. Second, much depends on the timing of conciliatory offers in the broader sequence of coercive action; if conciliation is tried before a defender's resolve is credible to a challenger, it is likely to be perceived as weakness.[65] Third, it is entirely possible that the incompatibilities that divide a challenger and defender are so fundamental and all-encompassing that no accommodation is possible.

My examination of the bargaining relationship between Egypt and Israel since 1948 suggests that not much more than a tactical accommodation between the two was possible until after the October War.[66] Even in the period examined here, the two did consider a limited agreement in 1971, for example, whereby Egypt would have reopened the canal and rehabilitated the cities along the waterway in return for a withdrawal of Israel's forces. If they had reached agreement, it is at least plausible to argue that Egypt would not have chosen to resort to force in 1973. But Egyptian and Israeli leaders could not agree: they argued about the scope of the withdrawal, the demilitarization of the territory that was to be evacuated, and the duration of the proposed agreement. Egypt would not concede despite its pessimistic evaluation of the military balance, and Israel saw no reason to conciliate, no military or diplomatic imperative to accommodation.

The war changed the negotiating environment, although not precisely in the way President Sadat anticipated when he chose to use force for political purposes. Despite the optimal conditions of the Egyptian attack—a two-front attack for the first time in Arab history, a military operation that benefitted from meticulous planning, repeated rehearsal, and surprise—the Egyptian army came perilously close to disaster. For this reason Sadat was not prepared to risk his hard-won political gains in a further use of force; the only alternative was the political concessions he had been unprepared to make two years earlier. Israel, sobered by the enormous costs of the use of force and alarmed by the fragility of deterrence, now preferred the option of reducing Egyptian frustration through concession. The challenge to deterrence, on the one hand, and the asymmetrical outcome of the fighting, on the other, acted together to reshape leaders' perceptions: the one would not have sufficed without the other. In a deterrent relationship extended over time, both the challenger and the defender finally learned.

This empirical examination of deterrence emphasizes not only a challenger's estimate of relative military capabilities but also the political, economic, and diplomatic imperatives that inform the broader set of calculations. It also underlines the pervasiveness of misperception by both the challenger and the defender. Defenders must take cognizance of both these factors. Insofar as they focus on the broader grid of a challenger's perceptions, they can at least identify the grievances that inflame an adversary and consider the appropriateness of conciliation. The obstacles to successful conciliation are legion: mutually reinforcing misperception, reciprocal fear, the timing of accommodative action within the broader context of a coercive relationship, and the appropriate mix of accommodation and coercion in any given sequence of action. The evidence shows, however, that exclusive reliance on deterrence over time is itself a high-risk strategy. Deterrence may be necessary, but it is not sufficient.

5

■

MISCALCULATION IN THE SOUTH ATLANTIC: THE ORIGINS OF THE FALKLANDS WAR

Richard Ned Lebow

I thought and we thought we were old enough to make our own decisions. ■ *Leopoldo Galtieri, 7 June 1982*

It would have been absurd to despatch the fleet every time there was bellicose talk in Buenos Aires. ■ *Margaret Thatcher, 3 April 1982*

■ The recent war in the South Atlantic broke out because of two serious and mutually reinforcing misjudgments: the belief in London that Argentina would not invade the Falkland Islands and the expectations in Buenos Aires that Britain would accommodate itself to a military takeover of the islands.* The former illusion made British policy makers unresponsive to warnings of invasion while the latter encouraged the Argentine *junta,* dissatisfied with the progress of negotiations, to seek to resolve the question of sovereignty once and for all by force.

This study was written under the aegis of the Frankfort Peace Research Institute. I am indebted to Ernst-Otto Czempiel, Gert Krell, Harald Mueller, Reinhard Rode, and Bernd Kubbig for their encouragement and support.

*I have used the term *Falklands* as opposed to *Malvinas* or *Falkland-Malvinas* as a matter of convenience. It should not be construed as an indication of preference for either side in this controversy.

Any analysis of the Falklands War must start by accounting for these two misjudgments; only then can we hope to explain the air of unreality that characterized the behavior of the two protagonists throughout the prewar period and, in the case of Argentina, well into the actual war. No doubt, there are lessons here for other policy makers as well. For miscalculation in this instance may have led to what some have described as an *opéra bouffe* conflict in a remote corner of the world, but the causes of the conflict are not likely to prove so arcane or idiosyncratic.

Any kind of definitive treatment of the crisis must obviously await the emergence of the relevant documents.[1] This would include intelligence estimates, diplomatic correspondence, and memoirs of the principal actors. In the absence of these documents the investigator can only piece together the outlines of the story from the evidence available at this time. This consists principally of speeches, newspaper accounts, interviews and, above all, the visible actions of the protagonists. As such evidence is not only fragmentary but possibly misleading, the following analysis is of necessity speculative in nature. The hypotheses it advances concerning miscalculation cannot be documented conclusively. They can, however, be shown to be consistent with the existing evidence. Only time and subsequent study will reveal the extent to which they are valid. A preliminary examination is nevertheless a valuable exercise to the extent that it identifies the attributes of the case that have significant theoretical or policy relevance and, by doing so, directs later research to these questions. This study is offered with such a purpose in mind.

Self-deception in London

On 3 March 1982 Argentina disavowed the negotiations that had just taken place with Britain in New York over the future status of the Falkland Islands. On 2 April Argentine marines stormed ashore near Port Stanley, overwhelmed the small British garrison, and raised the Argentine flag over the Falklands. The month between these two events was marked by steadily escalating tensions between Argentina and Britain as well as obvious Argentine military preparations for an invasion. However, from the vantage point of London the danger looked remote. It was not until 29 March, four days before the invasion, that the Cabinet Office and the government judged the situation to be serious. In response, they ordered a submarine and support vessels from the Mediterranean to the

South Atlantic. Prime Minister Thatcher did not summon her first cabinet meeting on the crisis until the night of 31 March. By then, the *Economist* rightly observed, it was too late to deter with anything but words.[2]

As is so often the case with intelligence failures, Britain's inability to foresee the Argentine invasion cannot be attributed to simple lack of information. The British government had ample intelligence about Argentine intentions and military preparations. From 3 March onward, Buenos Aires had done its best to signal both its dissatisfaction with the status quo and its intention to do something about it. The Argentines also made efforts to publicize rather than conceal their military preparations in the hope that this demonstration of resolve would elicit a British concession on sovereignty that would make military action on their part unnecessary. Beyond this, London was in receipt of a wide range of information about Argentina from both open and clandestine sources. The Joint Intelligence Committee (JIC) of the Cabinet Office, whose task it is to warn the government of impending foreign threats, had before it all the cable traffic from the British embassy in Buenos Aires. This included reports from political officers, military attachés, and secret intelligence sources run through the embassy. The JIC also had access to naval and other relevant intelligence.

Britain participates in a worldwide naval intelligence network together with the United States, Canada and Australia. A Fleet Ocean Surveillance Information Center (FOSIC), run by the United States Navy in London, analyzes data from their combined intelligence sources in the Atlantic, and routinely passes its reports on to the Royal Navy. A major source of FOSIC's information is the global ship radio monitoring system run by the four powers. Another is the U.S. navy's four ocean surveillance satellites (OSUS) which use radar and infra-red cameras to detect ships. They can also monitor their radio and radar signals.[3] Close-up photo-reconnaissance can be provided by SR 71s. The United States, in response to a British request, flew such a surveillance mission in the South Atlantic prior to the Argentine invasion.[4]

Britain also receives signal intelligence from a variety of U.S. and jointly operated listening posts, one of them on Ascension Island in the South Atlantic. According to Ted Rowlands, a Labour Member of Parliament (M.P.), who handled the Falkland question in the Foreign Office until 1979, Britain had successfully broken the Argentine diplomatic code. He told the House of Commons that in terms of intelligence Argentina was an open book for the British.[5] No one in the Thatcher government has disputed his claim.

There can be little doubt that the government had enough information to suggest the very real possibility of a military confrontation in the South Atlantic. By its own admission in various statements to the press and in Parliament, the government was aware of the following:

2 March: The Argentine Government terminates negotiations with Britain and announces that it reserves its right to "seek other means" of regaining the Falklands.

3 March: *La Prensa,* known to have good connections with the *junta,* announces its dissatisfaction with the negotiations and predicts the liberation of the Falklands by force within three months unless Britain agrees to cede sovereignty.

Junta members begin dropping hints to diplomats that they are contemplating some kind of unilateral military action in the absence of a commitment by Britain both to speed up negotiations and to put sovereignty of the islands formally on the agenda.

Clarin and other newspapers begin talking about the prospects for an invasion of the Falklands.

14 March: An Argentine air force Hercules 130, claiming technical difficulties, makes an emergency landing at Port Stanley airport.

19 March: Employees of an Argentine scrap firm land on South Georgia Island and raise the Argentine flag.

22 March: A group of Argentines occupies the Port Stanley office of the Argentine state airline and unfurls the Argentine flag.

25 March: Three Argentine warships arrive in South Georgia to give "full protection" to the landing party.

27–28 March: British intelligence sources learn of the impending departure of the Argentine fleet with wartime stocks.

28–29 March: The Argentine fleet puts to sea a force that includes an aircraft carrier, two missile destroyers, a battleship, and two corvettes, ostensibly to conduct maneuvers with Uruguay.

29 March: The Argentine press is put on a worldwide alert by the government; diplomatic leaves are cancelled; DYN, the Argentine news agency, citing unnamed military sources, announces that the marine regiment with the fleet has been issued food rations,

              arms, and ammunition; Uruguay asks the British government if any Falklanders wanted to be airlifted to safety "before the invasion."

31 March: London learns that the Argentine naval units on maneuver have broken away from the Uruguayan force and are steaming toward the Falklands.

1 April: Argentina's foreign minister tells Britain's ambassador in Buenos Aires that "the diplomatic channel as a means of solving the dispute is closed." The Buenos Aires magazine *Siete Dias* publishes a fictitious front page of the *Times* with the headline "Argentine Navy Invades Falkland Islands" alongside a photograph of Argentine marines allegedly storming ashore.

2 April: Argentina invades the Falkland Islands.

In fairness to the Foreign Office, the JIC and the prime minister, all of these "signals" only became clear in retrospect. At the time, they were also consistent with a strategy of bluff, as British ministers hastened to point out. Lord Carrington told the House of Lords: "Had this been the first time over the past 20 years that some allusion to the use of force had been made from the Argentine side it might have struck Britain as more significant than it did.[6] Prime Minister Thatcher put her finger on the dilemma that a situation of repetitive threat created for the government. On 4 April, she explained to her critics in the House of Commons that "several times in the past an invasion had been threatened. The only way of being sure of preventing it would have been to keep a large fleet close to the Falklands, 8,000 miles away from base. 'No government has ever been able to do that,' she insisted, 'because the cost would be enormous.' "[7]

One must feel some sympathy for policy makers caught in this bind. However, the problem of repetitive threat neither excuses nor fully accounts for the poor judgment of the British government. Faced with the prospect of recurring crises, it was incumbent upon the British to develop indicators to help distinguish bluff from the real thing. This they failed to do. Instead, London waited for indisputable evidence of impending attack. Due to what Robert Jervis has called the "masking effect," the fact that moves associated with bluff and preparations for attack are generally indistinguishable until the very last moment, Argentine intentions only became clear after it was already too late to do anything to influence them.[8]

A useful analogy can be drawn to the situation faced by Israel in October 1973. Israeli military intelligence had devised a series of tactical indicators to predict the possibility of an Egyptian attack. Their principal indicator was the deployment and reinforcement of troops along the cease-fire lines. Also deemed significant were the mobilization of reserves, construction of ramps and bridging equipment along the Suez Canal, and the imposition of wartime security measures at military bases throughout the country. On three occasions prior to the October attack, in December 1971, December 1972, and in April–May 1973, the Egyptians did all of these things without going to war.

The Israelis, who had braced themselves for war in each instance, understandably lost confidence in their tactical indicators. They fell back upon strategic indicators of attack. Their hypothesis was that Egypt would not attack unless two conditions were met: that the Egyptian air force be capable of striking at Israel in depth, in particular at Israeli airfields, and secondly, that Egypt be joined in the attack by Syria. Israeli military intelligence accordingly considered an Egyptian attack highly unlikely before 1975, the earliest possible date they believed the Egyptian air force capable of absorbing enough Soviet equipment to achieve the requisite strike capability.[9]

The Agranat Commission, established by the Israeli cabinet to investigate the 1973 intelligence failure, attributed much of the fault to the fact that Israel's strategic indicators were based on the flawed assumptions that Egypt would only go to war together with Syria, and then to seek Israel's destruction. Israeli intelligence ignored the possibility of a limited war, fought for less ambitious objectives, a conflict in which Egyptian equality in the air was not an essential precondition of success. Egyptian forces relied instead upon a missile screen in the vicinity of the canal to keep the Israeli air force at bay. The erroneous Israeli fixation on general war, for which the Arabs were clearly not ready in October 1973, combined with Israeli disillusionment with tactical indicators, encouraged Jerusalem to dismiss Sadat's escalating threats of war in the summer and late fall of 1973 as bluff initiated in the hope of winning diplomatic concessions. For the same reason, Israel's leaders did not become particularly disturbed by the build-up of Egyptian forces along the canal, the evacuation of Soviet dependents, and the subsequent warnings of attack. All of this they had seen before.[10]

If the Israelis were led astray by a faulty conception of the strategic objectives of their principal adversary, they at least had such a conception. The British by contrast gave no evidence of having developed any express notion of the political-military conditions under which Argentina might attack the Falklands. At best, they seem to have developed a misleading tactical scenario that presupposed that any Argentine escalation of the conflict would be gradual, begin with suspension of air services, and not lead to an invasion until the end of the year.[11]

The Agranat Commission faulted the very existence of a strategic conception, as it inevitably biased information processing. Janice Gross Stein, in her perceptive study of Israel's intelligence failure in 1973, argues that such conceptions can function as useful aids to policy makers concerned with developing indicators of warning. The important question, she believes, is not the use of an organizing concept but rather "its logical coherence and completeness, its relationship to other concepts in a larger analytical system, and the way it is used."[12] According to Stein, a strategic conception concerning deterrence, defense, and miscalculated escalation must analyze and relate at least five issue areas to be considered coherent and complete. It ought to include an evaluation of the interests at stake, specify the challenge to be deterred, evaluate the adversary's calculation of the conditions and options for challenge, consider the credibility of a commitment to respond, and describe appropriate responses to deterrence failure.

It is not the purpose of this chapter to develop a strategic conception for Britain concerning her commitment to defend the Falkland Islanders' right of self-determination. It is rather to make the case that, had such a conception been developed by the British, it would have made them very much more sensitive to the possibility of Argentine military action. Such a conception would of necessity have required an examination of the Falkland question from the Argentine perspective. Any moderately sophisticated effort in this regard, based only on the information already at hand, would have highlighted striking differences between the situation in 1977, the last time Argentina appeared on the verge of invading, and in 1982. All of these differences should have been seen as having had the effect of increasing the attractiveness to Buenos Aires of an invasion while at the same time reducing its perceived military cost.

Perhaps the most important difference between 1977 and 1982 was that in the interim Argentine leaders had lost faith in negotiations with Britain and had concluded that they would never achieve sovereignty over the Falklands by diplomacy.

Since 1965, at Argentina's insistence, the two countries had been conducting almost yearly negotiations with regard to the future of the Falkland Islands.[13] These talks were often preceded by saber rattling in Buenos Aires, but serious violence had always been forestalled by Argentine expectations that negotiations would ultimately lead to a transfer of sovereignty. Step by step, the British appeared to be moving in that direction. The Wilson government recognized the legitimacy of Argentina's de facto claims to the islands. The Heath government signed a communications agreement that gave Buenos Aires control of air transportation to and from the Falklands. Subsequently, Argentina was permitted to lengthen the Port Stanley runway, increase tourist traffic with the mainland, and take over management of the Falklands' energy supplies. Islanders made growing use of Argentine hospitals and schools. Both sides assumed that sooner or later some mechanism could be found that would enable Argentina to "recover sovereignty" yet still permit Britain to protect the rights and life style of the inhabitants.

Progress in this direction had continued, if at a snail's pace, until the "lease-back" debacle of 1980–81. Nicholas Ridley, the new junior minister put in charge of the Falklands question following the Conservative victory of 1979, settled upon the lease-back proposal, first broached by his predecessor, as the most promising solution to the sovereignty dilemma. His goal was to placate both Buenos Aires and the islanders by transferring formal sovereignty to Argentina while leasing back British administrative responsibility for them. Although backed by Lord Carrington, Ridley failed to generate enthusiasm for the lease-back proposal either in the cabinet, sensitive to the chauvinism voiced by many backbenchers on the question, or in the islands, where public opinion regarded the scheme with suspicion. Ridley's report to the House of Commons on 2 December 1980 was greeted with derision and hostility from right-wing Tories who wanted to know why the Foreign Office could not leave the matter alone.[14]

Two months later the talks resumed in New York. This time Ridley brought islanders with him to meet directly with Argentina's representative, Carlos Cavandoli. According to Adrian Monk, one of the islanders included on the delegation, Cavandoli held out the promise of a "democratic form of government, a different legal system, different customs, and a different form of education." The only thing Argentina wanted, Cavandoli insisted, was sovereignty. The islanders declared that they could agree to nothing before their council elections in November.[15]

After this round of inconclusive negotiations, the Argentine press, and, privately, government officials as well, began to accuse the British of stalling and voiced considerable pessimism about the prospects of a diplomatic solution. Two subsequent developments appeared to lend credence to their view. In September 1981, Thatcher removed Ridley from the Foreign Office and replaced him with Richard Luce, a politician with a reputation for caution. In November, the Island Council elections were held with Ridley and the lease-back proposal the principal issue. The anti-lease-back forces won a clear victory: two moderate representatives who had attended the talks in New York were defeated by hardliners adamantly opposed to any further concessions to Argentina.

The *junta*, now headed by General Leopoldo Galtieri, who had assumed power in December, made a final attempt in February 1982 to reach an agreement with Britain. Enrique Ros, the negotiator sent by Argentina to New York, demanded the concession of sovereignty before the year's end. The most the British would agree to was the creation of a negotiating commission to work toward this goal. Moreover, Richard Luce, representing the British, now insisted that any agreement would also have to meet the approval of the islanders. The Thatcher government in effect gave the islanders a veto power over the negotiations, something that all but precluded any transfer of sovereignty. The significance of this development was not lost to the *junta*. Upon his return home, Ros was disavowed by the generals, and the talks were broken off. The Argentine press began to speculate about an invasion.

As Argentine leaders became convinced of the impossibility of obtaining sovereignty over the Falklands through diplomacy, they also came under increasing pressure at home to achieve that elusive but immensely popular goal. The political vulnerability of the *junta*, the result of its poor performance on a range of important domestic issues, made this pressure all the more difficult to ignore.

The excesses of Peronism had been such that five years earlier, in March 1976, the *junta*'s accession to power in a bloodless coup had been greeted with a nearly universal sense of relief. By the spring of 1982, however, the generals had succeeded in alienating almost all of their earlier backers. Their repression of the left, expected to be a short-lived operation, turned into an extensive and often indiscriminate reign of terror directed not only against *Montoneros* but any element of the society too free-thinking for the military. Estimates of the victims run as high as 20,000 and include entire families tortured and killed, sometimes without any apparent motive.[16]

Economically, the picture was also bleak. A country of 28 million people, and with the highest standard of living and the highest rate of literacy in Latin America, Argentina had been brought to the brink of economic disaster by thirty years of political instability and economic mismanagement. The *junta* had vowed to reverse this trend through free market policies but had only succeeded in intensifying the pace of economic decline. After an initial improvement, economic growth dropped from a high of 7.1 percent in 1979 to below 1.0 percent in 1981. In 1980, Banco de Intercambio, a leading financial institution, collapsed along with twenty-seven other banks, as did Sasetru, the country's leading conglomerate. Ninteen eighty-one was even more disappointing. Continuing failures of banks and businesses forced the *junta* to abandon its economic program. This in turn led to a run on the peso and a series of devaluations. The inflation rate shot from 87 to 149 percent. Real wages declined by 18 percent, and unemployment may have climbed as high as two million.[17]

The precipitous economic decline had its political consequences. Independent farmers and entrepreneurs, originally among the *junta*'s supporters, openly voiced criticism of its economic programs. Organized labor, emasculated by the generals in 1976, also began to reassert itself. The General Confederation of Labor (CGT) slowly rebuilt its grass-roots organization and on 30 March 1982 defied the ban on union political activities by filling Buenos Aires' Plaza de Mayo with thousands of protesting workers. The demonstrators, shouting for "bread, freedom and work," were only dispersed after four hours of battle with police armed with water cannon and tear gas. In Mendoza, the same day, police are reported to have fired on union demonstrators.[18]

Political parties also began to become active again. In June 1981, the five largest parties, led by the Peronists and the Radicals, formed the *multipartidaria* (common front) and demanded a new electoral law that would permit open party activity and competition. The *junta* did not feel strong enough to reject these demands outright. In November, the generals issued guidelines for a new electoral law that, while restrictive, was nevertheless interpreted as an important step toward the ultimate restoration of civilian rule.

The *junta* also had to permit a substantially freer press. After 1976, newspaper editors had become very restrained in their criticism of the military. In 1981 they became more outspoken, taking the generals to task both for their mismanagement of the economy and for their apparent failure to secure Argentine sovereignty over the Falklands. The most vocal critics of the *junta*, *La Prensa* and the English-language *Buenos Aires Herald*, began to call for an end to military rule.[19] These editorials were an indication of the *junta*'s growing isolation. In the aftermath of the 30 March labor demonstration the generals faced a stark choice: step down or do something dramatic to restore public confidence and their own legitimacy. The obvious choice in the latter regard was recovery of sovereignty over the Falklands.

Well before the spring of 1982, the *junta*'s vulnerability on the Falkland question was obvious. During the summer 1981 round of talks, Carlos Cavandoli, the Argentine negotiator, had pleaded for some concessions that would demonstrate progress on sovereignty. Time and again he is reported to have told Nicholas Ridley: "Just give me something to take back home."[20] When Cavandoli's successor, Enrique Ros, failed to obtain such a concession, he was abandoned by the *junta,* anxious for domestic political reasons to dissociate itself as much as possible from his mission. Spurned by London, facing growing opposition at home, the distraught, anxious men of the *junta* must have found the idea of military action more and more attractive.

If London was insensitive to the *junta*'s fast waning freedom of action with regard to the Falklands, the South Georgia incident should have made the problem apparent. A barren wasteland 800 miles south of the Falklands and over 1,000 miles east of the southernmost tip of Argentina, South Georgia is inhabited only by scientists at the British research base at Grytviken. On 19 March, an Argentine naval transport ship on long-term contract to a private company landed a team of workmen at Leith Harbour. Their ostensible purpose was to cart away old equipment sold to them by the British company that had formerly operated whaling stations on the island. The director of the Argentine scrap company had received permission for his men to land on the island from the British embassy in Buenos Aires with the proviso that they obtain permits from the base commander in Grytviken. The landing party ignored the stipulated procedure and instead raised Argentina's blue and white flag and sang the national anthem. The action seems to have been carried out without the connivance or perhaps even the prior knowledge of the *junta.*[21]

When apprised of the situation, the British Foreign Office protested to Buenos Aires. London also quietly dispatched HMS *Endurance,* an Antarctic survey ship then in the vicinity of the Falklands, to South Georgia. Niconor Costa Méndes, Argentina's foreign minister, assured the British that his government would send a ship to take the men off the island. In response, the British kept *Endurance* with its complement of twenty-one marines from the garrison at Port Stanley at sea awaiting the arrival of the promised vessel. Instead, three Argentine warships appeared and *Endurance* had to beat a hasty retreat. Meanwhile, the Argentine government announced that its navy would give "full protection" to men on South Georgia. Clearly, the *junta,* once it realized the extent to which this private initiative had caught the country's imagination, no longer deemed it prudent to dissociate itself from the flamboyant gesture.

The South Georgia episode occurred in a climate of escalating tension that had begun on 3 March following the repudiation of the New York negotiations by Buenos Aires. The events of the next four weeks indicated a shift to a harder line by the *junta,* the further arousal of Argentine public opinion in expectation of military action, and finally, actual preparations for the invasion of the Falklands. This pattern of events, when seen against the political background just described, did not indicate with any certainty that an invasion would actually occur. However, it certainly should have made it appear a very real possibility. British passivity in light of these developments was really quite extraordinary.

According to Janice Gross Stein, the Israelis committed a second major error in 1973; they insisted upon near certain knowledge of an Arab attack before they were prepared to initiate any military countermeasures themselves. Their concern to avoid what they feared might be a premature mobilization derived in the first place from the tremendous economic and social cost to Israel of calling up its citizen army. Beyond this, it reflected Israel's experience in 1967. Many senior Israeli military and intelligence officers had concluded that war at that time had arisen only because of miscalculation. Israel, the argument went, had misjudged Nasser's strategy, which was probably one of bluff, and had initiated an unnecessary preemptive attack. Stein points out that the Israeli commitment to avoid a possible repetition of this situation also reflected relative satisfaction with the status quo. The policy implication of this position was obvious: no mobilization or preemption unless the leadership was absolutely convinced that the adversary was itself on the verge of attacking. Such a restrictive criterion of warning, linked to a requirement for certainty, reduced the attractiveness of any markedly significant defensive option during the crisis.[22]

Once again, there seems to be an analogy between the Israeli and British cases. British policy makers, for many of the same reasons as the Israelis, appear to have insisted upon evidence of the near certainty of an Argentine invasion before they were willing to authorize the kind of military preparations that might have been successful in deterring it or at least in limiting its chance of success.

Like the Israelis, British officials were fearful of the consequences of miscalculated escalation. This concern had dominated the British response to the 1977 crisis. At that time, diplomatic relations had been severed, Argentina had fired on a British ship, occupied the dependency of Southern Thule, and cut off fuel supplies to the Falklands. The Callaghan government, despite strenuous opposition from the Ministry of Defense, sent a hunter-killer submarine to the Falklands as a precautionary measure. As the ensuing negotiations were encouraging to Argentina, the threat of invasion receded and the submarine was withdrawn after a month.

The most remarkable thing about the 1977 crisis was the secrecy that surrounded the mission of the submarine. Its presence was hushed up in order to avoid precipitating the very invasion the vessel was sent to forestall. In doing this, Callaghan and his advisors were willing to sacrifice whatever deterrent value the submarine might have had, for that clearly required Argentine knowledge of its presence.

For the British, the lesson of 1977 was that caution was likely to reap a handsome dividend. Not surprisingly, therefore, the consensus in both the Foreign Office and the Cabinet Office in March 1982 was for the need to avoid any public display of British resolve. The fear was that this would only elicit a similar response from the *junta* concerned about protecting its *machismo* in the eyes of Argentine public opinion. There was also concern, Lord Carrington explained in Parliament, that moving ships into the area would prove counterproductive by strengthening the hand of the extremists within the *junta*. "Nothing," he argued, "would have been more likely to turn the Argentines away from the path of negotiations and towards that of military force."[23]

The proclivity to do nothing unless invasion appeared imminent was almost certainly reinforced by political and economic considerations. The Thatcher government had met with little success in lifting Britain from its economic doldrums and faced discouraging electoral prospects. Its foreign and defense policies had also come under increasing attack from the burgeoning peace movement. War, under almost any circumstances, must have seemed a loathsome idea to Downing Street. But all the more so to the extent to which the Thatcher government could in any way be made to appear responsible for it. This would almost certainly have made the Tories that much more vulnerable at the next general election. Military restraint no doubt appeared the best way to avoid this problem.

Sending a tripwire force would also have cost money. By most accounts, the climate in Whitehall was totally inimical to the authorization of extra expenditure. This penny-pinching mentality is said to have been particularly marked in the Ministry of Defense, barely able to fulfill its various commitments on what it believed to be a penurious budget. For Lord Carrington or John Nott, the defense minister, to have asked the Overseas and Defence Committee of the cabinet for authorization for a naval force for the South Atlantic, they would have had needed some very compelling evidence of the likelihood of Argentine attack. This was lacking until 29 March, four days before the invasion. The concern for saving money was so pronounced, the *Economist* asserts, that a request from the foreign secretary for a naval force any time before 29 March "would probably have been laughed out of court."[24]

As the Israeli and British situations illustrate, there are almost always trade-offs to be made between escalation and passivity in pre-crisis or crisis situations. Escalation, while it conveys resolve, if premature or miscalculated, risks provoking the outcome it was initiated to forestall. Often, it also carries economic and political costs. Military passivity, on the other hand, is decidedly unprovocative but may weaken or even undermine deterrence by conveying an inappropriate signal to an adversary. It too can have serious military and political costs if war breaks out and finds the nation unprepared.

Decisions regarding escalation are among the most difficult leaders can face. The problem is extraordinarily complex because it has political, military, and psychological components that must be considered with regard to both foreign and domestic audiences. It is also anxiety provoking, as the wrong decision entails significant, perhaps even catastrophic loss. Moreover, there are no decision-making rules that can be followed. Rather, policy makers must consider and weigh a number of situational attributes, among them the interests at stake, their confidence in deterrence, the political vulnerability of the adversary's leaders, and the possible military cost of inaction. Perhaps the most important consideration in this regard is the judgment policy makers must make about the other side's intentions. To the extent that a challenge of an important interest or commitment is deemed likely, some kind of military preparations are usually implemented as both a demonstration of resolve and a means of putting the nation in a better position to wage war if the crisis is unresolved. Conversely, when the challenge appears remote, policy makers are more likely to prove responsive to the possible costs of miscalculated escalation.

The importance of assessing the probability of a challenge brings us full circle by highlighting the need for strategic indicators that offer some insight into this question. In the absence of some kind of strategic conception from which these indicators can be derived, policy makers must of necessity fall back upon tactical indicators, the dangers of which we have already described, or rely upon their personal assessment of the situation. Such judgments may be haphazard, ill informed or even quite arbitrary. They are also likely to escape the kind of scrutiny given to institutionally developed strategic conceptions, whose assumptions must normally be articulated and defended before colleagues.

One danger of personal or informal assessments is that they can all too easily, even unconsciously, be made consonant with the politico-military needs of the policy makers who form them. By doing this, policy makers may finesse the need to make trade-offs between the sometimes incompatible objectives of buttressing deterrence and avoiding miscalculated escalation. They can convince themselves instead that all, or almost all, of the "facts" of the case and their own interests point to one or the other of the options open to them. Some wishful thinking of this kind may have occurred in London. Civil servants in Whitehall and members of the government believed that military preparations on their part were likely to provoke, not deter, a confrontation with Argentina. For this reason among others they decided not to initiate any military preparations until late in the crisis. As this left them vulnerable in the case of an invasion, they accordingly had every incentive to believe that Argentina was bluffing. This could in turn be expected to bias British receptivity to information about Argentine intentions.

The psychological approach to decision making may in fact hold the key to understanding the British intelligence failure in the South Atlantic. For the remarkable British passivity in light of all the danger signals coming from Argentina still seems to defy ordinary institutional explanations. Perhaps it is best understood as a form of collective "defensive avoidance," an attempt by British policy makers to shield themselves from threatening realities which they were unprepared for and unable to face.

According to Irving Janis and Leon Mann's formulation of defensive avoidance, a policy maker searches for an alternative to his current course of action when he perceives serious risks to be inherent in it. If the search reveals a feasible alternative, he will adopt it without inner conflict. If, however, the policy maker is unable upon first assessment to identify an acceptable alternative, he experiences psychological stress. He becomes emotionally aroused and preoccupied with finding a less risky but nevertheless viable policy alternative. If, after further investigation, he concludes that it is unrealistic to hope for a better strategy, he will terminate his search for one despite his continuing dissatisfaction with the current policy and other available options. This results in a pattern of defensive avoidance, which is characterized by efforts to avoid fear-arousing warnings.[25]

Janis and Mann identify three forms of defensive avoidance: procrastination, shifting responsibility for the decision, and bolstering. The first two are self-explanatory. Bolstering is an umbrella term that describes a number of psychological tactics designed to allow policy makers to entertain expectations of a successful outcome. Bolstering occurs when the policy maker has lost hope of finding a satisfactory policy option and is unable to postpone a decision or foist the responsibility for it onto someone else. Instead, he commits himself to the least objectionable alternative and proceeds to exaggerate its positive consequences and minimize its negative ones. He may also deny the existence of his aversive feelings, emphasize the remoteness of the consequences, or attempt to minimize his personal responsibility for the decision once it is made. The policy maker continues to think about the problem but wards off anxiety by practicing selective attention and other forms of distorted information processing.[26]

Bolstering can serve a useful purpose; it helps the policy maker forced to settle for a less than satisfactory course of action overcome residual internal conflict and move more confidently toward commitment. But bolstering is detrimental when it blinds the policy maker to the possible adverse consequences of his course of action. It lulls him into believing that he has made a good decision when in fact he has avoided making a vigilant appraisal of the alternatives in order to escape from the conflict this would engender.

For years, the British government had been committed to twin goals of a negotiated settlement of the Falkland dispute with Argentina and protection of the liberties and interests of the islanders. Superficially, each round of talks in New York seemed to bring these objectives closer to realization. However, the negotiations also made apparent the full extent of the differences that separated the parties. The islanders, never pleased with the prospect of absorption by Argentina, became even more hostile to the idea when the *junta*'s bloody suppression of the Argentine left revealed its utter disregard for the most fundamental human rights. The Argentines were also dissatisfied with the negotiations. They came increasingly to believe, and not without reason, that they were behaving like the proverbial donkey, tricked into pulling the cart by a carrot on a stick dangled before him.

Some time before Argentina's repudiation of the New York talks, British officials had begun to recognize that a negotiated settlement of the dispute was very unlikely given the seemingly unbridgeable gap between the interests of the islanders and the demands of the Argentines. This realization prompted a gradual but significant shift in the British strategy for dealing with the Falkland question. The Thatcher government began to move away from the objective of actually finding a solution to the problem and instead sought merely to forestall a crisis by keeping the negotiations alive. Ridley, who made a serious and even courageous effort to confront the problem head on, had elicited for the most part the scorn and even antagonism of his colleagues. His report to the House of Commons on 2 December 1980 was greeted with "howls of outrage." The *Economist* reported that he appeared at the dispatch box shattered and uncertain and many observers were astonished that he should have wrecked his political career on such a hopeless little venture.[27]

The impractical goal of trying to continue the talks from year to year was probably motivated in part by the illusory hope that some future development would facilitate a settlement. A less charitable explanation is that British officials had come to view the Falkland dispute as a "hot potato," something that could only burn their fingers if they picked it up. They sought instead to pass it on to their successors for resolution. In either case, a strategy that substituted procedure for substance was doomed to failure, as sooner or later Britain would run out of new proposals or Argentina would tire of the game. As we have observed, this critical juncture was reached with the failure of the lease-back proposal, and not long afterwards the negotiations stalled.

The Thatcher government was to a certain extent responsible for the dilemma in which it now found itself. Supporters of Ridley insist that between a third and half of the islanders did not oppose the lease-back proposal when it was first broached to them. They argue that more islanders would have come around had London made it clear that it supported the idea and was prepared to compensate residents who wished to leave rather than live symbolically under the Argentine flag.

We will never know whether or not government pressure on the islanders would have succeeded in bringing about a consensus in the form of recognizing de jure Argentine sovereignty, for the policy was never tried. Margaret Thatcher was unprepared to put any pressure on the islanders. No doubt, she viewed such a policy with loathing. Another reason for her caution may have been the strength of the Falkland lobby among Conservative Members of Parliament. This small but outspoken group of Tories portrayed the Falkland Islands as a test case of the government's commitment to uphold traditional British freedoms. They allied themselves with left-wing Labourites who also opposed any concessions to the *junta* on the grounds that it was a fascist dictatorship. Both groups are reported to have kept in close touch with the islanders and to have encouraged them to keep up their pressure on the government. The prime minister, already in trouble within her own party, and her popularity sagging in the polls, would have been reluctant to antagonize backbench opinion on this issue.

The prime minister's solicitousness toward the islanders signaled to them that a harder line on their part was likely to be rewarded, as indeed it was when they received what was in effect a veto power over the negotiations. The whole affair was reminiscent, on a much smaller scale, of the successful effort earlier in the century by Orangemen to gain a stranglehold over successive British governments in order to forestall a settlement of the Irish question. They too had a powerful lobby in Parliament that successive prime ministers were reluctant to defy.

The two mediating conditions for defensive avoidance are: a state of relatively high decisional conflict resulting from two clashing types of threat that make easy resolution impossible; and the loss of hope of finding a better solution than the defective ones already considered. This was precisely the situation the British government confronted in 1982. The failure of the lease-back proposal left the government with only two clear policy alternatives. The first of these, to put pressure on the islanders to accept Argentine sovereignty, was unpalatable to the government and entailed serious political costs at home. The other option, telling Buenos Aires that a transfer of sovereignty was out of the question for the time being, was something the British had all along been unwilling to do because it would have required them to garrison the Falklands with forces sufficient to deter an Argentine invasion.

Rather than face this unpleasant reality and the unappealing and costly choices associated with it, the British government sought escape in the illusion that its existing policy of stringing Argentina along could be continued. Despite all the indications that this objective was no longer realistic, Luce and other British negotiators in New York returned to London in March convinced that they had "bought another year."[28] They were surprised by the *junta*'s disavowal of the talks.

The British sense of helplessness in the South Atlantic seems to have elicited all three forms of defensive avoidance. The overall British policy objective of keeping negotiations alive was in effect a form of procrastination designed to postpone the need to make a choice between the Scylla of islander interests and the Charybdis of Argentine nationalism. It can also be seen as an attempt by the Thatcher government to avoid altogether the responsibility for such a decision by passing it on to their successors. Finally, the government and the intelligence community engaged in bolstering. They convinced themselves that the course of action to which they were committed would succeed and became insensitive to information that indicated otherwise. Toward this end, British leaders may unwittingly have encouraged their intelligence organizations to provide them with reassuring estimates. It would not be at all surprising to find that intelligence officials shaded their evaluations to bring them in line as much as possible with expectations of their superiors. Air Commodore Brian Frow, director general of the Falkland Island Office, has openly charged the Foreign Office with ignoring the warnings he passed on from islanders because they were found inconvenient.[29] Some middle-level intelligence officials have also confided to the press that "their raw material was far more alarmist than the much blander assessment of it reaching ministers," assessments that are known to have played down the threat of invasion.[30] The failure of senior intelligence officials to insist upon the development of a strategic conception could also have been, at least in part, an expression of the same phenomenon.

We must return to the original justification given by both Margaret Thatcher and Lord Carrington to explain their failure to predict the Argentine invasion. This was that they were victims of the cry-wolf phenomenon. As such threats had been made before without resulting in invasion, they had become relatively immune to them. Given the obvious difference between 1977 and 1982, one is left wondering the extent to which this argument was really a rationalization used by British leaders throughout the month of March to convince themselves that the very outcome they feared the most but were unprepared to confront would not actually come to pass.

Self-deception in Buenos Aires

In May 1982, James Reston, the doyen of mainstream U.S. political commentators, declared: "The problem in Buenos Aires is not that the calculations of the generals went wrong . . . but that they did not think or calculate at all."[31] Reston's observation is typical of the instant analysis that proliferated in the British, European, and

North American press. The media in these countries for the most part portrayed the Argentine *junta* as ignorant, short-sighted, and even foolish men who went to war oblivious to its likely consequences for their nation. While there is certainly some validity to this judgment, it also helps to justify London's failure to foresee the Argentine invasion. For if the *junta* behaved irrationally, indeed unpredictably, then British leaders might to some extent be excused for not foreseeing the invasion. The truth is more complex. The British, as we have seen, were themselves guilty of a number of errors and illusions. Nor were Argentine leaders quite so unsophisticated in their approach to the Falklands problem as is commonly alleged.

After the termination of the New York negotiations, the generals set out upon a deliberate course of escalating tensions with Britain. Their strategy was to commit themselves step by step to military action in the expectation that this would succeed in eliciting some kind of British concession on sovereignty before they were compelled to act. Such strategy had worked in 1977.

The *junta* first burned its bridges with public opinion. On 2 March, the generals announced that Argentina reserved its right to "seek other means" to regain the Falklands. At the same time *junta* representatives briefed the press on the unsatisfactory outcome of the New York talks. This prompted bellicose editorial comments, which continued throughout the month and culminated in predictions of invasion. *Junta* members also began dropping broad hints to diplomats in Buenos Aires that they were considering military action unless the British displayed willingness to cede sovereignty. The Argentines even communicated the precise concession they had in mind: a public statement by London that it would resume negotiations with the purpose of reaching an agreement to transfer sovereignty before the end of the year. Later in the month, the *junta* increased the pressure further by sending three warships to South Georgia to give "full protection" to a small party of Argentines who had unfurled the national flag on that island in defiance of the British.

That this strategy was a form of political coercion is made apparent by the fact that the generals made no effort to disguise their intentions, nor later to hide their military preparations for invasion. The latter were well publicized and meant to be taken by London as palpable indicators of Argentine commitment and resolve. DYN, the Argentine news agency, carried accounts of extensive naval preparations including a report on 29 March that the marine regiment attached to the task force had been issued food rations, arms, and ammunition in expectation of an invasion of the Falklands. Even more telling was a query from Uruguay on 30 March, in all likelihood with Argentine approval, asking Britain if any Falklanders wanted to be air lifted off the islands before the invasion.[32]

The Argentine strategy, while deliberate, was not altogether a matter of choice for the *junta*. The generals were to a great extent the prisoners of passions they themselves had helped to arouse and to which they had subsequently become increasingly vulnerable by virtue of their faltering legitimacy. In this sense, the March policy of the generals represented something of a desperate gamble; it was the last card they could play from a bad hand that held out any prospect of success.

During this month of crisis London was probably in a position to have eased the *junta*'s dilemma in one of two ways. Thatcher could have made a concession on sovereignty, as Buenos Aires certainly hoped she would, or she could have assembled a naval armada that was sufficiently imposing to permit the *junta* to back down without necessarily losing face. The British government did neither.

After the invasion, David Owen, Labour's former foreign secretary, suggested that the proper policy would have been to have deployed hunter-killer submarines without any publicity.[33] However, this would have done nothing to insulate the *junta* from the domestic political repercussions of appearing to shy away from the use of force. The only naval action that had any hope of success was a visible and intimidating display of force, say a carrier task force with a contingent of Royal Marines to augment the meager Port Stanley garrison. This might just have allowed the generals to justify passivity as the only possible policy in light of the adversary's overwhelming military superiority. Such an outcome might not have been at all disadvantageous to the *junta* because it could have rallied considerable political support at home and elsewhere in Latin America by portraying itself as the victim of colonial oppression. Moreover, by compelling Britain to assemble and send a naval armada all the way to the South Atlantic it would unquestionably have succeeded in giving the Falkland question much greater salience in London. This in itself might even have helped to break the diplomatic logjam by convincing the Thatcher government that the cost of ignoring Argentine claims was at least as great as that of antagonizing the Falkland lobby.

Unfortunately for the *junta,* it was dealing with an adversary who was insensitive to so many of the political storm warnings blowing from Argentina. The generals' strategy thus failed in the first instance because their desperation went unrecognized in London. Argentine leaders were in effect trying to compel their British counterparts to make the very choice they were trying so hard to deny. In the end, the British capacity for self-delusion triumphed over Argentine efforts to instill a sense of urgency in the British consciousness.

By the end of March the *junta* accordingly found itself in a position where it had to make some kind of decision about military action. To back down, after having raised public opinion to a feverish pitch, invited a political backlash that was likely to sweep the generals from power. However, to carry through their strategy to its logical conclusion, an invasion of the Falkland Islands, risked war with Great Britain.

Like the British before them, they found themselves in the kind of decisional dilemma that prompts defensive avoidance. Not surprisingly, they too procrastinated and deferred a decision as long as they could. The evidence indicates that Galtieri did not actually pluck up his courage and authorize Admiral Anaya to break away from maneuvers with Uruguay and steam to the Falklands until 31 March, three days after the fleet had put to sea.[34]

In weighing their decision, it seems likely that Galtieri and his colleagues in the *junta* were in the end swayed by the consideration that backing down entailed near certain political disaster whereas invasion, if it did not lead to war, held out the prospect of substantial gains for little cost. In this regard, the labor demonstrations against the regime on 30 March, the very day before the decision to invade was apparently made, could reasonably have been expected to have brought home their vulnerability to the generals. They may even have tipped the scales in favor of invasion. By contrast, there were a number of reasons, some convincing and some much less so, why the *junta* could bring itself to believe that the policy to which it was committed would succeed. General Galtieri himself later confessed to Oriana Fallaci that he downplayed the likelihood of a British military response. "I'll tell you," he replied to her query, "that though an English reaction was considered a possibility, we did not see it as a probability. Personally, I judged it scarcely possible and totally improbable."[35]

The principal reason why Galtieri may have discounted the possibility of a strong British reaction was London's obvious failure to communicate resolve. To the best of our knowledge no strongly worded warnings, even private ones, emanated from London until 31 March, when the invasion was all but a *fait accompli*. Nor, *Endurance* aside, was any effort made to strengthen Britain's naval presence in the South Atlantic until quite belatedly. On 20 March, a submarine and support ships were ordered south from the Mediterranean. Even then, this deployment was not announced publicly but remained an unconfirmed press report. The ships did not reach the Falklands until after the invasion. *Endurance* itself, sent to South Georgia in the aftermath of the unauthorized flag raising incident, was withdrawn when three Argentine warships appeared on the scene despite Lord Carrington's earlier promise in Parliament that "it would remain on station as long as necessary." This episode did nothing to enhance British credibility.

The avowed reason for London's passivity was, of course, concern for miscalculated escalation. In retrospect, it is apparent that this was quite a mistaken emphasis. The British should have been more fearful of a deterrence failure. Argentine leaders, propelled toward invasion by the series of events I have described, were probably predisposed to interpret British passivity as a sign of lack of resolve. Tony Emerson, the *Times* correspondent in Buenos Aires, reported that many Argentine officials had actually formed the impression that the British failure to respond to Argentine provocations could only be attributed to their desire to be rid of the Falkland problem once and for all by means of an invasion.[36]

A second consideration that may have influenced Argentine calculations was the *junta*'s apparent belief that there was little or nothing in a military sense that Britain could do to dislodge Argentina from the Falklands once they had actually occupied it. The time for Britain to have acted was before an invasion, when a reinforced garrison in Port Stanley could have opposed the Argentines with some expectation of success, or better yet when the British fleet, had it been in Falkland waters, could have interdicted the invasion force. Having missed this opportunity, Britain's only logical military recourse was to try to dislodge the invaders, a very risky and exceedingly complex operation that required forces and a national commitment of an altogether different magnitude. Rear Admiral John F. Woodward, commander of the Royal Navy task force, himself agreed that recapture of the Falkland Islands could be "a long and bloody campaign." There was, he admitted, "no simple, short, quick military solution . . . while the Argentine resisted."[37]

Galtieri confided that the *junta* thought such an amphibious operation "inconceivable." When the British subsequently prepared to carry it out he gave it little chance of success.[38] Galtieri was not alone in this opinion. Many naval experts, among them Americans, who were presumably well informed on the subject, doubted Britain's ability to liberate the Falklands even after the Thatcher government had committed itself to this course of action. "The British aren't going to be able to do it," predicted a senior American general. "They will control the seas but not the air."[39] The *Washington Post* reported a similar expectation among high-ranking naval officers. The consensus was that the British task force would not be able to do much when it arrived in Falkland waters because it lacked sufficient air power and logistical support. A retired U.S. admiral told the *Post:* "The British made the decision to structure their navy to only certain NATO tasks and have lost their ability to conduct independent operations in the process."[40] Drew Middleton, one of the most respected U.S. military analysts, offered an only slightly less pessimistic assessment in the *New York Times*.[41]

Subsequent events proved predictions of failure to be quite unfounded, although the British did pay a heavy price for their inability to provide adequate air cover for their fleet. The point, however, is that, if knowledgeable authorities doubted Britain's ability to recapture the Falklands, the Argentines might to some degree be pardoned for their failure to foresee first the scope and then the success of military operations against them.

A third consideration, which some commentators suggest influenced the Argentine decision to invade, was the change in U.S. policy toward Argentina initiated by Ronald Reagan. Stanley Hoffmann, for one, has taken the line that U.S. policy "twice fueled" the Falklands crisis. The Administration, he argues, first helped to start it by leading Argentina to believe it could get away with seizing the islands, and then made matters worse by trying to mediate a settlement instead of immediately condemning the Argentine aggression.[42]

It is certainly true that even before Reagan took office he actively sought to reverse the Carter approach to Latin America. Transition team members journeyed to Buenos Aires and advised the *junta* to clean up its act in order to pave the way for closer relations with the United States. In Washington, administration intellectuals devised a farcical distinction between "totalitarian" and "authoritarian" regimes and used it to justify their circumvention of Carter's human rights policy. In the United Nations, the United States delegate to the Human Rights Commission supported Argentina's effort to block disclosure of its abysmal human rights record in opposition to the efforts of all the European democracies to make it public. In March 1981, then President designate of the *junta*, General Roberto Viola, who had commanded the army during the reign of terror, was entertained at the White House by President Reagan, who called him "a majestic personality." He was similarly feted by bankers in New York.

The reasons for Reagan's courtship of Argentina were both ideological and geopolitical. The Administration, impressed by the *junta*'s strident anticommunism, sought to enlist its cooperation against leftist regimes and guerilla movements in Central America. Argentina was encouraged to speak out against the Mexican-French initiative for a negotiated settlement in El Salvador. Cooperation between the two countries was later broadened to encompass a wide range of activities including the dispatch of Argentine "advisors" to the Salvadoran and Guatemalan armies and to *Somocista* camps in Honduras. Argentina also withdrew its ambassadors from Havana and Managua in support of Reagan's policy and proved receptive to the possibility of participating in the Sinai peace-keeping force.

The United States had always remained aloof from the dispute over the Falklands' sovereignty. The Reagan administration, despite its closer relationship with Buenos Aires, did not publicly deviate from this line. It is not known what, if anything, General Vernon Walters, Reagan's sub rosa intermediary with "authoritarian" regimes, said about the Falklands on his several trips to Argentina. It may be, as some critics of the Administration allege, that he whispered words of sympathy into the ears of the *junta*.[43] Even if true, this could hardly be taken as license for an invasion. Nor should the Reagan administration's efforts to woo the generals have necessarily provided any assurance that Washington would turn a blind eye to Argentine aggression. After all, the United States also had a long-standing and far more intimate relationship with Britain, who was in addition a mainstay of her most important military alliance. Washington was also opposed on principle to the unilateral use of force to resolve territorial disputes. President Reagan belatedly attempted to make this point clear in his fifty-minute telephone call to General Galtieri on the morning of 1 April. He tried unsuccessfully to persuade Galtieri to call off the invasion, telling him that Britain was certain to respond with force and that an invasion "would wreck relations between the United States and Argentina."[44]

From the perspective of Buenos Aires, the U.S. record could at best be seen as ambiguous. The Argentine military attaché in Washington is nevertheless reported to have informed the *junta* that the Reagan administration was so eager for Argentina's support in Central America that "in a crunch it would tilt toward Buenos Aires, not London."[45] Galtieri admitted to Oriana Fallaci that he shared this view. "I didn't expect his [Reagan's] approval or support," he said, "but I was sure that he would behave with balance and neutrality." It is significant that Galtieri was unwilling in this interview to face up to his own miscalculation. Instead, and with obvious emotion, he portrayed Haig's mediation and Reagan's subsequent support for Britain as "a tremendous deception" in light of his close personal relations with the president and the importance of Argentina for U.S. global strategy. "Both the Argentines and I," he asserted, "see this as a betrayal."[46] Such a paranoid response, indicative of severe disappointment, is another sign of the importance U.S. neutrality seems to have had in the *junta*'s calculations.[47]

One further and on the whole more convincing explanation for Argentina's miscalculation should be considered. This is the very different cognitive contexts in terms of which Buenos Aires and London conceived the Falkland problem. The different contexts encouraged quite divergent estimates of British resolve.

From the Argentine perspective the Falkland Islands were national territory that had been occupied by a colonial power since 1833. Continued British sovereignty over the islands was an atavism in a world that had witnessed numerous wars of national liberation to bring the age of colonialism to an end. General Galtieri gave voice to this sentiment in his address to the Argentine nation on 1 May. "Our cause," he insisted, "has ceased to be an Argentine problem. It has become a cause of America and of the world, which does not acknowledge colonialism as a situation which can be tolerated in this century."[48]

Galtieri's claim was more than mere rhetoric. Opinion throughout Latin America was strongly supportive of Argentina's claim and on the whole, understanding of the *junta*'s exasperation with diplomacy.[49] Within Argentina, feeling was even stronger. Every newspaper in the country greeted "the recovery" of the "Malvinas" with banner headlines. All the political parties, including those who had been the most strident in their criticism of the *junta,* issued statements celebrating the reconquest. Deolindo Bittel, leader of the Peronists, whose views on just about everything were at odds with the generals, publicly embraced Galtieri. Not to be outdone in this orgy of nationalism, the CGT, which had demonstrated against the *junta* the week before, called upon its members to return to the Plaza de Mayo to voice their approval of its foreign policy. What linked these disparate and antagonistic factions together was the belief on the left as well as the right that the British occupation of the Falklands represented, as *La Prensa* put it, "an intolerable insult to Argentine independence and nationhood."[50]

Viewed in this light, it must have seemed a far-fetched notion indeed that in 1982 a "colonial" power would try to reimpose its rule on a liberated colony by force of arms, let alone succeed in doing so.

World opinion, international morality, and, most important of all, the constellation of international political forces, all appeared to militate against it. The analogies that might have sprung into Argentine minds were Goa and Suez—an early invasion scenario prepared by the navy was actually called Plan Goa. The original Goa operation, a possible model for the Argentine operation, resulted in a colonial power, Portugal, accommodating itself to the loss of its colonial enclave on the Indian subcontinent when it was overrun by India. Suez, of course, remains the best example of how an attempt to reimpose colonial domination failed for all of the reasons already alluded to.

The British conceived of the Falklands controversy in an altogether different way. Politicians, the press, and public opinion for the most part dismissed the colonial metaphor as inappropriate because the population of the islands was of British stock and wished to remain under the protection of the crown.[51] Majority opinion did not see the Argentine invasion as an effort at national liberation but as an act of naked aggression carried out by a dictatorship against a democratic and peaceful people. For the major parties and most factions within them, even those who admitted some legitimacy to Argentine claims, the military means Buenos Aires had used to achieve its end were repugnant and unacceptable. There was, however, considerable disagreement as to the best way of effecting an Argentine withdrawal.[52]

For British opinion, the dominant historical analogy was Hitler and the origins of World War II. Newspapers and politicians made frequent, if not incessant, reference to the events and lessons of that period. Chief among these lessons was the need to stand up to aggression lest failure to do so further whet the appetites of would-be aggressors everywhere. The day before the invasion, the *Times* drew the parallel between the two situations when it warned the government that "it would be wrong to give Argentina the impression that any sudden *Anschluss* would be unopposed."[53] The Thatcher cabinet later pursued the same line of reasoning. On 7 April, Francis Pym began his first speech in Parliament as foreign secretary with the declaration that "Britain did not appease dictators."[54] The prime minister herself justified the cost in lives and money of retaking the Falklands with the twin arguments that "aggression must not be allowed to succeed" and "freedom must be protected against dictatorship."[55] Probably the most succinct statement of the essence of the analogy appeared once again in the *Times*. The first editorial following the invasion declared: "We defended Poland because we had given our word and because the spread of dictatorships across Europe had to be stopped for our own sakes. . . . As in 1939, so today, the same principles apply to the Falkland Islands. We have given our word, and we must, where we can, prevent the expansionist policies of a dictatorship affecting our interests."[56]

If it was inconceivable for Argentina that Britain would ever go to war to regain the Falklands, it was equally inconceivable to most Britons that they would not if it proved the only way to effect an Argentine withdrawal.[57] The different cognitive contexts in terms of which the two countries conceived of the problem led not only to contrasting visions of justice but also to quite different imperatives for action. Unfortunately, policy makers in both London and Buenos Aires, while not altogether ignorant of the other's conceptualization of the problem, seemed unable to grasp its implications for that country's behavior.

Having reviewed the likely reasons for the *junta*'s failure to foresee Britain's reaction to the invasion of the Falklands, one must still assess the extent to which this judgment could be considered reasonable based on the information on hand at the time. Such an assessment cannot be made in terms of the outcome of the crisis because there can be situations in which an adversary proves willing to go to war in defense of a commitment but his precrisis behavior nevertheless made it reasonable to assume that he would back down or remain passive when challenged. The North Koreans, for example, clearly misjudged the U.S. response to an invasion of South Korea, but their expectation of U.S. nonintervention was not an unreasonable expectation. U.S. statements and actions prior to June 1950 had given them good cause to believe that Washington would not commit its few forces in the Pacific to the defense of South Korea.[58]

Like the United States in Korea, Britain had sent misleading signals to Argentina, signals that I have shown could have been interpreted as indications of lack of resolve. It was also far from clear that Britain had the means to recapture the Falklands even if it had the resolve. Considering only this information, the *junta* might be said to have acted with reasonable expectation of success. However, there were other equally important attributes of the situation that should have dictated caution in Buenos Aires.

It did not require sophisticated political analysis to grasp the fact that an invasion of the Falklands dealt a severe blow to British honor and prestige and that the British government and people would probably be moved to do something about it. The Argentine government should have been particularly sensitive to this reality given its problem in this regard. What reason did the *junta* have for believing that Thatcher and her government would be that much more able than it had been to ignore the demands of what was certain to be aroused if not enraged public opinion?

The extent of public outrage in Britain became apparent immediately following the invasion. In a three-hour emergency parliamentary debate, the first on a Saturday since the Suez crisis in 1956, Margaret Thatcher, Lord Carrington, and John Nott were subjected to a "verbal battering," the *Times* reported, "of a savagery reserved by the House of Commons for occasions of national humiliation."[59] The prime minister faced a possible revolt among Tory backbenchers and the prospect of a near total loss of confidence in her by the electorate.[60] A national public opinion poll published in the *Daily Mail* on 6 April revealed that 80 percent of the British people blamed the government for the invasion and 36 percent blamed Thatcher herself. Twenty-five percent believed she should resign.[61] A week later the *Times* featured a Gallup report with the stunning finding that the public thought Thatcher the worst prime minister in British history. She topped the list with 48 percent of the vote. Neville Chamberlain, usually the winner in such contests, only received 12 percent.[62] It was clear that only a forceful and successful response would have any hope of restoring the government's credibility. One member of the cabinet confessed to an American journalist: "To be frank, I don't see how she [Thatcher] can survive if she shrinks from a military showdown."[63]

Domestic politics aside, Britain had important interests and commitments throughout the world that would have been seriously compromised by passive acceptance of the Falklands invasion. Many of these interests, as were the Falklands themselves, were carryovers from the days when Britain had ruled a great empire. Concern for Gibraltar probably headed the list, for the invasion had touched off an onrush of nationalism in Spain.[64] "If we can't get the Argentinians out of the Falklands," a senior British defense official observed, "how long do you think it will be before the Spaniards take a crack at Gibraltar?"[65] The *Economist* voiced the same concern and thought it sufficient grounds for retaking the Falklands.[66]

Within Latin America, Guatemala and Venezuela stood out as particularly vocal backers of Argentina's action. Both coveted former British territory. Guatemala hoped to annex Belize, which had been granted independence in September 1981. The country was protected by a small British force that the Thatcher government had been seeking to withdraw because of its cost. Venezuela in turn had laid claim to about two-thirds of Guyana for eighty-three years but in 1970 had agreed to a twelve-year moratorium, which was due to expire two months after the invasion. In March, the Guyanese had reported military activity along their border and were worried that the Argentine invasion would strengthen factions within the Venezuelan armed forces who favored a harder line.[67]

Loss of the Falklands might also have been expected to have weakened Britain's position in both Diego Garcia and Hong Kong. Diego Garcia, an important Western naval base in the Indian Ocean, had attracted the increasing attention of the left-wing electoral alliance in Mauritius that won the general election of 13 June 1982, and which previously had vowed to launch an international campaign to regain sovereignty over the atoll.[68] Hong Kong, which had been subjected to Chinese intimidation in the past, was soon to be the subject of negotiations because the British lease on the New Territories expires in 1997. Finally, there were the questions of economic rights in South Atlantic waters and territorial interests in Antarctica to be considered. Argentina and Britain had extensive clashing claims with regard to both. In Parliament and in the press concern was expressed that British interests would be prejudiced, if not irreparably harmed, by continuing Argentine occupation of the Falklands.[69]

Argentina should also have taken into account a less tangible but nevertheless important consideration: the personality of Britain's leader. Throughout her term as prime minister, the "iron lady" had actively cultivated an image of toughness. To the delight and occasionally the dismay of her supporters, she had a tendency to treat defiance of government policy as a personal challenge. Her series of clashes with the unions, which had pitted her against them in a highly confrontational manner, were well-publicized cases in point. Given her government's standing commitment to the islanders, an invasion of the Falklands was almost certain to be conceived of by her as the kind of challenge to which she had to respond.

There were, therefore, good and for the most part perfectly obvious reasons why it was unlikely that Britain would accept an invasion of the Falklands. There is no evidence that Argentina's leaders considered any of these reasons. Even after Britain's naval armada had laid siege to the islands, General Galtieri, if he is to be believed, was still amazed by London's response. "Why" he asked, "should a country situated in the heart of Europe care so much for some islands located far away in the Atlantic Ocean; in addition, islands which do not serve any national interest? It seems senseless to me."[70]

Galtieri's apparent difficulty in comprehending Britain's motives must be attributed, at least in part, to his lack of international experience and political sophistication. Like most of the other members of the *junta*, his education had been narrowly technical, his professional experiences entirely within his own branch of the service, and his political horizon limited to Latin America. The *junta* as a body was poorly equipped to understand the differences between the political systems of Argentina and Britain or to put itself in the position of its adversary in order to see the world through his eyes.

Lack of sophistication is, however, an insufficient explanation for the *junta*'s failure to consider some of the more obvious motives for intervention. Here we must fall back upon our earlier hypothesis of defensive avoidance, which makes its selective attention to information more readily explicable. Galtieri and his colleagues, compelled for internal political reasons to go forward with the invasion, sought to insulate themselves from information that suggested their policy would lead to war. At the same time they played up any circumstance, however uncertain its import, that might indicate a successful outcome. Seen in this light, the range of reasons we have explored for the *junta*'s miscalculation—lack of apparent British resolve, the difficulty of recapturing the Falklands, expectations of U.S. neutrality, and differing cognitive conceptions of the controversy—were rationalizations for a policy to which the generals were committed. They constituted a psychological shield behind which the *junta* could protect itself from threatening realities that lay beyond the barrack walls. The perceptual distortion this engendered was the real cause of the miscalculation that led to war.

Conclusion

In an earlier study of international crisis I defined brinkmanship as a confrontation in which one state knowingly challenges an important commitment of another with the expectation that its adversary will back down when challenged.[71] In such a confrontation the initiator is not attempting to start a war but rather to achieve specific political objectives by means of coercion. Brinkmanship succeeds only if the initiator achieves his goals without provoking war.

The Falkland confrontation clearly conforms to this pattern of crisis. Argentina's leaders certainly had no desire to provoke a war with Great Britain but rather expected the Thatcher government to retreat from its commitment to maintain sovereignty over the Falklands when Argentine marines occupied Port Stanley. Like many initiators of brinkmanship crises, they miscalculated their adversary's response, an error that resulted in war.

Crisis strategies are predicated on a set of expectations about the behavior of other international actors. These expectations are often derived from the analysis of a large number of indices and signals, many of which are ambiguous or contradictory. Nevertheless, one of the most striking findings of my study of brinkmanship was the extent to which initiators of these crises frequently misjudged their adversary's resolve. The expectation that the adversary would back down when challenged, a defining characteristic of brinkmanship, proved justified in only three of the fourteen cases I examined. In every other instance, the initiator had to back down or go to war.

The Argentines also remained insensitive to the full extent of their miscalculation well into the crisis. In the month between the invasion on 2 April and the sinking of the Argentine cruiser *Belgrano* on 3 May, the *junta* received ample indications of British resolve to use force to recapture the Falklands. The Argentines also had several opportunities to reach a negotiated settlement. Nevertheless, Haig's shuttle diplomacy, the United Nations initiatives, and the mediation of Peru's President Fernando Belaunde Terry all failed to bring about a peaceful withdrawal. Until Washington's announcement on 31 March that it would support Britain, the *junta* gave every appearance of confidence in a diplomatic outcome. Argentine Foreign Minister Nicanor Costa Méndez kept expressing his optimism in this regard and even claimed that "the danger of war with Britain was fading."[72] When these several attempts at settlement fell through, Argentine leaders took refuge in the belief that the British task force would fail in its attempt to dislodge Argentina from the islands. Throughout, they continued to insist, quite unrealistically, on some nod by London in the direction of recognizing Argentine sovereignty as their minimum condition for withdrawal.

It is always difficult to know the extent to which public statements actually reflect the thinking of the officials who make them. In the Argentine case they may have done so, for Costa Méndez's statements were given substance by an unrealistic policy that appeared to be based on those judgments. Once again, psychology and politics were intertwined. The generals were caught between the military facts, which dictated a settlement, and the political facts at home, which indicated that neither the honor of the military nor their tenure as Argentina's leaders was likely to survive any settlement they had any chance of reaching. The *junta*'s dilemma was, if anything, more acute after the invasion than before by reason of the commitment this action entailed. One Argentine editor commented: "Galtieri and the generals are cornered. They have nowhere to go but forward. If they go backwards, they will be swept away."[73] They thus stayed locked into their suicidal collision course with Britain until the very bitter end.

The Falkland crisis was complicated by the fact that there was serious miscalculation on both sides. The British, as we have seen, also took refuge in illusions when it helped to reconcile their clashing political and strategic needs. This perceptual sleight of hand was abetted by the failure of British intelligence officials to develop a strategic rationale from which useful indicators of warning could be derived. British political leaders also insisted upon almost certain knowledge that Argentina actually intended to invade the Falklands before they were willing to buttress deterrence. By the time they received this information it was too late to influence Argentine behavior.

We can surmise that the contrasting cultural temperaments of the two societies, one given to hyperbole and visible displays of emotion, the other to understatement and the public suppression of feeling, complicated the problem of prediction even further. Despite all the difficulties attendant upon the task, the problem of facing recurrent crises compelled the British to develop a conception of strategic and political conditions that might encourage or even necessitate an Argentine attack. Such a conception, we have argued, would have pointed to some very important differences between 1977 and 1982 and could have alerted British policy makers to the gravity of the situation they faced.

Strategic conceptions, important as they are, are no panacea to the problem of fathoming an adversary's intentions. They can be misleading, as was true for Israel in 1973. They are nevertheless the only practical means of attempting to decipher an opponent's intentions in a situation of recurrent threat short of a reliable source with access to its opponent's most secret deliberations.

The Israeli failure illustrates some of the difficulties inherent in constructing a strategic rationale. By virtue perhaps of decades of extreme Arab hostility and rhetoric superimposed on Israel's own "holocaust mentality," Israeli military intelligence could not imagine an Arab attack that did not have the destruction of Israel as its objective. The conditions they posited for such an attack, equality in the air and Syrian participation, were largely irrelevant to the limited war envisaged by Sadat.

Israel's strategic indicators were also strictly military ones; they ignored the political context of Arab-Israeli relations. In practice, relative military advantage, while it is an important consideration, is rarely the determining factor in foreign policy challenges. It was not decisive for Egypt in 1973 nor was it for Argentina in 1982. In fact, had Buenos Aires waited one more year, it might well have gotten away with its invasion. HMS *Invincible* would have gone to the Australian navy, *Hermes* would have been paid off. *Intrepid* and *Fearless*, the two amphibious assault ships, would have been scrapped together with some of the supporting frigates. Britain, which barely had the means to retake the Falklands in 1982, would have been very hard put, perhaps unable, to do so in the absence of these vessels. Both these cases illustrate the importance of political as opposed to military calculations in the decision to go to war. This puts a premium on devising strategic conceptions that specify not only the military preconditions of a challenge but also the political conditions that encourage or necessitate them in the first place. This requires close collaboration between military intelligence and its civilian counterpart because the latter can be expected to be more sensitive to the political dimension of the problem.

The other British error I have identified was the government's misplaced concern for avoiding miscalculated escalation. As a result, the British government insisted upon absolute certainty of Argentina's aggressive intentions before it was willing to act. Its passivity contributed to a deterrence failure since it appears to have been interpreted by Argentina as lack of resolve.

The British failure in this regard had two dimensions to it. The first we have already noted. In the absence of a strategic rationale the government had little guidance in making an appropriate trade-off between the need to guard against miscalculated escalation and deterrence failure. The second concerned the actual cost of making a trade-off between these two somewhat contradictory objectives of crisis management.

Action designed to buttress deterrence, in this instance visible naval preparations coupled with warning to Buenos Aires, would have entailed an immediate cost. A significant naval presence in the South Atlantic was both expensive and politically embarrassing, for the government had recently cut the budget for precisely the kind of conventional naval forces it would now have utilized. It seems likely that concern for these immediate costs contributed to the reluctance of the government to act and made it insistent upon near certain knowledge that Argentina was going to invade before it was willing to do so.

If this analysis is correct, it points to the importance of immediate as opposed to deferred costs for policy makers in crisis situations. Both miscalculated escalation and deterrence failure would have grave consequences. Either could lead to war and in circumstances that would be particularly embarrassing to the British government. If war arose from miscalculated escalation, the government could readily be portrayed by the Opposition as having been responsible for it. If, on the other hand, war was the result of a deterrence failure, as was in fact the case, the government had to account for its apparent intelligence failure to predict and prevent the attack and then for the necessity of organizing a risky expedition to recapture the Falkland Islands. These costs, great as they were, were difficult to assess in magnitude and probability. No doubt the inability to determine with any certainty which of the two problems posed the greater and more likely threat made it difficult to choose between competing courses of action. The costs may even have tended to cancel each other out in the minds of policy makers. Calculations of immediate costs, although hardly comparable in consequence, would have accordingly loomed larger in the deliberations of the government. They may even have had a decisive impact upon the decision to opt for passivity.

The general principle that emerges from this argument is that policy makers, not only in crisis situations, but across a whole range of decisions, are probably inordinately influenced by immediate and predictable costs regardless of their dimensions. The relative importance of short-term considerations is likely to increase in proportion to the difficulty of determining the magnitude or likelihood of the longer-term costs that might be associated with any particular course of action. In the case of the British government, short-term consideration, unfortunately and quite arbitrarily, pointed to what we now know was the wrong policy choice. In retrospect, it was a tragedy that the prime minister, a person of unquestioned courage when she perceives matters of principle to be at stake, seemingly failed to rise above narrow calculations of short-term interests when formulating Falklands policy.

The short-term interests that presumably influenced Thatcher's Falkland policy were political in nature: concern for maintaining backbench support and the desire to avoid the embarrassment associated with a precautionary naval demonstration after her government had recommended deep cuts in funding for conventional naval forces. As we have seen, Argentine policy also appears to have been heavily, perhaps decisively, influenced by domestic political concerns. The motive here was the *junta*'s need to do something to restore its faltering legitimacy.

The Falkland crisis is by no means unique in the extent to which domestic political concerns, often short-term in nature, shaped foreign policy decisions, including those entailing high risks. This was the case with many crises included in my earlier study of brinkmanship. In so many of these crises, policies determined principally by domestic considerations had disastrous consequences for both the state and political leaders involved. This is also true of the Falklands. The Argentine military leaders responsible for the war were forced out of office in the aftermath of their defeat, and the *junta* itself was quickly replaced by a civilian government. In Britain, Margaret Thatcher's popularity increased following Britain's victory, but that victory was a costly one. It was also a very near thing. The war could easily have resulted in disaster for Britain and her prime minister.

The principal policy lesson of the Falklands is clear. Political leaders, especially in democracies, must respond to public opinion and other domestic pressures. However, leaders who allow themselves to shape foreign policies *primarily* in terms of these internal considerations court disaster at home and abroad because such policies are likely to bear only a chance resemblance to the needs of the nation.

6

■

SAVING FACE FOR THE SAKE
OF DETERRENCE

Patrick M. Morgan

■ Deterrence is undoubtedly a psychological phenomenon, for it involves convincing an opponent not to attack by threatening it with harm in retaliation. To "convince" is to penetrate and manipulate the thought processes of the opposing leaders so that they draw the "proper" conclusion about the utility of attacking. This gives the effectiveness of deterrence a psychological dimension that is only partially related to the deterrer's retaliatory capabilities, for it is the persuasiveness of the message about those capabilities rather than the capabilities themselves that determines success or failure. Thus it is possible for a state to achieve a degree of deterrence at variance with its ability and willingness to retaliate. It may threaten retaliation, be quite capable of inflicting the harm it threatens, be prepared to carry out the threat, and yet experience the attack it hoped to forestall because the opponent did not perceive the threat or (more likely) did not believe it. On the other hand, a state may pose a retaliatory threat it cannot or will not carry out but that the opponent perceives and believes, in which case more deterrence is achieved than the state is, in some "objective" sense, entitled to obtain.

It is apparent that deterrence succeeds or fails in the mind of the potential attacker, and that this is therefore the proper starting point for a theory of deterrence. The objective would be to elucidate the ways in which, and the conditions under which, a potential attacker can be induced to take a retaliatory threat seriously. This has in fact been a central objective of deterrence theory, but in this connection the theory developed in a somewhat peculiar fashion, primarily because it concerns cognitive processes, and they are a notoriously difficult subject for study and analysis. When the relevant cognitive processes are in the heads of foreigners, that makes things all the worse. As a result, the theory in its initial formulation turned out to be less than satisfactory. Broadly speaking, there were two possible ways to proceed. One would have involved attempting to construct a typology of potential attackers in terms of cognitive processes typical of their decision makers and a set of guidelines setting forth the conditions under which—depending on the type of attacker one faced—various sorts of deterrence threats would be likely to succeed or fail. We have nothing of the sort.[1] Merely stating what it would look like conveys some sense of the difficulty of ever successfully doing it, undoubtedly the reason it has never been seriously attempted. The resulting theory would have been far from elegant or parsimonious. And with such a theory in hand, the analyst (or policy maker) would still have faced the daunting prospect of constructing a map or image of an opponent's cognitive processes sufficiently accurate to show where the defender fit in the typology, how to apply the theory, and how to reach the proper interpretation of the opponent's prospective behavior when confronted with deterrence threats.

The alternative was to assume that all potential attackers were, in terms of cognitive processes, much the same—in this case to view them as, relatively speaking, rational.[2] That eliminated the need for a typology of attackers and cleared the way for the theory to focus on the nature of commitment, the dynamics of which would then be essentially the same irrespective of the opponent in whose mind it was to be established. It was at this point that the development of the theory took on its peculiar aspects. For one thing, as the whole point of the theory was to explain, and thus predict, the behavior of a government once it had been subject to a deterrent threat, the logical next step would have been to study instances when deterrence was attempted in order to see what went through the mind of the threatened party and what it did as a result—that is, to investigate the decision making of a government facing threats of retaliation if it chose to attack. This would have provided some evidence relevant for testing the theory. But almost no one set about systematically investigating the theory and practice of deterrence in this fashion. The most elaborate study available of the practice of deterrence concentrates primarily on the government (the United States) doing the deterring; as for the decision-making processes of the other side, the analysis is often (and necessarily) conjectural and is usually in keeping with the assumption that the opponent was rational.[3]

What the theory needed more of is exemplified in a recent study of major crises in this century. Lebow's *Between Peace and War* does look at the decision processes of states that forced a major confrontation in the face of deterrence threats and reaches some disturbing conclusions. He finds that such states, when strongly motivated to challenge the vital interests of opponents, found ways of convincing themselves—in spite of readily available and impressive evidence to the contrary—that their adversaries would back down, abandoning their commitments. They fell victim either to factors that distort perception or to cognitive patterns that can induce a departure from reality, and they thereby acted at variance with deterrence theory's assumption of rationality. "The existence of this phenomenon suggests that efforts to impart credibility to commitments may have only a marginal impact on an adversary's behavior."[4] Lebow concludes that the United States has devoted too much attention to trying to ensure the credibility of its commitments and not enough to ascertaining what conditions might prompt challenges to them.[5]

Lebow's good advice reiterates a conclusion reached by Alexander George and Richard Smoke, and it runs contrary to the theory and practice of deterrence as it emerged in this country. Deterrence theory had its greatest impact in focusing on the problem of attaining credibility in deterrence, of the ways that establishing a firm commitment in the mind of a rational opponent might be attained. As the objective was to avoid ever having to uphold a commitment, particularly by nuclear retaliation, it seemed vital to concentrate on what made commitments, and the accompanying threats of retaliation, believable.

Here we come to the second peculiarity in the development of deterrence theory. As Schelling's elegant analysis demonstrated,[6] it was difficult to make a commitment believable when, as is the case with many deterrence threats, it would be very costly to carry it out and when a state had enough freedom of action to choose to not do so. How was such a commitment to be made credible to an opponent? It was pointed out that it would be useful for the deterring state to find ways to restrict its freedom of action, or at least to convey the impression that this was so, so that it would appear to have no choice. Or it might find ways of demonstrating that it was impervious to the costs of upholding its commitment. Finally, it might benefit from the fact that while, in strictly logical terms, it would be foolish to carry out the commitment, no government—

particularly in a tense crisis or confrontation—could guarantee not to do foolish things. I have argued elsewhere that all such tactics involve a retreat from the assumption of rationality;[7] either the deterrer is trying to suspend its capacity for rational choice or demonstrating that it does not exist, or the opponent's capacity for rational assessment of the situation is so incomplete that it can be deceived about these things. This is hard to make compatible with the assumption of rationality as the departure point for the theory.

Of the various ways in which a government could attempt to make its commitments appear firm, a number were related to that government's reputation or image on such matters. A reputation for upholding commitments would, it seemed, make each one adopted appear credible. By the same token, reputation becomes an important resource in dealing with opponents, and this means a state can appear to circumscribe its freedom of action and bolster its incentives to live up to its word by attaching its reputation to a commitment, for failure to uphold it would then carry the added cost of weakening the credibility of all of its current and future commitments. A reputation for bearing the costs of fulfilling commitments—no matter how severe those costs might be—would also enhance credibility. Or an image of irrationality might be useful for conveying the impression of being impervious to the costs of carrying out commitments. All this is familiar. Deterrence theory came to place considerable emphasis on reputation or image as an important aspect of the art of commitment. With the right sort of image, a state might be successful in practicing deterrence whether or not it deserved to be (in terms of its true willingness to retaliate if challenged); with the wrong sort of image it could have difficulty deterring attacks even when its retaliatory threats should be taken seriously.

Which brings us to the third peculiarity. If deterrence often rests on the ability of deterrers to limit, inhibit, or suspend their rationality or their inability to promise not to do irrational things in the heat of the moment, then it would seem unlikely that the way governments practice deterrence is much the same from one case to the next and is adequately captured by a rational decision maker model. This would seem to call for careful study of the behavior of states that practiced deterrence, to see how they went about establishing commitments, constructed deterrence threats when necessary, and tried to sustain the credibility of those threats. For a long time no such investigation was attempted. When it was finally done, for one government at least, the massive study by George and Smoke demonstrated that to practice deterrence was much more complicated than the theory suggested. It turned out that the U.S. government often had difficulty in deciding just when and to what extent it was committed, that this led to all sorts of difficulties because ambiguous messages were conveyed to opponents, and that commitments might be challenged in many ways that complicated the business of sustaining a credible deterrence posture. Though George and Smoke offered refinements of deterrence theory that they hoped were of universal validity, one implication of their study was that the difficulties and complexities experienced by the United States in the practice of deterrence might be, to a considerable extent, a product of the idiosyncracies of U.S. decision making.

The last thought provides the point of departure for this study. The aspect of deterrence in practice selected for examination is the U.S. attitude toward reputation. Let us suppose that in the postwar era we find the United States government has been persistently concerned about its reputation for purposes of deterrence and has manifested a fear that its image might prove insufficient to sustain the credibility of its commitments. Would the way in which deterrence theory analyzes the relationship between reputation and credibility provide the better part of an explanation for this? I think the answer is no, both on reflection and by reviewing some of the available evidence. If so, then it is likely that an emphatic concern about the national image is a more subtle and complex matter than deterrence theory would suggest. In turn this would be an illustration of the existence of more facets to deterrence as a psychological relationship, facets that pertain not to the mind of the potential attacker—the primary focus of classic deterrence theory—but to that of the deterrer. Thus we must see if, in reviewing the U.S. approach, it turns out that there is more to saving face for the sake of deterrence than we can encompass with our existing theoretical tools.

Reflections on Reputation and Credibility

The analysis may begin by giving further consideration to the way in which, in the fashion outlined above, classic deterrence theory handles the matter of national reputation or image as it bears on credibility. As has been fairly widely noted, the theory came to place particular emphasis on technique, both in the structuring of a deterrence situation and in communicating the retaliatory threat. Not much attention was paid to the intrinsic merits of the commitments a nation undertook to uphold. There was much more concern about the possible ways in which credibility could be sustained, which included steps to create and maintain a reputation for upholding commitments and techniques for attaching such a reputation firmly to any particular one.

The major criticism of this approach is that it is distinctly apolitical and thus ignores the fact that the essence of commitment is the application of political judgment in assessing national interests. As the critics would have it, the most important factor that should shape a government's commitment is whether it has weighty interests involved. This, in turn, determines the extent of its credibility problem. If a commitment does not reflect major interests, then there will be difficulty convincing others that it should be taken seriously, and it may well be challenged. Technique is no substitute for having the national interest at stake.[8]

Classical deterrence theory treats commitments as exceedingly interdependent; how one behaves with respect to any of one's commitments affects the credibility of all the rest via the image of reputation that is projected. One implication of the critics' view is that commitments are not fully interdependent. A state may think it better not to uphold a commitment where it finds it has little of importance at stake, without necessarily harming its credibility vis-à-vis commitments where its vital interests are obviously concerned. From here it is but a short step to the conclusion that some of a state's interests are so intrinsically vital that it will be seen as having a commitment, and the commitment will be perceived as credible, whether the state does anything to assert this or not. It can be argued that Europe is of such importance to the United States that Washington cannot escape being committed to resisting any Soviet attempt to overrun it; the commitment is there and is recognized as such whether the North Atlantic Treaty Organization (NATO) and other formal expressions of it exist or not.[9] Jervis explores the same idea with his distinction between intrinsic interest, strategic interest, and commitment—the first is one for which commitment is taken for granted.[10]

There is a serious problem with this argument. It derives from a cast of mind characteristic of political realism as an approach to foreign policy making, in that it perceives states as having logical (and hierarchical) structures of political interests. Some are clearly so vital that a state will fight for them; others are not; and some fall in between, so that an exercise of judgment is called for. It is the structure of interests that has much to do with the credibility of a particular commitment. The problem is this. Deterrence theory was developed to improve our understanding of the burdens of statecraft in the nuclear era. And the fact is that where nuclear weapons might have to be involved in upholding a commitment, *there are no intrinsic interests of sufficient value to make that commitment inherently credible.*[11] This is not to say that there is nothing for which states will fight with nuclear weapons, only that there is no logical way of deciding in advance what it is by referring to national interests. Nor is there any empirical way of doing so. States may be quite capable of fighting nuclear wars, on a nonrational basis or on some basis that they believe to be rational at the time, but one cannot learn from the past behavior of states just when they will, and one cannot predict the emotional predictions of any particular government toward the use or nonuse of nuclear weapons when the time for choice is at hand.

Many analysts believe that nuclear weapons markedly enhance the effectiveness of deterrence, as indeed they do, but the tendency is to see their effect as one of strengthening credibility,[12] which they do not do. They boost the possible stakes in a confrontation to a point where all parties are very likely to behave with great caution. But this is not the same thing as bolstering the credibility of the state doing the deterring—it, too, is subject to increased fear, uncertainty, and caution as it contemplates possible reactions to challenges. Nuclear deterrence "works" to inhibit war in spite of its corrosive effect on the credibility of commitments. We are fortunate that there has not yet been a confrontation involving a government so incautious, self-confident, or feverishly motivated as to be willing blatantly to test a nuclear power's willingness to retaliate with nuclear weapons, that no state has yet chosen to exploit to the fullest the barriers to the use of such weapons.

It has been suggested that nuclear deterrence won intellectual acceptance in this country in the post–World War II era because it fit within the dominant political-realism tradition in foreign policy analysis.[13] Actually it did not fit very well at all. Just prior to his retirement from the State Department, George Kennan, that most eminent realist, put down his views on nuclear weapons and reached conclusions that have remained essentially unchanged in his commentaries to this day.[14] Much like Bernard Brodie, Kennan contended that if war was to be fought within a Clausewitzian framework—for political purposes meaningfully reflected in the means used—then war with nuclear weapons was next to impossible. The destructiveness of the weapons overrode any possible political objective. At best one would hold such weapons for use against a state that had launched a nuclear attack. They had no other utility.

It might be argued that this still leaves room for nuclear deterrence; that, if a state has nuclear weapons, no other state, acting from a realist perspective, would challenge its vital interests because the risks of nuclear war would outweigh any possible political gains; and that this would be particularly true of a direct attack on a nuclear-armed state. Instead, however, the realist perspective more or less eliminates the existence of national interests so compelling as to make nuclear deterrence commitments credible. To take the United States as an example, this is clearly true of even its most profound commitments. On either rational or highly emotional grounds, a case can easily be made for the view that the United States should not (and therefore would not) deliberately choose strategic or theater nuclear war in response to a Soviet invasion of Western Europe. From Kennan's perspective, which insists means be proportionate to ends, the case could have been made even when the United States enjoyed a nuclear monopoly or vast nuclear-strategic superiority; it certainly can be made at a time when both monopoly and superiority have been erased. Notice that this does not mean that the United States would not fight for Western Europe, up to and including use of nuclear weapons, or that in doing so U.S. officials would not have worked out a conscious, calculated reason for doing so. It simply means that there is an excellent case for not doing so, on the perfectly rational grounds that millions of American, European, and Russian lives—to say nothing of major elements of Western civilization—would far more likely be saved.

As for the instance of a direct attack on a nuclear power, consider the frequently voiced Soviet-attack-on-U.S.-silos scenario under which a Soviet counterforce strike does not lead to a U.S. retaliatory response. The point of the scenario is that if it is not rational to retaliate, the President might do so. Even critics of the scenario do not say retaliation would be a rational decision—they cite nonrational motives and factors to explain why it would occur. As for the scenario's champions, when they advocate developing more nuclear war options to ensure a decision to retaliate, they ignore the logic of their original argument. As I have tried to explain elsewhere, where the objective is to minimize damage to one's country and retaliating might bring further destruction on it, there is no rational way to choose whether or not to retaliate. The effectiveness of nuclear deterrence does not rest on the rationality of retaliating: thus even a direct attack on the nation might be insufficient to provoke it.

The argument up to this point is as follows: one cannot discard the emphasis in classic deterrence theory on the interdependence of commitments and hence the overwhelming importance of a reputation for upholding commitments by reference to national interests as the key to credibility, because this breaks down when it comes to nuclear deterrence. (In fact, the same is true for large-scale conventional warfare in some instances.) This leaves two possibilities. The first is that it is a political-realist world in fact, if not in logic. The second is that classical deterrence theory was on the right track. I will take up each in turn.

Suppose governments do, in fact, assume that the credibility of commitments is linked to the underlying national interests at stake even where nuclear weapons would be involved, no matter what some theorist says. Does this mean that reputation need not be such a paramount concern? Let us assume that the most potent factor shaping the credibility of a commitment is the interest involved. This cannot be true in some fixed, invariable way in the real world of states, for credibility is then dependent on two characteristics pertaining to the opponent. The first is the strength of the potential attacker's interest/motivation that drives it to consider challenging the commitment. Various studies have demonstrated that the more strongly motivated the attacker, the more likely it is to doubt the credibility of the commitment and to believe that the defender will yield. Perceptions and misperceptions along these lines are all too familiar in international crises.[15] The second factor is the potential attacker's political assessment of the nature and scale of the deterrer's interests. It is not enough to have vital interests at stake for deterrence purposes, for the opponent must perceive that this is the case. But regimes vary in appreciation of the interests of others. They are subject to serious perceptual errors on this score, particularly when strongly motivated to challenge another state's commitment, as we know from some case studies of crisis.[16]

This being so, a guide to or typology of the cognitive processes of opponents to operate deterrence effectively is necessary. The statesman would need a clear sense of, for example, how a particular opponent perceives the statesman's commitments and what the opponent's political judgment is like, in order to tailor his deterrence posture properly. And the same objection applies: suitable cognitive maps of opponents are seldom, if ever, available. The available clues in the opponent's previous behavior will be insufficient and ambiguous. This will tend to drive the deterrer into giving constant attention to the nation's reputation vis-à-vis commitments, as a second-best solution to the problem, particularly when nuclear war might be involved. If one knows too little about the opposing leadership to be sure it understands when one will fight, a reputation that should minimize misjudgment will seem rather important. Lacking certain understanding of how the opponent sees things, the deterrer will face great pressure to try to reinforce that reputation in whatever way possible. The deterrer has no reliable way of knowing when concern on this score may be relaxed.

This suggests that Schelling and others who stressed technique, such as a preoccupation with reputation through the inter-dependence of commitments, as the crux of credibility were on the right track. Returning to the point made earlier, commitments involving the use of nuclear weapons can hardly be made credible by anything other than technique. Some way must be found to signal to opponents that one will do things not fully justifiable on rational grounds. But this still leaves a puzzle when it comes to developing a reputation for upholding commitments. It is believed that credi-bility is enhanced by cultivating the right image. But of what use is the right image when built, as it must be, on responses to lesser challenges to minor commitments? Or rather, can one be certain that it is useful? How does one translate that into credibility vis-à-vis major commitments that could involve truly awful weapons and monstrous costs to uphold? The circumstances are so different that behavior in the one kind of case can hardly be guaranteed to be reiterated in the other.

It would seem more appropriate to reverse what is, in the stan-dard view, the relationship between lesser commitments and those reflecting preeminent national interests. This is the contention that states defend the former so as to maintain a reputation that fore-stalls miscalculations with regard to the latter, the latter being ones for which they most assuredly fight (even with nuclear weapons). Instead, nuclear powers may uphold lesser commitments because *they are the only ones they can certainly decide to fight for*. Challenges to minor commitments may be met because of a rarely expressed but deeply felt uncertainty by decision makers that they would retaliate after challenges to major ones. A reputation is thus eagerly sought that will forestall challenges, but not because a government seeks to avoid the costs of a commitment it cannot help but uphold. Instead it seeks such a reputation because those costs will make it doubt whether to meet the commitment should it ever have to decide. A challenge is to be avoided because what one will do is awesomely unclear, not because what one will do is quite clear but very un-palatable. This converts a concern for reputation from a rational extension of the art of commitment into a pretense used to hide a pervasive insecurity over what to do if one's most important com-mitments are challenged. A vigorous response to attacks on lesser commitments might even be an index of this insecurity; that is, a state confident in its readiness to use nuclear weapons may well take a more relaxed attitude toward lesser challenges.

Earl Ravenal makes roughly the same point when he critiques the "paradox of destruction." Credibility rests on exaggerating the probability that the United States would retaliate with nuclear forces, but fear of the consequences of a deterrence failure works in the opposite direction. The result is that, "in order to buttress its credibility, a nation should intervene in the least significant, the least compelling, and the least rewarding cases, and its reaction should be disproportionate to the immediate provocation or the particular interest at stake." The result is a "paradox of credibility: the less the occasion, the greater the response."[17]

It would seem that a preoccupation with reputation can be explained by a refinement of both the classic deterrence theory approach to commitment and the rejection of that approach as apolitical. If a state is highly uncertain about how it might respond to challenges to its greatest commitments, then a reputation built on responses to lesser provocations looks exceedingly important, and if it cannot be certain how an opponent perceives that reputation and the commitments it shields, then the state will be sorely tempted constantly to attend to or worry about its image. Commitments will be seen as interdependent in the hope that opponents see them that way, but leaders will not wish to have occasion to find out if they will act on that basis. A disturbing aspect of this is that a concern for image has no natural bounds. It may readily extend to actions other than responses to provocation. The objection to seeing commitments as interdependent is that this invites a loss of perspective and judgment; excessive defense of unimportant obligations is likely to prove debilitating. This may readily apply to other matters. If the objective is to look militarily competent, resolute, and steadfast, then almost anything may come to seem relevant. Rhetoric might be important, or keeping up in an arms race, or perhaps appearing tough in personal encounters at summit meetings. A state will have no certainty that these things are important, just a gnawing concern that they might be.

But at this point the available theory is no longer of much use, which opens up a further dimension of deterrence as a psychological phenomenon, in this case with respect to the behavior of the deterrer. Tracing the factors that shape a state's sense of the importance of reputation, its conception of what to do about it, and its approach to conveying deterrence threats would require going beyond an abstract analysis of the logic of conflict situations. Many of these factors must be domestic in nature and, one suspects, a product of such things as culture or decision-making patterns. Deterrence as a psychological relationship cannot, then, be adequately comprehended without treating the behavior of the deterrer as an extension of its nature and character. How a state practices deterrence would tell us as much or more about the state itself then it does about the state's opponents and the threats they pose. It is possible that deterrence behavior is not primarily a reflection of opponents and threats, which would help explain why deterrence is sometimes inappropriately practiced. If internal factors drive the specific application of deterrence as much as or more than external threats, there is apt to be a frequent mismatch between the external realities with which deterrence is expected to cope and the ways in which it is undertaken. Deterrence is already burdened by an unavoidable incidence of misperception. Only further complications can arise if the design and implementation of deterrence has domestic roots and varies from state to state.

Application to the United States

One of the distinctive features of the post–World War II behavior of the U.S. government in managing its long-term deterrence relationship with the Soviet Union (and Moscow's allies) has been a recurring, compulsive concern about its reputation for being ready and willing to follow through on its commitments. Why has this concern been so persistent, and why has it had a bearing on so many aspects of national security policy?

It may be instructive to begin by reviewing examples of the many ways in which this concern for image has affected postwar policy making. One can see its imprint on at least four sorts of national security decisions:

1. decisions to intervene in military conflicts on behalf of friends and allies; and to disengage from such interventions;
2. decisions on the development of weapons systems;
3. decisions on the proper design of the overall U.S. force posture; and
4. decisions on when and how to negotiate with adversaries.

In the years after World War II, as the conflict with the Soviet Union grew, U.S. policy makers gradually began to see that conflict as having an important psychological/political dimension; indeed, many came to view the Soviet threat as chiefly psychological in nature, consisting of Soviet propaganda and communism's political appeal in many countries plus an image of growing Soviet strength. It must be recalled that the original objectives of NATO and the Marshall Plan were to bolster Western Europe's morale so as to counter this threat. From these institutions, perhaps inevitably, a widespread feeling emerged that in this psychopolitical contest the image of the United States was fragile and subject to damage by all sorts of unfortunate events. Part of this was the growing sense that events were interconnected in terms of their psychological impact, making U.S. commitments—formal and informal—interdependent. In turn this was a product of seeing the world increasingly in bipolar terms.

The effects of this way of thinking appear in the rhetoric of the Truman Doctrine, with its suggestion that freedom is indivisible and the United States will support struggle for it everywhere. Then it helped shape the U.S. decision to sustain the West's position in Berlin in spite of the Soviet blockade. "American policy-makers had come to believe that the international system was an increasingly polarized, unstable one in which a setback in one locale could have profound destabilizing effects in other locales as well."[18] In the debate over whether to develop the hydrogen bomb, one of the more persuasive arguments by its supporters was that failure to do so while the Russians went ahead would convey an image of weakness, and that Soviet achievement of the "super" first would provide Moscow with an enormous psychological boost.[19] As a recent study notes, "The intangible attraction of 'psychological' superiority subsequently assumed a dominant place in the military's advocacy of the super-bomb." And in mid-January 1950 the Joint Chiefs of Staff (JCS) urged that President Truman support its development because it would "grossly alter the psychological balance between the United States and the USSR."[20]

NSC-68 was a watershed in the development and forceful expression of this way of thinking. It insisted that "the assault on free institutions is worldwide now, and in the context of the present polarization of power a defeat of free institutions anywhere is a defeat everywhere," and it offered the "loss" of Czechoslovakia as a case in point.[21] It was particularly preoccupied with the possibility that shifts in the international balance of power could come through determined Soviet efforts to intimidate and humiliate the United States, leading to a loss of U.S. credibility. As John Gaddis points out, by perceiving the reputation of the United States to be at stake whenever a Soviet threat to encroach on some area arose, NSC-68 in effect made vital U.S. interests a function of Soviet threats.[22]

When North Korea struck in June 1950, the powerfully felt need to sustain the reputation of the United States came as a surprise even to U.S. policy makers, but it was the decisive consideration. Acheson describes his support for U.S. intervention in his memoirs in this fashion: "To back away from this challenge, in view of our capacity for meeting it, would be highly destructive of the power and prestige of the United States. By prestige I mean the shadow cast by power, which is of great deterrent importance."[23] Of a particular concern was the debilitating effect that little or no response was expected to have on the credibility of the U.S. commitment to NATO. A few months later, similar considerations helped bring about the decision to cross the 38th parallel. Failure to do so was held likely to project an image of timidity and weakness. Gaddis concludes that the decision was made mainly "for reasons of credibility and prestige."[24]

Throughout this period the United States was reluctant to pursue negotiations with the Soviet Union for much the same reason. Dean Acheson referred to the need for "positions of strength" from which to bargain, and NSC-68 discouraged talks until alleged U.S. military weaknesses had been corrected. What is interesting is that it was felt unwise even to invite negotiations because this would suggest weakness. During the Korean War, when the British sought to ease the direct confrontation between Washington and Peking, U.S. officials resisted on grounds that merely proposing negotiations would threaten credibility.[25]

In the Eisenhower, Kennedy, and Johnson administrations, a common policy theme was that "victories to communism anywhere represented losses for the United States,"[26] and the resulting decline in prestige would encourage further communist expansion and aggression. In the Eisenhower era this was illustrated in the Taiwan Straits crises, where Washington acted on the basis of "a rigid conception of containment that sought to exclude loss on any territory, even islands . . . admittedly not necessary for the defense of Taiwan and not easily defensible."[27] This attitude invited a continued expansion of U.S. commitments, and it was a major factor in U.S. unhappiness with the French withdrawal from Vietnam and the serious consideration given to direct intervention against the Vietminh.

Yet the Eisenhower administration was bitterly criticized for failing to be sufficiently attentive to matters of prestige, thereby weakening deterrence. It was said that the United States was losing ground to the Soviet Union in terms of projecting a vigorous, progessive, national image. There was the unflattering comparison of U.S.-Soviet rates of economic growth and the national soul-searching in the wake of Sputnik, coupled with the fears about the "missile gap." The Kennedy administration then responded to this concern with great vigor, not only in defense spending but also in areas like the space program, because its leading members shared the view that power in international policies was very much shaped by perceptions.[28]

Both Kennedy and Johnson felt the United States had too many commitments, but neither saw a feasible way to pare those obligations without conveying a sense of weakness and retreat, something they rejected because both administrations feared, above all else, "the threat of embarassment, of humiliation, of appearing to be weak."[29] This attitude dominated the U.S. response to the presence of Soviet missiles in Cuba; it was felt that failure to react was certain to shatter U.S. prestige and influence. Kennedy's initial speech on the crisis charged that the Soviet move was a deliberate shift in the distribution of power "which cannot be accepted by this country if our courage and our commitments are ever to be trusted again by either friend or foe."[30]

The emphasis on image as the essence of managing deterrence reached extreme levels and had the most serious consequences for U.S. policy during the war in Vietnam. Successive administrations invested South Vietnam with great significance almost entirely because what happened there would affect the credibility of U.S. commitments elsewhere. That was the dominant refrain in the official rationale for the war. "The security of the United States, indeed of the entire noncommunist world, was thought to be imperiled wherever communist challenges came up against American guarantees. Vietnam might be insignificant in itself, but as a point of intersection between threat and commitment, it was everywhere."[31] The Pentagon Papers clearly indicate this was not simply a posture for public consumption. As an illustration, at one point John Mc-Naughton summarized U.S. aims in Vietnam as "70%—to avoid a humiliating U.S. defeat (to our reputation as a guarantor). 20%—to keep SVN (and the adjacent) territory from Chinese hands. 10%—to permit the people of SVN to enjoy a better, freer way of life."[32] As U.S. involvement and sunk costs mounted, so did the potential humiliation of a defeat—the preoccupation with reputation thus became self-reinforcing.

Kissinger was sensitive to this even before entering the government,[33] and the Nixon administration embraced the view that U.S. credibility was the key stake in Vietnam. The president expressed this view most strikingly in his justification for the 1970 incursion into Cambodia. "If, when the chips are down, the world's most powerful nation, the United States of America, acts like a pitiful, helpless giant, the forces of totalitarianism and anarchy will threaten free nations and free institutions throughout the world."[34]

This concern overpowered the Nixon-Kissinger assertion that it was the overall balance of power rather than the outcome of specific contests that was important. Like its predecessors, the Administration was unable to regard any communist triumph with equinimity, which dictated the reaction to Allende in Chile, to the civil war in Angola, and to the emergence of Eurocommunism. "The administration was not prepared to tolerate further victories for communism, even when it took indigenous, and independent, forms. The dangers of humiliation, of conveying the appearance of weakness to real adversaries, were too great to permit acquiescence in the triumph even of apparent ones."[35] The ultimate expression of saving face in Southeast Asia was the *Mayaguez* incident, a clumsy attempt to demonstrate resolve and the ability to react militarily.

One other illustration of the scope of this concern for image is provided by a New York *Times* report of a conversation between Kissinger and Egyptian leaders in the wake of the 1973 war in the Middle East. Kissinger stressed that U.S. support for Israel was a geopolitical necessity. "Do not deceive yourself, the United States could not—either today or tomorrow—allow Soviet arms to win a big victory, even if it was not decisive, against United States arms. This has nothing to do with Israel or with you."[36] In other words, the image was on the line even in the actions of allies and client states.

It was also in the Nixon administration that greater emphasis was placed on the psycho-political dimensions of the strategic balance. It was asserted that nothing less than "perceived equivalence" would do, which meant not only avoiding inferiority in simple indexes of strategic forces but also ensuring a rough parity in the range of strategic options and missions. That objective has dominated the design of the deterrence posture ever since. James Schlesinger promulgated this view in his annual reports as secretary of defense,[37] insisting that settling for less might lead opponents to miscalculate U.S. resolve and assume they enjoyed a degree of political leverage that would be dangerous. The JCS chairman, Admiral Moorer, concluded that "the mere appearance of Soviet strategic superiority could have a debilitating effect on our foreign policy and our negotiating posture . . . even if that superiority would have no practical effect on the outcome of an all-out nuclear exchange." Secretary Laird, in pushing the Trident program, stressed that it would be "diplomatically and politically unacceptable" to permit Soviet numerical superiority in strategic forces.[38]

The Carter administration proved in the end to be quite sensitive on this score. It reaffirmed the importance of perceived equivalence and offered this as partial justification for the multiplication of targeting options endorsed in PD-59. It proposed MX in part as a way of matching Soviet counterforce options, and it is difficult to reject the conclusion that the concern about the counterforce gap and the resulting desire to deploy MX had primarily psychological roots. "The attention devoted to this matter could be taken as a reflection more of the crisis in American self-confidence and confusion over what made deterrence 'work' than any serious movement in the military balance."[39] Concern for the U.S. image played a role in the decision to attempt the rescue of the hostages in Iran, and of course the entire hostage crisis was widely considered an episode of national humiliation damaging to U.S. credibility. It was also during this administration that steps were announced to close the gap in European theater nuclear forces, lest the impression be conveyed that the Soviet Union could get away with a unilateral adjustment in the military balance, which would suggest weakness.

Finally, the Reagan approach to national security policy reflects the conviction that our reputation has slipped badly and needs to be restored on every level from rhetoric to strategic forces. Many in the Administration or closely associated with it had been actively promoting this view for years prior to the 1980 elections.[40] The shift to a more confrontational stance toward the Soviet Union has been a part of this, and it has been one of the principal justifications for the defense buildup. The Administration did much to provoke the early confrontation with Libya, which resulted in the downing of two Libyan fighters, as one way of establishing a more forceful U.S. image. It also seems clear that the invasion of Grenada was more than a little motivated by the Administration's sense that here was a very suitable opportunity to restore the U.S. reputation for being ready to use force boldly and decisively. The Administration's reaction to the nuclear freeze idea has been, in part, that such a step would have the unfortunate effect of weakening the U.S. image of resolve, sending the wrong message to Moscow. Also relevant is the obvious reluctance of the Administration over its first two years to consider arms control negotiations seriously for fear this would suggest weakness.

While numerous additional examples could be cited, it is clear that this country has been deeply concerned with saving face for the sake of deterrence. Anxiety on this score has sometimes been eased but never stilled, even when it has resulted in heavy costs and burdens. In line with the argument set forth earlier, to explain this adequately requires some refinement of our understanding of how deterrence works, for the anxiety has been present in eras of U.S. strategic superiority and great conventional strength, as well as in periods of declining relative strength. It helped freeze containment into inflexibility despite criticisms of the costs involved. It was largely responsible for the folly of Vietnam and the severe damage to the credibility of U.S. commitments that resulted. The obvious question is, How is this behavior best explained?

It is possible that such behavior can be explained as an inevitable consequence of nuclear weapons. This would suggest that other states that have such weapons for purposes of deterrence experience a similar compulsion. While no extended discussion is possible here, this is not a point that is easy to sustain. First, one would think that a state would be most concerned about reputation when its nuclear weapons are small in number and inferior in such things as survivability. But Britain and France have not displayed the same preoccupation with credibility vis-à-vis the USSR, either for themselves or for this country. Neither they nor most other U.S. allies were every fully in sympathy with the predominant U.S. rationale for involvement in Vietnam. There was no grave concern in Europe that U.S. credibility was at stake in the 1973 Middle East war or in a variety of earlier East-West crises. The same was true on Iran and Afghanistan during the Carter administration. The initial European alarm over the SS-20 soon gave way to a more modest reaction, leaving the United States with far less support for its insistence that an offsetting deployment was vital for purposes of credibility and the conveying of resolve. More broadly, the internal tensions in NATO have for years reflected, in part, a divergent view as to what is important for the credibility of deterrence and why, with the United States generally seeing far more situations and actions as potentially relevant.

Nor does the Soviet Union seem to have been as concerned as the United States about these matters. Moscow has often accepted the necessity for a retreat without apparently fearing that a disasterous erosion of its credibility would follow—in Iran in 1946, over Berlin in 1949, 1959, and 1961, in the Cuban missile crisis in 1962. It has been willing to see defeats of Soviet arms by U.S. arms—in Korea in 1950 the Soviets showed no inclination to intervene as the Chinese did, and in several Middle East wars (most recently in Lebanon) it has seen its clients go down to defeat. Prior to Nixon's first Moscow summit, the U.S. blockade of North Vietnam was not seen as an assault on Soviet credibility. There is little in the Soviet literature on deterrence that emphasizes the importance of reputation and the delicacy of credibility.[41] The Soviet conception of deterrence seems to rest on expectation that it is the objective factor of available military strength to which governments eventually respond, which appears to be the source of the Soviet military build-up for the past two decades and the assertion that it is Soviet strength that induced the West's interest in detente. In other words, reputation or image takes care of itself, as does deterrence.

It would be incorrect to see other nuclear powers as completely unconcerned about sustaining their credibility for nuclear deterrence by the way they attend to other threats and problems. For instance, the Soviets would about certainly view direct "imperialist" involvement in the collapse of the communist government of a member of the Soviet bloc as alarming in its implications for Soviet credibility if allowed to proceed. President de Gaulle had a well-developed sense of the necessity to attend to France's reputation on a wide variety of foreign policy matters in order to strengthen his nation's credibility. The point is that such judgments are not the same from one state to the next—what is important in the context varies in the perceptions of states, even when they are close allies. The judgment may also vary with the leadership changes in a particular state to some extent. If one then has to look to a nation's diplomatic tradition, domestic political situation, or ideological framework, and to the personalities or perceptions of the particular leaders in order to explain when that state will see its credibility deeply invested in a particular decision or action, then the relevant psychological dimensions of the practice of deterrence are considerably enlarged.

Attempting an Explanation

If one recalls Lebow's suggestion that the U.S. approach to deterrence has put too much emphasis on trying to ensure the credibility of commitments, it is hard to explain this by looking at the military facts. Since 1945 the United States has had an enormous military capability at its disposal. It is the only state that has ever proven that it can use nuclear weapons. It has, unlike the Soviet Union fought two sizeable wars since 1945. It has directly confronted the Soviet Union and other states with the distinct possibility of war on a number of occasions. It has had the most powerful allies, enjoyed clear strategic superiority for years, and has always had more flexible strategic and conventional forces than the Soviet Union. With all this in mind, why is the United States not inclined to treat its credibility problem as distinctly less serious than that of any other great power and certainly not, in perspective, an overwhelming one?

Some possible explanations present themselves. It can be argued that a status quo power has the greater difficulty here; those with the initiative in undertaking provocations have a greater psychological and political flexibility in this regard. There may be something to this, but why does it not seem to rub off on our major allies, as they have a similar orientation but seemingly less concern? Even in the case of the SS-20, early European concern that the Soviet deployment, if unmatched, would weaken NATO's image seemed to recede a good deal and leave the United States with an unmatched preoccupation on this score.

Second, there is the often referred to "engineering approach" that Americans are said to display on military and foreign policy matters. Is it this that has made deterrence appear to be an exercise in problem solving, a matter of technique in which one manipulates reputation amidst interdependent commitments with no reference to the political subtleties involved? But this would ignore the equally often noted pragmatism of Americans, which should predispose the United States to eschew an abstract approach to deterrence.

However, this second argument does have the virtue of calling our attention to the national style, which seems to be a potentially profitable way to think about the problem. It is quite useful to start with the assumption that the design and implementation of deterrence varies from one nation to another, that there is a national style in this.[42] States do not practice deterrence in the same way. The reliance placed on deterrence as opposed to other means of influence, the commitment process, the timing and delivery of retaliatory threats, and so on, will vary. There is nothing earthshaking in this idea; it just broadens the meaning of deterrence as a psychological phenomenon. It calls attention to the varying behavior associated with attempting deterrence, something not readily captured by assuming rational decision making and focusing on the techniques of commitment.

For the United States, a highlight of its approach to deterrence has been its great sensitivity to sustaining its reputation, with that reputation believed to bear heavily on its credibility. Based on the earlier discussion, a start at an explanation can be made through deterrence theory. A state with commitments must look to its reputation, and in the nuclear age the government dearly wishes to project an image that prevents miscalculation by opponents. An elaborate explanation along these lines could be constructed—

nearly every action is weighed very carefully for the image it helps convey—and indeed has been.[43] Again in line with the earlier discussion, I think this approach oversimplifies. It rationalizes compulsions that have bordered on the irrational and neglects important aspects of U.S. behavior.

It would be better to begin from the very different perspective offered in the first section. Nuclear weapons are frightfully difficult to use, under even the most extreme circumstances. Commitments that rest on them are, therefore, of dubious credibility in the minds of those who assert them. They cannot know what they would do if those commitments were challenged, and this deep-seated insecurity is at the root of deterrence posturing. This invites policy makers to seize upon reputation as a possible way to manage this situation, to keep away from having to contemplate doing something one has promised to do but may not be able to bear doing.

How has this uncertainty and resulting insecurity shaped the U.S. practice of deterrence? There are two broad ways in which this has happened. Earlier it was suggested that it is hard to fit deterrence into a pure realist perspective, for it is very difficult to identify national interests that would be worth a nuclear war. At most a state would "use" nuclear weapons to deter an outright, direct attack on itself, particularly one that employed nuclear weapons. This perspective was adapted to become the basis for one U.S. school of thought on deterrence, ranging from minimum deterrence to mutual assured destruction (MAD). The adaptation involves turning a liability into an asset by assuming that the great uncertainties afflicting U.S. leaders on the use of nuclear weapons must similarly affect Soviet leaders. This makes nuclear deterrence relatively straightforward and profoundly stable—the Russians are at least as scared of nuclear weapons and nuclear war as we are. To fret constantly about the U.S. image and be aroused by any sign of Soviet superiority, such as the exact state of the strategic balance, is silly. Thus these people find it totally implausible, for example, that any Soviet government would seriously consider a disarming strike at U.S. ICBMs—no Soviet interests would justify the enormous consequences and risks, and therefore the inhibitions would be too great to be overcome. Critics of this view often charge that it assumes Soviet strategic doctrine mirrors that of the United States, which can be shown to be untrue. It would be more correct to say that it is the *feelings* of Americans about nuclear war that have been projected onto the other side, and the accuracy of this is both plausible and more difficult to falsify. Hence advocates of MAD or something like minimum deterrence do not bow in the face of evidence of a Soviet preoccupation with war fighting in strategic deployments, for this does not disturb the reality that fear of nuclear war is and must be the overwhelming consideration in the Soviet foreign policy.

The weak spot in this approach has always been it does nothing to ease the deterrer's insecurity at the prospect of actually resorting to nuclear weapons. One must count on deterrence working in spite of having weapons to make it work that induce great reluctance about their use. In effect, one has to count too much on the Russians being restrained and prudent in a competitive relationship that, by its existence, arouses fear that they are not. Essential to this approach, therefore, is great confidence—in the Russians, in the basic stability of nuclear deterrence, and in one's own judgment on these matters. Clearly U.S. officials have seldom had such confidence or vanity (perhaps only in the Eisenhower administration), one reason being that relying on nuclear weapons tends to undermine it. This gave rise, relatively early in the nuclear era, to an alternative school of thought. Here the inner uncertainty has shaped deterrence by leading to projection of exactly the opposite feelings onto the opponent. Where we feel hesitant, uncertain of our response to a grave challenge, we picture the opponent as feeling strong and decisive. Lacking confidence, we perceive the opponent as imbued with it. Deterrence then becomes more complicated and delicate because U.S. reservations about nuclear retaliation and war are coupled with a heightened sense of the power, purpose, and threat of the Soviet Union. The national response must be to bolster military resources and options, moving quickly to eliminate weaknesses so as to stand up to an overbearing Soviet Union. Gaining options is particularly crucial, for it is believed this will ease the decision makers' reluctance actually to use the weapons at their disposal. From this is to flow the necessary confidence to manage deterrence.

This is what characterizes the feelings and reactions of the champions of flexible response, as opposed to minimum deterrence, massive retaliation, and MAD, down through the years. The author of NSC-68 drew a picture of a Soviet Union growing in military strength, confidence, and boldness—probably prepared to attack the West as soon as the necessary degree of military superiority had been achieved. In contrast, "instead of appearing strong and resolute we are continually at the verge of appearing and being alternately irresolute and desperate."[44] In the wake of Mao's triumph in China, the Soviet atomic bomb, consolidation of Soviet control in Eastern Europe, and the outbreak of the Korean War, the feeling spread within the government that the Soviets were bounding ahead militarily, politically, and psychologically. A reassessment of NSC-68 the following year concluded that: "review of the world situation shows that the danger to our security is greater now than it was in April 1950. It is greater now than it was then thought it would be. . . . It now appears that we are already in a period of acute danger which will continue until the United States and its allies achieve an adequate position of strength."[45]

The surge of support for what became the Kennedy administration's military build-up and flexible response posture was accompanied by exactly the same picture of the Soviet Union—increasingly assertive and confident, bold, pulling ahead in the strategic arms race (the missile gap) and quite likely to attack when its lead was sufficient—an impression reinforced by Kennedy's meeting with Khrushchev in Vienna. As noted earlier, there was a distinct parallel in the thinking of the authors of NSC-68 in the fear of being intimidated and made to appear weak.

Nothing was more characteristic of the long campaign waged against MAD and SALT II, culminating in the Reagan defense build-up, than depicting the Soviet Union as confidently pursuing an imperial strategy and resolutely gaining the military superiority to implement it, while manipulating SALT accordingly. U.S. weakness has been contrasted with Soviet strength and assertiveness. There has been the same fear of Soviet military action at some point in the near future. One of Nitze's essays neatly summarizes this view by asserting that "we have to deal with the fact that at least for some years we will be conducting strategy from structural weakness."[46]

And always this approach has been preoccupied with the reputation of the United States. Why so? While it is hard to be certain, this is what seems to have happened. To return to an earlier point, the U.S. shift to an emphasis on deterrence, in and around 1950, took place within an intellectual/emotional context that reflected the declining influence of the realist perspective, for deterrence did not rest comfortably within it. Officials were grappling with the idea of deterrence as a psychological phenomenon against the backdrop of the steadily more influential view that the communist challenge was ultimately psychological in character. That view made image or reputation quite an important matter, for deterrence as well as other aspects of the Soviet-U.S. rivalry, and this was strongly reinforced by the fact that nuclear weapons had such awful potential consequences that officials could not help but wonder if they could ever bring themselves to use them. Thus the conception of the true nature of the Soviet challenge had a profound effect on the U.S. approach to deterrence by helping to build into it an emphasis on reputation.

The full effect of this was delayed for a decade. That the reputation of the United States was the bulwark of deterrence, to be constantly nurtured, became widely accepted and was fully shared by the Eisenhower administration. But that administration turned to relying on the pervasive uncertainty surrounding the use of nuclear weapons to make deterrence work. The flexible response solution of trying to contain and reduce that uncertainty by multiplying the options for nuclear, and non-nuclear, retaliation had to await the Kennedy administration.

Nitze has been the person most closely associated with seeing the struggle with the USSR as psychological in nature, from NSC-68 to his recent writings ("the political-psychological contest is at the heart of the struggle.")[47] The crux of this is that perceptions of power and images of strength are often as important as the material factors of power highlighted in realist analysis. This was transferred to the heart of the U.S. understanding of deterrence; image was crucial. When this was coupled with great uneasiness about ever using nuclear weapons, its primary expression came to be flexible response doctrine and postures.

The particular U.S. approach to deterrence was adopted because it was congenial, because it fit feelings and needs that arose early in the post–World War II years in the government and persist to this day. It was not enough that this country possessed enormous strength, had vast military power at its disposal, and exercised influence on a scale unparalleled in its history. That was insufficient to induce full confidence in deterrence and a steady appreciation of the fact that U.S. welfare was relatively immune to modest adjustments in the strategic balance or in the political makeup of small states far away. Reputation made everything important and deterrence fragile. Policies reflecting the opposite view have always proven politically vulnerable, in the end, to the charge that they conveyed an image of weakness, that the Soviets were outracing and outmaneuvering us, and that some gross strategic threat in yet another corner of the world was going unattended. The origins of these feelings and needs, amounting almost to compulsions, cannot be easily tracked down, but in a preliminary way it is possible to suggest factors that are almost certainly relevant.

The first is a persistent fear that the public would not sustain a resolute, responsible posture for this country in world affairs. Policy makers in the early post–World War II years worried about the

return of isolationism, of divisive internal debates that would para-
lyze U.S. foreign policy, of a loss of morale. Negotiation as a way out
of the Cold War was never an appealing option, for it would incite
such debates and multiply the resistance to doing what was necessary to strengthen the country. Losing ground to the communist
world could provoke mania on the right. Such fears revived in
connection with Vietnam. "There was, within both the Kennedy and
Johnson administration, a strange dread of American irrationality—of the unpredictable and uncontrolled reactions that might
ensue if the United States was perceived to have "lost" Vietnam."[48]
One of those reactions was isolationism, or "neo-isolationism" as its
liberal variant came to be called. Another was right-wing backlash
on the order of McCarthyism. Dean Rusk, Robert McNamara, and
Walt Rostow were warning of this with respect to Vietnam as early as
1961; it bothered Lyndon Johnson a good deal; and it was a major
consideration for Richard Nixon and Henry Kissinger. More recently, the pursuit of strategic arms control has been strongly
criticized in some quarters for having the effect of undermining
domestic support for defense spending.

This raises the intriguing possibility that U.S. deterrence posturing has often been aimed at domestic, not just foreign, targets, that
we have often sought credibility abroad when a major objective was
to reassure ourselves. Part of this would be the political containment
of those ready to pander to U.S. insecurities by charging that we are
weak and ineffectual. Another part would be outmaneuvering those
who would sharply reduce defense efforts and U.S. involvements
abroad, achieved by citing the vital necessity of keeping up our
reputation. This may be an unavoidable aspect of practicing deterrence when one has an open, democratic society.

A second factor has been a constant lack of confidence on the part
of the United States in friends and allies, a feeling that they were
fair-weather supporters, that any sign of U.S. weakness would cause
them to suffer domestic political disarray and to adjust their foreign
policies toward accommodation with the Soviet Union. This was in
keeping with the declining influence of the political realism approach. States with a profound interest in avoiding Soviet domination were seen as quite unlikely to be willing and able to act
accordingly if the United States appeared to be faltering. The policy
debates in and around the shaping of NSC-68 were shot through
with fears for morale in Western Europe if the United States was not
seen to be acting decisively. In the debate over development of the
hydrogen bomb, Pentagon analysts argued that the allies were
already wavering because of the passing of the U.S. nuclear monop-

oly.[49] NSC-68 rejected a no-first-use doctrine on nuclear weapons not only because it would be seen as "great weakness" by Moscow, but also because allies would take it "as a clear indication that we intended to abandon them."[50] This has been very much the response to the recent proposal by four distinguished former officials that we adopt a no-first-use posture now.

Typical of this pattern was the suggestion by John Foster Dulles, writing to Dean Acheson in May 1950, that the communist triumph in China had led numerous governments to suspect the United States was retreating because it did not dare to risk war. To bolster the confidence of friends and allies he urged that a "dramatic and strong stand" be taken to show "confidence and resolution" by acting to neutralize Taiwan, allowing it neither to be captured nor to be used as a base against the Peking government, advice soon taken to heart with the outbreak of war in Korea. Charles Bohlen was moved by early loses in Korea to urge a rapid military build-up because morale and support among friends and allies was slipping.[51] Washington resorted to vague threats of nuclear retaliation to deter a feared communist Chinese incursion into Vietnam in 1953 in part to stiffen French morale and will to continue the struggle with the Vietminh. The joint chiefs supported defense of the offshore islands in the Taiwan Straits because their loss, while militarily unimportant, would seriously damage the Nationalists' morale. The Eisenhower Doctrine was designed in large part to strengthen the confidence of pro-Western governments in the Middle East.[52]

The concern about how the loss of Vietnam would affect other governments in Southeast Asia was a significant feature of the U.S. approach to the war. Kissinger's defense of the objective of securing peace with honor reflects concerns in the same vein extending around the world. "Scores of countries and millions of people relied for their security on our willingness to stand by allies, indeed in our confidence in ourselves. No serious policymaker could allow himself to succumb to the fashionable debunking of 'prestige,' or 'honor' or 'credibility.' . . . We could not revitalize the Atlantic Alliance if governments were assailed by doubts about American staying power."[53]

James Schlesinger's pursuit of perceived equivalence in nuclear war options included numerous references to the beneficial effect this posture would have on allies' perceptions, a consideration that influenced the development of PD-59. The Carter administration was very much concerned, as is the Reagan administration, that a failure to match Soviet counterforce capabilities would undermine the confidence of NATO allies in the United States.[54] The Carter administration was vigorously criticized for the effect on our friends abroad of failing to prevent the collapse of the Shah in Iran. Other examples could be cited, but the point is clear.

What is striking, then, about many occasions when officials acted to maintain the U.S. image for purposes of deterrence is that the target has often been friends and allies as much as opponents. As one analyst has noted, this has led to much of NATO's approach to nuclear weapons being more for "mutual reassurance than warning the Soviet Union."[55] Why the felt need for this constant, sometimes expensive, reassurance? George and Smoke are undoubtedly correct in citing geographical distance as a handicap. The United States is often far away, and distance renders it more difficult to make commitments convincing.[56] To this can be added the historical record of U.S. neutrality and isolationism. The United States is not only far away; it has also in the past often seen itself as too far away to have to be bothered. This presents a credibility problem with one's friends, a problem nuclear weapons just reinforce, which could induce a fainthearted response.

But it would seem that underlying this worry about the inconstancy of friends is a deeper doubt about ourselves, once more projected onto others. It has been suggested that U.S. policy makers have been strongly influenced by the failures of appeasement in the 1930s and the Munich analogy, an influence leading to determination not to appear weak, for this tempts aggressors. The impact on the policy makers can be readily documented in terms of rhetorical references to the "lessons" of that period. But is this simply learning from experience or more like a convenient way to rationalize policies resting on the insecurity induced by doubts about being able to use nuclear weapons? Is not the Munich analogy so compelling because, deep down, one can never escape feeling that in the nuclear age the same thing could easily happen again?

Conclusion

The analysis offered here can be taken as an elaboration of the argument by George and Smoke that looking at how a state actually practices deterrence makes it appear more complex. It would seem that one must take into account the nature of the government that attempts deterrence in ways the available theory does not encompass. By reference to the U.S. preoccupation with image, it has been suggested that one cannot fully understand the U.S. approach to deterrence without extending the psychology of deterrence to embrace the deterrer. It has been customary to treat the specific force posture decisions and weapons development processes that generate the military basis of deterrence as driven by domestic processes as much as (or more than) considerations of how to shape an opponent's perceptions. We should extend this to the actual conduct of deterrence itself.

7

■

PERCEPTIONS OF THE
SECURITY DILEMMA IN 1914

Jack L. Snyder

■ A dispute about the effect of threats and concessions lies at the heart of much U.S. theorizing about national security policy. Robert Jervis has laid out this dispute starkly in his analysis of "deterrence theory" and "the spiral model."[1] Deterrence theorists stress the role of credible threats in deterring potential aggressors. They fear that concessions on any issue will be taken as a general sign of weakness and consequently will undermine the credibility of one's resistance to future demands. In contrast, spiral theorists warn that most conflicts are rooted in mutual security fears, which are aggravated by unyielding, "deterrence" policies but assuaged by concessions. Eclectic theorists admit both possibilities and rely on a case-by-case analysis of the intentions of the specific adversary to determine whether threats or concessions are appropriate.

The case of World War I presents a puzzle for both the deterrence and the spiral theories, however, and points to the existence of a more fundamental dilemma in world politics. As 1914 approached, the European powers found themselves locked in an increasingly vicious "security dilemma"—a situation in which each state believed that its security required the insecurity of others. The Germans believed that they needed a capability to defeat Russia and France quickly and decisively, because the Entente's superior resources

The author wishes to acknowledge the support of the Center for International Affairs, Harvard University, where he was a research fellow in 1981–82. Robert Litwak, John Mearsheimer, Glenn Snyder, and Stephen Van Evera provided especially helpful comments.

were expected to dominate a prolonged contest. The Russians, naturally, could not tolerate a decisive German advantage in a short war, and so they planned a 40 percent increase in their standing forces by 1917. As a consequence, German authorities began to view a preventive war as the only alternative to unilateral vulnerability. Given the prevailing strategic assumptions that Germany would be at a disadvantage in a long war and that offensive strategies were inherently preferable to defensive ones, the simultaneous security of the Entente and of Germany was logically impossible. Either Germany would be able to win a short war, which the Entente could not allow, or the Entente would be able to win a prolonged war, which Germany could not allow.

Neither deterrent nor spiral axioms can resolve this kind of security dilemma. Unyielding, "deterrent" policies may be stabilizing when they defend a balanced status quo, because they induce caution in those who would overturn the balance. Given the circumstances and presuppositions of 1914, however, balance was unobtainable. There could be only an imbalance favoring one side or the other. As a consequence, threats did not produce caution; rather, they, underscored the zero-sum nature of the strategic competition, the dangers of inferiority, and the virtual inevitability of war. Directed toward the inferior party, threats heightened its resolve to redress the imbalance. Directed toward the superior party, threats encouraged it to strike before the balance was redressed. Thus, as a result of the deterrent diplomacy of the Moroccan crisis of 1911, all of the continental powers came to believe that a European war was likely. Under the pressure of the security dilemma, this did not make them cautious but rather led them to seek an advantageous occasion to start the conflict.

It has been suggested that Germany could have been deterred in July 1914 if Britain had made clear its commitment to fight.[2] Given the logic of the security dilemma, however, this would have given Germany all the more reason to strike before the balance shifted any further against it. Indeed, Britain's unyielding posture in 1911 helped to convince the Germans that a preventive war was the only alternative to encirclement.

If threats could not resolve the security dilemma, neither could concessions. The European states did try to defuse their conflicts on peripheral issues like the Baghdad railway. On major issues, however, meaningful concessions were impossible because a stable, mutually acceptable bargain could not exist, given the prevailing strategic assumptions. Appeasing the security fears of one's neighbor would have entailed accepting one's own insecurity. Although the security dilemma was in some sense a spiral process, it was not a spiral that could be unwound by the concessionary policies that spiral theorists usually advocate.

In a security dilemma, the adversary's malign intentions are caused by the incentives provided by its own strategic circumstances, as it understands them. Its intentions can be made more benign by another state only by changing those circumstances—or the adversary's assessment of them—and not by the use of threats or concessions. Consequently, to defuse or prevent the development of an acute security dilemma, it is necessary first to analyze the source of the perverse incentives that are constraining the entrapped states.

Alternative Explanations for Aggressive Behavior

To this end, it will be helpful to distinguish four ideal types: the structural security dilemma, the perceptual security dilemma, the imperialist's dilemma, and deadlock.

The Structural Security Dilemma

Assumptions. This ideal type assumes that security is the overriding goal of all states. Each state's choice of a strategy for maximizing its security is determined solely by the structural incentives created by military technology, geography, and the relative power of states. The intentions of others can be inferred only from these structural factors.

Hypotheses. A security dilemma, defined as a situation in which the security of each state requires the insecurity of others, will occur when offensive military operations are easier than defensive operations and/or when the relative power of two states is changing, such that, for one of the states, attacking now is better than defending later.

The Perceptual Security Dilemma

Assumptions. Security is still the overriding goal of states, but the choice of a strategy for achieving it may be influenced by perceptual biases. Technology, relative power, and the intentions of others may all be misperceived.

Hypotheses. A security dilemma occurs when decision makers overrate the advantages of the offensive, the magnitude of power shifts, or the hostility of others.

The Imperialist's Dilemma

Assumptions. At least one of the states in the system desires to expand, even if this entails some risk to its security. At the same time, no state seeks expansion at all costs. All states prefer compromise to a major war, assuming that the compromise guarantees the minimum objectives of each state, including its security. The problem facing expansionists is to achieve their limited imperial aims without provoking a major war, which would entail disproportionate costs and risks. The problems facing status quo states are to prevent expansion that would overturn the balance of power and, at the same time, to avoid a major war.

Hypotheses. Security dilemmas arise from the dynamics of limited competition over nonsecurity interests. In order to prevail in the competition for political, economic, or ideological influence in disputed areas, states develop offensive military capabilities, engage in arms races to shift the balance of power, and threaten their adversaries with war unless they abandon the disputed prize. These competitive activities are likely to create or intensify a security dilemma and may force one of the states to choose between war and unilateral vulnerability.

Deadlock

Assumptions. The nonsecurity interests of the states are incompatible and non-negotiable. Even if security guarantees could be devised, there is no compromise that both sides would prefer to a major war.

Hypotheses. Even in deadlock,[3] war may occur in circumstances that are reminiscent of a security dilemma, especially on the eve of a major shift in relative power. This is merely the occasion for war, rather than the cause of it. Even without the dilemma, war will occur as soon as coercive bargaining between the adversaries fully clarifies ιne zero-sum nature of their conflict of interests.

Recent theorizing about international politics has stressed the structural characteristics of the system that promote conflict: anarchy, unstable distributions of power, and offensive military technologies.[4] Whether intentionally or not, these theories convey the impression that statesmen are frequently so entrapped by perverse structural incentives that wars are likely "even in the extreme case in which all states would like to freeze the status quo."[5] This impression is highly misleading. Strictly structural theories, like the structural security dilemma, are very weak explanations for international conflict, primarily because defensive military operations are almost always easier than offensive ones. Given this fact, structural configurations that could cause war among status quo states will be rare. Consequently, structural factors must usually be supplemented by perceptual biases or nonsecurity aims that exacerbate the dilemma.

The following theoretical section will explain how each of the four ideal types tries to account for international conflict and why the strictly structural explanation is deficient. A subsequent section will examine the causes of World War I in light of the same ideal types. Finally, some observation on the implications of this analysis for contemporary national security policy will be advanced.

The Structural Security Dilemma

Two variables create and intensify the structural security dilemma: military technologies and geographical circumstances that give an advantage to the offense, and "windows of opportunity," that is, fluctuations in the military balance that make attacking now preferable to defending later. If these conditions obtained, it would be impossible to make all states secure simultaneously. Even if all states sought only security, wars would be common. Fortunately, structural incentives for conflict are rarely, if ever, this strong.

Offensive Advantage

Jervis has argued that "an increase in one state's security decreases the security of others" whenever "offense has the advantage"—that is, when "it is easier to destroy the other's army and take its territory than it is to defend one's own."[6] If offense were literally easier than defense, an equal balance of military power would leave each side vulnerable to whichever took up the offensive. To be secure, a state would have to strike first and remain constantly on the offensive until it had shifted the military balance decisively in its favor. Only when it enjoyed a margin of superiority sufficient to offset the advantage of the offensive could the state be secure and at peace. Until the hegemony of one side was achieved, international politics would be a constant struggle to capture strategic positions and resources and to destroy the armed forces of the adversary by offensive means.

Status quo powers would have to behave like expansionist powers if they valued their security. If they neglected opportunities to strike first and maximize their relative power, there would be no guarantee that their neighbors would reciprocate this restraint. In a strictly structural theory, this kind of trust would be irrational; all security-seeking states would have to be distrustful aggressors. In short, offensive advantage would create a Hobbesian world in which the payoffs were loaded against cooperation.[7]

These deductions are sound; the only trouble is that offense is virtually never easier than defense.[8] Here it is important to distinguish between the operational "advantages" of offense and incentives for the offensive resulting from an adverse trend in the balance of power. When a state anticipates a major, irreversible decline in its relative power, it may launch a preventive attack despite the operational disadvantages of the offense. This phenomenon should not be confused with the operational notion of "offensive advantage."

Appropriately, Jervis's discussion of the offense-defense balance focuses on the operational implications of technology and geography (meaning terrain features and distance). He gives two related criteria for determining whether offense or defense enjoys the technological-geographical advantage. "First, does the state have to spend more or less than one dollar on defensive forces to offset each dollar spent by the other side on forces that could be used to attack? . . . Second, with a given inventory of forces, is it better [that is, easier?—JS] to attack or defend?"[9]

Intuitively, the conditions for offensive advantage seem implausible. In this upside-down world, the weaker army should always be the attacker, using offense to compensate for its weakness. In the real world, weak armies stay on the defensive because defending is easier. Defense acts as a multiplier of the strength of an army.[10]

Of course, attackers often win, but this is because they are stronger, not because offense makes their task easier. People who believe that the offense confers a net advantage are simply failing to control for the effects of the quantity and especially the quality of the opposing forces. European observers of the Russo-Japanese War made this error, for example. Since the Japanese attacked and won with fewer forces, people inferred that the offense had the advantage. In reasoning this way, they ignored the only available control for quality: namely, the fact that the Russians did even worse on the few occasions when they attacked than they did when they defended.[11]

Both the attacking state and the defending state enjoy some advantages, but on balance the advantages of defending are greater. The attacker's advantage lies in holding the initiative. This gives it the chance to achieve surprise in the time or place of the attack. The defender's forces must guard all possible avenues of attack, whereas the attacker can concentrate its forces on a small number of main axes. In this way, the attacker can achieve local superiorities, which may allow it to turn the defender's flank or break through its thinly stretched front. Once this occurs, the defender's lines of supply and communication may be disrupted. Disorganized defending units may be unable to coordinate their efforts in an efficient manner.

The problem is that the initiative is a wasting asset. If break-throughs are not achieved and exploited immediately, the defender can shift its forces to shore up the threatened sector. It can also counterattack where the attacker is weak. At this stage of the campaign, all of the advantages lie with the defending state, which can usually maneuver and supply its forces more easily than the attacker can. On its own territory, the defender enjoys the use of a transportation network that is relatively intact. In contrast, after the attacker crosses the frontier, it will usually find that the defender has destroyed bridges and railroads in the area it has evacuated. Distances from sources of supply to the front are normally shorter for the defender than for the attacker.

At the tactical level, the defending state enjoys the advantage of firing under partial cover, whereas the attacker must expose itself to advance. The defender can choose and prepare the terrain on which the battle will be fought. River barriers, high ground, trenches, and fortifications can be used to multiply the effective power of the defending units. The defender can man such barriers lightly in order to concentrate more forces in sectors where barriers do not exist.

It is an empirical question whether the material advantages of the defense outweigh the countervailing advantages conferred by seizing the initiative. No doubt there are combinations of circumstances where the offense has an overall advantage because its characteristic advantages operate strongly, whereas the defender's operate weakly. For example, if prevailing intelligence technologies make it difficult to anticipate the direction of the attack, seizing the initiative may pay big dividends. At the same time, if terrain barriers are few, if the theater of operations is wide but not deep, if the attacker is protected by effective armor, if supplies can be gathered from the countryside, and if the attacker and defender use the same means of transport in the defender's territory, then the characteristic advantages of the defender will operate very weakly. Normally, however, defending is easier than attacking, notwithstanding the advantages of the initiative.

In the search for examples of "offense dominance," people usually cite the German armored blitzkriegs of World War II by which a numerically inferior force rolled up rapid, decisive victories. Certainly the military technology of 1940 was more favorable to the offense than that of 1914, but the success of Guderian's blitz through the Ardennes does not necessarily show that technology had made it "easier to destroy the other's army and take its territory than to defend one's own." More likely, it shows that the French army was poorly deployed and that its commanders did not understand how to prepare a successful defense in the era of mobile armored warfare. After 1941, attackers found that they usually needed a substantial numerical superiority to succeed.[12]

For almost all cases, the question should be not whether offense or defense has the advantage but whether the defender's advantage is small or large. If this view is correct, one of the alleged engines of the structural security dilemma runs in reverse! The exigencies of military operations tend to mitigate the dilemma, not exacerbate it. The engine that winds the dilemma tighter must be found elsewhere.

Windows of Opportunity

States have an incentive to attack their neighbors whenever they anticipate an adverse shift in the balance of power. The literature distinguishes between two situations of this kind: preventive war, which forestalls the creation of new military assets, and preemptive attack, which forestalls the mobilization and deployment of existing forces. Both can be discussed under the common rubric of *windows of opportunity*.[13]

The security dilemma here is that a status quo state may choose to attack another status quo state, even though both would prefer a stable compromise to war. This can happen because the preventive or preemptive attack cuts short the diplomatic search for possible terms of compromise or because the declining power does not trust the other to adhere to the compromise in the future.

Whether the window constitutes a decisive incentive to attack depends largely on three factors: the magnitude of the shift, the offense-defense balance, and, at the most general level, the likelihood that other states will attack during the anticipated period of vulnerability. If the shift is expected to produce a situation of only slight inferiority and if the defense is dominant, then a status quo state should have no incentive to launch a preventive attack. Even if more substantial vulnerability is expected, the declining state may still shun preventive war unless it expects to be attacked during the period when it is vulnerable. Perhaps its neighbors have no desire to attack it. Perhaps they can be appeased until the window of vulnerability is closed. Even if the power shift is permanent, perhaps a geopolitical retreat could reduce international frictions and make the state's holdings more defensible.

For a status quo power, the security risks posed by preventive war have to be weighed against those associated with the alternative strategies. Even if a state assumes the worst about the intentions of its adversary, preventive war now may not be preferable to defensive war later.

Preventive war involves numerous disadvantages. In addition to the military-operational ones of the offensive, there are also the diplomatic ones of being the aggressor. As Bismarck told the elder Moltke, a clumsily prepared preventive strike would place "the full weight of the imponderables . . . on the side of the enemies we have attacked."[14] As a rule, states tend to balance against aggressors rather than jump on the bandwagon with them.[15] States facing a secular decline in their relative power will need allies in the future; attracting a reputation for behaving recklessly would spoil their best chance for survival. Even a successful preventive war poses the problem of indigestible gains. If the attacking state tries to keep control of its gains, it may become overextended. The cost of protecting its empire may rise faster than its resources. But if it retreats after destroying its neighbor's army, it will be leaving behind a suspicious foe.[16] In contrast, a defensive war later may not be so grim a prospect, even though the state's relative power has declined, since it will enjoy both the operational and the diplomatic advantages of the defensive.

Even worst-case assumptions about the intentions of the opponent may not produce a clear, decisive case in favor of preventive war. When the assumption of unalterable hostility is relaxed, the case for preventive war becomes still less persuasive. Consequently, although structural incentives for preventive war may exist, they will often be counterbalanced by other considerations.

The Perceptual Security Dilemma

Even if structural conditions produce only a weak security dilemma, those conditions may be misperceived in ways that tighten the dilemma. People may underestimate the operational advantages of the defensive or overestimate the likelihood of other states jumping on the diplomatic bandwagon. People may overestimate their prospects in a war now while underestimating them in a war later. People may underestimate the costs of war and overestimate its inevitability. Any of these misperceptions would intensify the security dilemma, making it a more plausible explanation for the ensuing conflict.[17]

Some sources of perceptual bias can either exacerbate or alleviate security fears, depending on the circumstances of the case. For example, superficial "lessons" of the last war may strongly bias perceptions of the offense-defense balance, but they can cut in either direction depending on the nature of that war. This kind of bias is important for understanding individual cases, but it has no bearing on the plausibility of the security dilemma as a major, endemic source of international conflict.

Other sources of bias do support that view, however. In particular, two biases consistently tend to tighten the security dilemma: the tendency of the military to overrate the advantages of the offensive and the tendency of states to overestimate the hostility of others.

Military Bias for the Offensive

Bernard Brodie believed that "military doctrine is universally, and has been since the time of Napoleon, imbued with the 'spirit of the offensive.' "[18] Although no definitive study of military attitudes on offense and defense has been attempted, three recent studies have argued that the interests and outlook of military organizations bias them in favor of offensive doctrines and strategies.[19]

A number of hypotheses might account for this bias:

Size and Wealth of the Organization. Offense is a difficult task that justifies large defense budgets. It is also a productive task in that decisive, offensive campaigns produce demonstrable returns on the state's investment in military capability. In the 1880s, for example, Field Marshal von der Goltz pushed the view that "modern wars have become a nation's way of doing business"—a perspective that made sense only if wars were short, cheap, and hence offensive.[20]

Prestige and Self-image. The quick, decisive Wars of German Unification turned the Prussian officer corps into demigods, whom the rest of the nation honored and emulated.[21] As Barry Posen puts it, offense makes soldiers "specialists in victory," defense makes them "specialists in attrition," and "deterrence makes them specialists in slaughter."[22]

Autonomy. The elder Moltke succinctly stated the universal wish of military commanders: "The politician should fall silent the moment that mobilization begins."[23] This is least likely to happen in the case of limited or defensive wars, where the whole point of fighting is to negotiate a diplomatic solution. Political considerations—and hence politicians—have to figure in operational decisions. The operational autonomy of the military is most likely to be allowed when the operational goal is to disarm the adversary quickly and decisively by offensive means. For this reason, the military will seek to force doctrine and planning into this mold.[24]

Uncertainty Reduction. Posen points out that "taking the offensive, exercising the initiative, is a way of structuring the battle."[25] Defense, in contrast, is more reactive, less structured, and harder to plan. People in charge of large organizations seek structure—or the illusion of structure. Hence Stephen Van Evera's hypothesis that the military will prefer a task that is easier to plan even if it is more difficult to execute successfully.[26]

Focus on Threats and Military Responses. The professional training and duties of soldiers force them to focus on threats to the state's security and on the conflictual side of international relations. Necessarily preoccupied with the prospect of armed conflict, they see war as a pervasive aspect of international life. Focusing on the role of military means in ensuring the security of the state, they forget that other means can also be used toward the same end. For these reasons, the military professional tends to hold a simplified, zero-sum view of international politics and the nature of war. In this kind of Hobbesian world, wars are seen as difficult to avoid and almost impossible to keep limited.

When the hostility of others is taken for granted, prudential calculations are slanted in favor of preventive wars and preemptive strikes. Indeed, as German military officers were fond of arguing, the proper role of diplomacy in a Hobbesian world is to create favorable conditions for launching preventive war. A preventive grand strategy requires an offensive operational doctrine. Defensive plans and doctrines will be considered only after all conceivable offensive schemes have been decisively discredited. Under uncertainty, such discrediting will be difficult, so offensive plans and doctrines will be frequently adopted even when offense is not easier than defense in the operational sense.

The assumption of extreme hostility also favors the notion that decisive, offensive operations are always needed to end wars. If the conflict of interest between the parties is seen as limited, then a decisive victory may not be needed to end the fighting on mutually acceptable terms. In fact, denying the adversary state its objectives by means of a successful defense may suffice. However, when the opponent is believed to be extremely hostile, disarming it completely may seem like the only way to induce it to break off its attacks. For this, offensive doctrines and plans are needed, even if defense is easier operationally.

Kenneth Waltz argues that states are socialized to the implications of international anarchy.[27] Because of their professional pre-occupations, military professionals become "oversocialized." Seeing the security dilemma as tighter than it really is, they make it still tighter by adopting offensive plans and buying offensive forces.[28] In this way, the perceptual security dilemma becomes a self-fulfilling prophecy.

Perceptions of Hostility

Military professionals are particularly prone to overestimate the hostility of other states, but even civilians seem to have some bias in this direction. This bias intensifies the security dilemma by making a stable, mutually acceptable compromise seem infeasible.

Two fairly similar explanations for this phenomenon are most prominent in the psychological literature. An ego-defense theory starts with the proposition that the ego protects its self-image by denying that its activities harm or threaten others. Consequently, when others behave in a hostile manner, this is seen as an indication of their aggressive intentions, not as a reaction to the threat posed by oneself.

A somewhat different explanation, proposed by attribution theorists, starts with the proposition that people are "naïve scientists" who fail to consider the biases that are inherent in information available to them. When analyzing their own behavior, states are highly conscious of the role of external constraints, the difference between intended and inadvertent consequences, and internal political processes that may produce inconsistent policies. States feel that they are not responsible for threatening or deceiving others, because they are under duress or because the threat or deceit is unintended. In contrast, it is intellectually more difficult to empathize with the constraints on others or to imagine the complex internal processes that might account for the vagaries of their behavior. It is much simpler to posit a unitary, purposeful actor, whose behavior is a reflection of innate character rather than of the problems faced. When the naïve scientist is inconvenienced by a sudden change in another's policy, he attributes it to purposeful guile; when he is threatened, he infers aggressive intent.[29]

In summary, the addition of perceptual factors makes the security dilemma a more powerful theory of international conflict. It breathes life into the concept of "offense dominance," and it helps to explain why people underrate the feasibility of cooperation. Conversely, the concept of the security dilemma makes perceptual theories more persuasive by showing how perceived hostility gets translated into decisions for war.

The Imperialist's Dilemma

The ingredients of a security dilemma are offensive advantage, incentives for preventive or preemptive attack, and the fear that the adversary will attack at the first opportunity. Among status quo states, these conditions are unlikely except as the consequence of a misperception. However, when one or more states are motivated by nonsecurity, expansionist aims, the natural dynamic of international competition tends to create these conditions. Even if states would rather limit their imperial competition than risk a major war, this competitive dynamic may confront them with the choice between war and unilateral vulnerability.

In order to achieve its expansive political, economic, or ideological goals, the aspiring imperialist state develops offensive military forces for the purpose of conquest or intimidation. When resistance is met, a testing of will and capabilities ensues. An arms race occurs as the imperialist and its opponent both try to prove that they have the capability to achieve their nonsecurity aims unilaterally, if necessary. Crises are staged as the states test each other's willingness to risk war rather than retreat. The conflict spiral may be punctuated by attempts at conciliation, especially if each side would prefer some compromise to the costs and risks of a major war. Indeed, the art of coercive diplomacy is to use threats to discover the adversary's minimum bargaining position short of war and then to conciliate it to consolidate a favorable compromise.[30]

The imperialist's dilemma arises when this process of intimidation and bargaining is interrupted by a window of opportunity. Until the bargaining process is concluded, the adversaries do not know whether a compromise will be obtainable—that is, whether each side would rather accept the other's minimum demands than fight. Consequently, they must constantly guard their relative power position in case the adversary decides to break off the bargaining and attack. When a window of opportunity intervenes, however, maintaining one's position of relative power may require a preventive or preemptive attack.

Windows that provide incentives for prevention and preemption are likely by-products of the process of intimidation and bargaining. Windows are particularly likely to appear during arms races, when changes in underlying power capabilities are quickly and dramatically manifested. A prudent state may decide to strike if it feels that its fortunes are declining, thus cutting short the search for a compromise. Windows are also likely to appear during crises, for two reasons. First, the crisis may convince one or both sides that war is inevitable and, consequently, that any preemptive or preventive advantages, no matter how slight, might as well be reaped. Second, military mobilization, which may be used as a tactic in the game of crisis intimidation, may threaten to close a window of opportunity. In 1914, for example, the Germans felt that they had to respond to Russian mobilization by attacking France immediately, since their whole strategy depended on the time-lag of the Russian offensive in their rear.

In sum, the imperialist's dilemma is a security dilemma that is a by-product of the competition over nonsecurity interests. It is a dilemma in the sense that both competitors may prefer some compromise to a major war, but they are unable to reach it because the dynamics of the arms race and brinkmanship make their security interests incompatible.

Like the security dilemma, the imperialist's dilemma can be considered either a structural or a perceptual theory. However, the latter's need for a perceptual boost may not be as great as the former's. The nature of the imperialist state's policy gives it a reason to buy offensive forces and seek offensive doctrines. It also makes mutual security guarantees more difficult to devise because they may rule out the kinds of capabilities that the imperialist needs for its campaign of limited expansion. Such factors are rooted in the structure of the nonsecurity competition and do not require misperceptions to be set in motion.

Deadlock

Not all conflicts result from dilemmas, of course. In some cases, there may be no compromise that both sides would prefer to war, even if ironclad security guarantees could be arranged. Under those conditions, there would be no dilemma, only a deadlock.

In practical terms, it may be difficult to distinguish an imperialist's dilemma from a deadlock. Even in deadlock, there is likely to be a period of competitive arming and brinkmanship, as the competitors test each other's capabilities and resolve. These are likely to create windows, which will be the immediate precipitant of the decision for war. For example, the U.S. decision to cut off petroleum shipments to Japan in 1941 confronted the Japanese with a closing window of opportunity. If Japan were to have even the slightest hope of success in a war against the United States, it would have to strike as soon as possible. Pearl Harbor was the result. Nonetheless, Snyder and Diesing call this a deadlock, not a dilemma, on the grounds that further bargaining would not have produced a compromise and that war would have occurred anyway. Thus the distinction between a deadlock and an imperialist's dilemma in any particular case may involve a speculative exercise in counterfactual history.

The European Security Dilemma, 1870–1914

Historians of World War I can be divided into two schools. Members of the first, typified by Sidney Fay, have portrayed the war as an unwanted, almost accidental by-product of the search for security.[31] For them, the nonsecurity disputes of the European powers seem insufficient to have caused the Great War. Instead, they believe that the explanation lies largely in the dilemma posed by Germany's vulnerable position in the center of Europe, the spiral logic of arms competition and alliance commitment, and runaway war plans. The concept of the security dilemma, including its structural as well as its perceptual version, adds theoretical support to the arguments of this school. The second school, typified by Fritz Fischer, has portrayed the war as the inevitable result of the ambitions or interests of the powers—in short, as a deadlock.[32] In particular, emphasis has been placed on the domestic factors compelling Germany's expansion and on the inevitability that her expansion would be resisted. A third explanation, based on the imperialist's dilemma, borrows from the insights of both schools. Germany's attempt to expand through intimidation created a security dilemma for both itself and its neighbors.

Explanations that focus exclusively on the security dilemma or exclusively on deadlocked nonsecurity interests are not fully convincing. The strictly structural version of the security dilemma explanation, for example, is undermined by the defensive advantage proffered by prevailing military technologies. The perceptual version of the security dilemma, which rests on a misreading of those technological incentives, captures part of the problem, but it may not be able to account fully for Germany's belligerent diplomacy between 1904 and 1914, which was often gratuitously aggressive in a way that jeopardized rather than enhanced German security. At the same time, there is no reason to label the European bargaining game a deadlock. If security guarantees had been available, compromise on economic, ideological, and prestige issues would not have been unthinkable. Only the imperialist's dilemma (or variants of it) capture the role of both the security dilemma and nonsecurity competition in causing World War I.

In order to examine these alternative explanations more closely, three topics will be discussed. An analysis of Germany's military situation from 1870 to 1905 will test the structural variant of the security dilemma explanation against its perceptual variant. An analysis of German diplomacy after 1904 will propose explanations based on the perceptual security dilemma, the imperialist's dilemma, and combinations of the two. Finally, a discussion of the July crisis will examine the competing claims of the imperialist's dilemma and deadlock explanations.

Germany's Military Dilemma

Germany's position and policy must lie at the heart of any analysis of the European security dilemma between 1870 and 1914.[33] After 1870 both Bismarck and the German chief of staff, the elder Moltke, considered Germany a satisfied power, interested only in securing the gains of the Wars of Unification. France and Russia, however, were not fully satisfied with the status quo. Germany's annexation of Alsace-Lorraine gave the French a motive for revenge, while Russia's encroachments into the Balkans risked a conflict with Austria that could upset the balance of power to Germany's detriment.[34] Germany could handle either of these threats separately, but a combined Franco-Russian effort would tax Germany's strength to the limit, even with Austrian help.

In planning for a possible two-front war, Moltke faced a classic dilemma: whether the incentive to attack offered by a window of opportunity outweighed the disincentive posed by the operational advantages of the defense. The comparative slowness of the Russian mobilizations opened a window of opportunity for Germany during the first month of a two-front conflict. Since Russia would be operating at partial strength, Germany had an incentive to seek decisive results during this initial period. Most decisive would be a rapid battle of annihilation in France, using the bulk of the German army. This was Moltke's preference during the 1870s.

By the 1880s, however, the improvement of the French fortress line made Moltke doubt the feasibility of such an operation. Consequently, he decided to use half of his army to defend against France and the remainder to encircle the relatively weak Russian force in

Poland during the first weeks of a conflict. Moltke realized that this would not be decisive in the same sense as the destruction of the whole French field army. The Russians could continue the fight with their late-mobilizing units, while the French could hammer away at the German defense line on the Saar. But using diplomacy and the advantages of the defense, Moltke believed the bloodied French and Russians might accept peace on the basis of the status quo ante. Moltke had been impressed by the holding power of the tactical defensive in the Franco-Prussian War, and, in any case, he came to believe that this stalemate strategy was Germany's least miserable option.

Toward the end of the 1880s, increased Russian peacetime deployments and improved fortifications in Poland threatened the viability even of Moltke's limited offensive around Warsaw. In 1887, in the context of a Russo-German financial war and continuing tension in the Balkans, Moltke and his deputy Waldersee urged a preventive war against Russia before the completion of the Russian build-up.

Here was a classic security dilemma fed by offensive plans and a closing window of opportunity. To Moltke, German security required the vulnerability of Russian forces in Poland. Without this vulnerability, both Russia and France could mobilize to full strength at their leisure and then attack in the second month of the conflict. To Russia, the security of Russian Poland required eliminating this vulnerability. In this situation, Russia's move to defend itself was an offensive threat to Germany. Conversely, Moltke's defensive motives led him to propose aggression against Russia. Offense and defense had become indistinguishable; for Moltke, at least, the security dilemma was operating at full force.

Underlying Moltke's preventive advice was an assumption that war between Russia and Germany was inevitable; therefore it should be undertaken while Germany could still capitalize on the window provided by Russia's slow mobilization. Bismarck did not share this assumption. Believing that a combination of appeasement and deterrence could hold Russia in check, he vetoed the preventive strike.

In the 1890s, Schlieffen took over the task of planning for a two-front war. His studies showed that frontal attacks on the French or Russian positions would not yield quick results. The only way to effect a decision before Russia completed its mobilization would be to outflank the French fortress line via Belgium. He and his successor, the younger Moltke, understood most of the pitfalls of this maneuver quite well: the gratuitous provocation of new enemies, logistical nightmares, the possibility of a rapid French redeployment to nullify the German flank maneuver, the numerical insufficiency of the German army, the tendency of the attacker's strength to wane with every step forward and the defender's to grow, and the lack of time to finish with France before Russia would attack. It is remarkable how well the German general staff anticipated all of the factors that contributed to the failure of the Schlieffen plan in August 1914.

As difficult as the attack through Belgium seemed, all other options seemed worse. The main alternative considered was a mirror image of the Schlieffen plan pointed toward the east. According to German staff studies, this was a poor option because the French would quickly break through weakly held German positions in the Rhineland. What the general staff refused to consider after 1890 was the possibility of an equal division of their forces between west and east, allowing a stable defense against France and a limited offensive with Austria against Russia. (This was the combination that Germany used successfully in 1915.)

Operationally, this would have been the easiest strategy available to Germany. Politically, its appeal would have been as a deterrent. If Germany had accepted the advice of its military engineers and fortified the gap between Metz and Strasbourg on the French frontier, the German security dilemma would have largely dissolved. Attacking Germany would have become obviously unattractive to France and therefore to Russia.

But the German military reasoned inside out. They took the inevitability of war for granted and reasoned that defense or limited offense could not end it. Particularly if a British blockade were imposed, a long war might hurt Germany more than her neighbors, they believed. Therefore, a decisive offensive was necessary, and the best chance for its success was to attack across Belgium before Russia was fully mobilized. German military planners failed to understand that a war might not occur if Germany drew an impregnable defense line around itself and Austria. Likewise, they arbitrarily rejected the idea that Britain would stay out of the war if Germany fought it defensively.

It would be convenient to argue that Germany adopted an offensive military strategy because it wished to conquer its neighbors' territory. This would parsimoniously explain the Germans' willingness to run the great risks inherent in the Schlieffen plan. However, there is little support for this view. The three chiefs of the general staff who dominated German war planning between 1870 and 1914 all considered Germany to be a satisfied power in Europe and thought primarily in terms of a war for security (or perhaps for national honor). Younger staff officers like Wilhelm Groener were sometimes imbued with a sense of German manifest destiny in *Mitteleuropa*, but the basic shape of the Schlieffen plan was formed before these ideas became current. Moreover, there is no evidence that expansionist civilians had any influence in war planning.

This chronicle of German military policy making includes a number of points of theoretical interest. First, some of the elements of a structural security dilemma helped to shape German policy. Although offense was operationally more difficult then defense, the window provided by Russia's slow mobilization gave Germany an incentive to develop offensive war plans. The danger that the Russian build-up in Poland would close this window gave Germany an incentive to carry out these offensive plans. This should not obscure the fact, however, that Germany also had reasonably good defensive options for solving its security problems. After 1890, these defensive options were probably superior to the offensive one that was adopted.

This raises the second theoretical issue: the perceptual aspects of the security dilemma. The German military overrated the hostility of their opponents, the inevitability of war, and hence the need for a preventive, war-fighting strategy rather than a deterrent strategy. The military was consistently more extreme in this view than were civilians, a fact that indicates that a military perceptual bias accounts for it. The German military was fairly realistic about the operational difficulties of the offensive, however. In this case, it was not that an overestimation of offensive capabilities led to a perception of a hostile world; rather, the perception of a hostile world led to a belief that an offensive capability was necessary. On the other hand, once offense was seen as necessary, there arose a tendency to see it as possible. The general staff stopped asking whether the Schlieffen plan would work; they asked only how they could make it work better.

A third theoretical issue is the temporal and causal relationship among four key variables: offense, windows, nonsecurity disputes, and expected hostility. In a structural security dilemma, offense and windows should come first, and hostility should grow as the consequences of these structural conditions become clear. In a perceptual security dilemma, this same pattern might hold, with the exception that offense and/or windows would be rooted in perceptual biases. Alternatively, a perceptual security dilemma might begin with an overestimate of the other's hostility, causing the subsequent adoption of offensive plans to take advantage of windows of opportunity. Finally, in an imperialist's dilemma, nonsecurity disputes should come first; offense, perceived hostility, competitive armament, and windows should follow.

For the German military, the assumption of hostility came first. As soon as the Franco-Russian war was over, the elder Moltke was announcing the inevitability of a Russo-German war. This was long before substantive disputes over economics or spheres of influence became acute and consequently supports the perceptual security dilemma explanation. For German civilians, however, the order was probably the reverse. Even though German military strategy created a security dilemma through its emphasis on offense and windows, German civilians refused opportunities for preventive wars in 1887 and again in 1905, when Russia was neutralized by the Russo-Japanese War and revolutionary upheaval. In neither case, did they believe that war was inevitable, and consequently they were not swayed by the argument that conditions would become less favorable if they waited.[35] Only later, after German imperial aims had expanded, did the German civilian elite become convinced that there was no acceptable compromise that could avoid the war.

In sum, there is no denying that the structure of Germany's security problem played a role in the creation of a security dilemma, in which attempts by states to defend themselves inherently threatened their neighbors. Nonetheless, German military planners could have extricated Germany from this dilemma by preparing a defensive alternative based on deterrence through denial. That they ignored this option had more to do with perceptions than with the structure of their dilemma. Despite the thinking of the German military, German civilians did not yet feel tightly bound by their security dilemma.

The Diplomacy of Expansion and Security

The evolution of German policy after 1904 can be explained plausibly as the result of a perceptual security dilemma, somewhat better as an imperialist's dilemma, and perhaps best as a combination of the two. The aim of this section is not primarily to argue for one or another of these intepretations but to trace the logic of each and to show how security and nonsecurity motives interact.

The perceptual security dilemma argument holds that the Schlieffen plan was rooted in a misperception of offensive advantage, but once in place it caused a real security dilemma for German diplomacy. The Schlieffen plan predicated German security on the maintenance of a war-winning capability—that is, on the inferiority and insecurity of others. This presented a hard task to German diplomats: to feel fully secure, they either had to break up enemy coalitions that might neutralize Germany's war-winning capability, or they had to authorize a preventive war before such a coalition reached full strength. It can be argued therefore that Germany's offensive diplomacy during this period is best explained by the expansive security requirements of the Schlieffen plan. However, since this diplomacy was clearly counterproductive in security terms, it may be easier to explain it as the result of a nonsecurity interest in expansion.[36]

In favor of the security explanation is the argument that Germany could not let the Triple Entente, existing in latent form since 1904, consolidate and grow in strength. Even if the Entente were satisfied to balance German military power, this would jeopardize the Schlieffen plan. Consequently, German attempts to break up the Entente by intimidation in the Moroccan crises of 1905 and 1911 can be understood in security terms. Even more easily, Austro-German ultimatums and *faits accomplis* in the Balkan crises of 1909 and 1914 can be explained as offensive means serving a defensive end, namely the preservation of Austria-Hungary as a stable factor in the European balance of power. Even if we accept that German leaders consciously sought war in July 1914, this can be explained as a preventive struggle for survival in circumstances in which either the Triple Entente or the Triple Alliance had to be insecure militarily. Germany's attempts to achieve security by splitting the Entente and by aggressively defending the declining Austrian Empire served only to tighten the Entente, provoke a "national reawakening" in France, and stimulate plans for a huge Russian arms buildup to be completed by 1917. Because German authorities doubted their ability to finance an unrestrained arms race, they began to see preventive war as the only way out.

While it is true that German policy had provoked the increases in the Russian army and the tightening of the Entente, a security dilemma argument would hold that Germany had no choice but to gamble on breaking up the incipient Entente. Moreover, in this view, it would have been dangerous for Germany to try to learn from her mistakes and become more conciliatory after 1911. By that time the mere memory of the Franco-German Agadir crisis had created a security dilemma mentality in France as well. Tepid Russian support during the Agadir crisis had led some French statesmen to believe that is was in France's interest to provoke a final showdown with Germany and Austria over an issue that was primarily of concern to Russia. In the fall of 1912, Austro-Russian tensions during the First Balkan War provided such an occasion.

Some French officials tried to goad the Russians into mobilizing, perhaps hoping that a war would ensue.[37] Although French motives were primarily defensive, a security dilemma forced them to adopt offensive diplomatic tactics. Whoever or whatever had created the European security dilemma, by 1912 there was no simple way out of it. Arguably, a state that gave its neighbor the benefit of the doubt in these circumstances would have come to regret it.

There are also arguments against the security explanation, however. Just as Schlieffen and the younger Moltke could have better solved Germany's military problem defensively, so too Holstein and Kiderlen could have better kept the Entente divided through blandishments and Bismarckian "reinsurance" than by threats. Even taking the Schlieffen plan as a given, it is hardly obvious that German diplomacy had to break up the Entente to ensure Germany's survival. Until the Agadir crisis, the Entente was a desultory affair. Military cooperation among the three powers was at best sporadic, and diplomatically their interests did not always coincide.

Even after Agadir, conciliation and restraint were probably as good a policy as the preventive implementation of the flawed Schlieffen plan. Why not, from a security standpoint, conciliate Britain on the fleet ratio, since the risk-fleet idea was preposterous anyway? Why dispatch General Liman von Sanders to Constantinople to organize a politico-military barrier to Russian expansion? Russian documents prove that the Czarist regime had a timetable for taking over the Turkish straits:[38] why not let them fritter away their strength on this project, which would have jeopardized the Entente more effectively than any German threats?

In many of these instances, it becomes tortuous to explain German behavior in terms of a security dilemma, which required offensive behavior to achieve defensive aims. The imperialist's dilemma often seems more straightforward: for reasons of domestic prestige, bureaucratic politics, or the perceived economic interests of various domestic groups, Germany was compelled to act in ways that threatened the interests and security of other states. The Junkers' demands for high tariffs on grain led to conflict with Russia; the demands of the bourgeoisie and the middle classes for a navy, colonies, and *Weltpolitik* led to conflict with Britain and France; the rising appeal of socialism had to be deflected by the counter-appeal of jingo nationalism. The weak ruling authorities could not impose rational priorities on competing claims, which created too many enemies at the same time, and had to maintain their prestige by means of cheap diplomatic victories at the expense of other powers. According to this analysis, Germany embarked on a more militant course after 1900 not because the security dilemma had become more acute but because domestic pressure for expansion had increased.

Arguably, those pressures did not foreordain a German policy of unlimited expansion at all costs. They did require Germany to engage in coercive diplomacy in order to force its neighbors to accept a German "place in the sun." Theorists of German expansion like Alfred Tirpitz and Kurt Riezler argued that brinkmanship and competitive armament could serve as a substitute for war, a way to measure power and will without actually fighting, as long as German aims were limited. They did not reckon, however, on the dynamics of the imperialist's dilemma. Recurrent crises and arms races led characteristically to tightening alliances, inferences that war was inevitable, power fluctuations producing windows of opportunity, and finally war. In this interpretation, what started as a limited competition over economic, imperial, and prestige issues evolved into a tight security dilemma because the instruments and tactics of limited, controlled expansion were indistinguishable from the means to achieve a decisive hegemony.

Still, this imperialist's dilemma explanation falls short in one respect. As I argued above, Germany's offensive strategy for land warfare was devised in response to the misperceived requirements of German security in Europe, not primarily as an instrument of coercive diplomacy to extract colonial or other nonsecurity concessions. Thus a major element of the security dilemma of 1914 was in place independent of any nonsecurity competition. A final possibility, then, is that both the perceptual security dilemma (in the form of the offensive Schlieffen plan) and the imperialist's dilemma (in the form of Tirpitz's naval arms races, Riezler's diplomacy of "calculated risk," and so forth) were needed to produce the tight security dilemma of 1914. The Schlieffen plan created a propensity toward instability in the system, and German coercive diplomacy and competitive armament turned that propensity into a dynamic security dilemma. Without the independent perception of offensive advantage, power shifts caused by the competition in land armaments might not have provided a sufficient incentive for preventive war. Likewise, it was in part the Schlieffen plan that made German bids for limited advantage indistinguishable from bids for hegemony, thus undercutting Riezler's theory of coercive diplomacy.

In short, a variety of explanations seems plausible for Europe's drift toward war in 1914, all of them relying on some variant of the security dilemma. The existence of nonsecurity sources of conflict rooted in economic, imperial, or domestic concerns is not necessarily incompatible with such explanations. On the contrary, limited competition over nonsecurity issues helps to explain the origins of some of the conditions producing an unlimited struggle for security in this period.

The July Crisis: Dilemma or Deadlock?

A final question is whether there was a dilemma of any kind in July 1914 or whether the interests of the two sides had simply become deadlocked. The argument for a dilemma can take two forms, the one focusing on preventive war and the other on pre-emption.[39]

For the former the dilemma for Germany was whether to launch a preventive war even though the conflict might eventually reach a satisfactory resolution without war. The preventive cast of German thinking on the eve of the war has been well documented.[40] Whether the war actually precluded the evolution of some mutually acceptable, peaceful outcome is more problematic. A few hopeful possibilities deserve mention: a continuation of the secular trend toward more pacific, socialist legislatures in France and Germany; a revolution or economic downturn in Russia; constitutional innovations allowing Germany to finance an open-ended arms race; diversion of Russian military deployments toward Turkey; implementation of a plan for slavic autonomy within the framework of the Austro-Hungarian Empire. With any or all of these long-run possibilities still outstanding, it seems fair to argue that a dilemma did exist. The July crisis was not just a cut and dried exercise. Bethmann-Hollweg and the Kaiser did have second thoughts after Russian restraint and British neutrality failed to materialize. How serious these second thoughts were is a matter of dispute, but even as late as 30 July there was anxiety that preventive war might be foreclosing some better option.

The case that World War I was a preemptive war is also commonly advanced. According to conventional wisdom, time pressure caused by incentives to mobilize or attack first cut crisis diplomacy short before all the options were explored and reflected upon.[41] While time pressure probably existed, historians often misunderstand and in some respects overstate it.

It is not true, for example, that the commanders believed that the army that mobilized and struck first would be able to disrupt the concentration of the opponent's army. Each side worried that the opponent might do this to it, so zones of concentration were protected from disruption by barriers or distance. Even so, no one wanted to be too late in mobilizing. Still, this was a reason only to mobilize shortly after the opponent, not to mobilize first.

The only exception to this rule was the Germans' need to attack the French fortress of Liège before the Belgians had fully prepared its defense. Liège sat astride a bottleneck in the path of the German army across northern Belgium. If the Belgians succeeded in reinforcing their garrison, the passage of the critical German First Army could be delayed and the Schlieffen plan foiled. Using German intelligence documents, Ulrich Trumpener argues that Belgian preparations around Liège were one of the main reasons for the "hardening" of Moltke's attitude on July 30.[42] When security depends on the success of offensive plans, even the self-defense measures of a weak power can be a provocation.

Another dubious argument is that German authorities believed that Russia's premobilization efforts had secretly given it a lead of several days. The only one who may have believed this unreservedly was the Kaiser.[43] Trumpener's research suggests that the general staff probably understood that the key act was the call-up and transportation of Russian reservists, which was unaffected by the premobilization measures.[44]

The time pressure inherent in the Schlieffen plan gave the Germans some incentive to mobilize before the Russians. All other things being equal, every extra day gave the Germans more time to finish with France before redeploying eastward. It does not seem that this incentive was decisive, however. Although time-lags and the Russian flirtation with partial mobilization serve to muddy an incomplete documentary record, it is most likely that the final German decision to mobilize followed confirmation of the news that Russia had switched to full mobilization.[45]

Ultimately, the case that World War I was preemptive rests on an analysis of the Russian decision to mobilize. Direct evidence about the motives and timing of the Russian general mobilization is extremely thin. The most likely source of time pressure on the Russians was the desire to gain a day or so on the Germans. The Russian general staff had promised the French that they would advance on East Prussia by the fourteenth day of mobilization. Everyone expected an early decision in the west, and the Russians—in their own interest as well as that of the French—wanted to attract at least five German corps to East Prussia, so that France might survive the German onslaught. An attack on the fourteenth day would mean advancing at partial strength and without supply trains, which would take another two or more days to organize. A head start of even a day or two would help to alleviate this extreme time pressure.[46]

While this time advantage was probably a factor, by far the most important element in the Russian decision was "the small probability of avoiding war with Germany."[47] The Russians had believed since 25 July that war was virtually unavoidable, and the Germans' lack of interest in negotiating about the substance of the Austro-Serbian dispute only confirmed this view. Under the circumstances, it would not be surprising if the Russians felt that they might as well grasp even a slight time advantage.

In sum, World War I can plausibly be viewed as a preventive and perhaps preemptive war in which decisions to capitalize on windows of opportunity foreclosed the search for solutions short of war. In this sense, the war can be seen as the consequence of a security or imperialist's dilemma, not just a deadlock of inexorably opposed interests.

Conclusions

World War I highlights two dangers in international politics. The first is the perceptual security dilemma. By overestimating the operational advantages of the offense, states may think incorrectly that the search for security is a zero-sum game, which offers substantial incentives for preventive or preemptive attacks.

The second danger is the imperialist's dilemma, a security dilemma that arises as a by-product of nonsecurity competition. Although all states may prefer compromise to a major war, the strategies that they pursue to gain advantages in the nonsecurity competition tend to make a stable, secure compromise impossible. To compete effectively, states develop offensive military capabilities, attempt to shift the balance of power through arms increases, and threaten war to test the adversary's resolve. These activities help to create the security dilemma syndrome, in which offense is feasible; both sides cannot be secure at the same time; attacking now is believed by one or both of the parties to be better than defending later; and war is considered virtually inevitable.

The perceptual security dilemma and the imperialist's dilemma are relevant not only to the pre-1914 era but also to contemporary problems. An understanding of these dilemmas may help U.S. strategists to solve puzzles that cannot be disentangled by either the deterrence or spiral models. Since concessions and intransigence are *both* dangerous when dealing with adversaries like imperial Germany and the contemporary Soviet Union, the deterrent-spiral debate may not be the most useful frame of reference for policy choices.

The mainstream interpretation of Soviet behavior is that of opportunistic expansion. The Soviet Union will not consciously run a high risk of war to expand its influence, but it will seize most opportunities to expand cheaply and safely. It will gladly pocket concessions and continue to look for more opportunities with unabated appetite. According to this view, its inclination to expand is limited primarily by prudential calculations of cost and risk, not by inherently limited aims. Thus the Soviet Union will never be satiated. If this is true, then a strategy of concessions will at best buy a little time before an unyielding deterrent strategy must be adopted. At worst, as deterrence theorists warn, short-run concessions will jeopardize the credibility of the ultimate switch to a deterrent strategy.

A strategy of uncompromising deterrence also involves dangers, however. Unless the imperialist state is extremely easy to dissuade, it will seek to overcome the resistance of status quo states through the build-up of a superior, offensive military capability and through coercive diplomacy. Deterrence theory prescribes a simple response: match all capability increases and yield no ground, so that the will to resist cannot be doubted. The imperialist's dilemma warns, however, that offensive arms races and competition in risk-taking are likely to create incentives for preventive and preemptive war, which might trap even prudent competitors. Deterrence axioms overlook this danger. Imperialists, by their nature, are unlikely to be highly attuned to the risks of "prisoner's dilemma" situations. If they were, their pursuit of expansionist goals would be tepid indeed, and there would be little difficulty in containing them. Consequently, the status quo power must normally bear a double burden: it must maintain its power and credibility at the same time as it works against the development of unstable, security dilemma conditions. In short, the status quo power must worry about everyone's security, not just its own.

In practical terms, this means that the status quo state must keep up its end of the power competition but do so by deploying defensive forces, forces that dissuade without the threat of escalation and create no first-strike advantage for either side. Moreover, it must avoid commitments and alliances that can be defended only by destabilizing means.

At first glance, this seems to demand that the status quo power compete with one hand—its offensive hand—tied behind its back. In fact, this disadvantage need not be crippling. It is more than outweighed by the operational and diplomatic advantages of the defender, which accrue primarily to the status quo state. Considered in this light, stability-enhancing security policies are not only a necessity, because of the dangers of the security dilemma, but also a great equalizer, because defense is almost always easier than offense.

8

■

THE DETERRENCE DEADLOCK: IS THERE A WAY OUT?

Richard Ned Lebow

■ Deterrence as an approach to regulating conflict has been widely criticized from a number of different perspectives. My own research into the origins of brinkmanship also calls the utility of deterrence into question; it indicates that deterrence fails to address what may be the common cause of aggression, the perceived need to pursue a confrontational foreign policy because of weakness at home or abroad.[1] This chapter will very briefly review these findings and build upon them to develop an alternative approach to conflict, a strategy of "reassurance." It will also explore some of the implications of this strategy for Soviet-U.S. relations.

The Origins of Brinkmanship

Between Peace and War studied the origins of thirteen brinkmanship crises—confrontations in which states challenge important commitments of adversaries in the expectation that the adversaries will back down—to determine why policy makers pursued policies that risked war. It found that almost without exception these crises could most readily be traced to grave foreign and domestic threats that leaders believed could be overcome only through an aggressive foreign policy.

The most important external threat was the expectation of a dramatic shift in the balance of power. In seven of the thirteen cases, brinkmanship was preceded by the widely shared perception among policy makers that a dramatic negative shift in the balance of power was imminent. Brinkmanship in these cases was conceived of as a forceful response to this acute and impending danger, a means of preventing or even redressing the shift in the balance of power before time ran out and such a response became unrealistic. The first Moroccan crisis (1904–1905), a confrontation between Germany on the one hand and France and Britain on the other, was provoked by German fears that the Anglo-French Entente would ultimately lead to Germany's military encirclement, is a case in point. So too is the Cuban missile crisis; the most widely held explanation of Khrushchev's decision to put missiles into Cuba attributes it to Soviet realization that the United States was capable of launching a first strike.

A second motivation for an aggressive foreign policy derived from weakness of a state's political system. In four of the cases— Korea (1903–1904), Bosnian annexation (1909), July 1914, and Arab-Israel (1967)—domestic political instability or the frangibility of the state itself appeared instrumental in convincing leaders of the advantages of provoking a confrontation. They resorted to the time-honored technique of attempting to offset discontent at home by diplomatic success abroad.

The political weakness of leaders as distinct from instability of the political system as a whole provided another incentive for brinkmanship. It can encourage leaders to seek a foreign policy victory in order to buttress their domestic position. Political weakness can also lead to confrontations because leaders feel too insecure to oppose policies they know to be very risky or otherwise ill conceived. One or the other of these manifestations of political weakness appears to have played a role in the origins of ten of the brinkmanship challenges.

A fourth incentive for brinkmanship is associated with intra-elite competition for power. This was a primary cause of three brinkmanship crises and probably a secondary cause of several others. A bureaucratic subunit or political coalition can engineer a confrontation with a foreign power in the expectation that it will enhance its domestic influence or undermine that of its adversaries. Intra-elite competition can also induce actors to pursue policies calculated to advance their domestic interests even though these policies have the side effect of provoking a crisis with another state. The Fashoda crisis between Britain and France in 1898 is an example of the former and the Russo-Japanese crisis in Korea (1903–1904) of the latter.

In practice, the expectation that an adversary would back down when challenged often proved unwarranted. The cases revealed that most brinkmanship challenges were initiated without any good evidence that the adversary in question lacked the resolve to defend its commitment. Available indications most often pointed to the opposite conclusion since the commitments at stake appeared to have met the four conditions normally associated with successful deterrence: they were clearly defined; their existence was communicated to possible adversaries; the states making them possessed the means to defend them; and they made reasonable efforts to demonstrate their resolve to do so. In only five cases—first Morocco, Bosnian, Rhineland (1936), Munich (1938), and Berlin (1948–1949)—did initiators have compelling reasons to suspect that their adversaries would back down when challenged. Even so, in two of these cases the initiators had to back down. In every other, the initiators had to back down or face war.

These findings indicate that the presence of a vulnerable commitment is not a precondition of brinkmanship. What counts is the perception by the initiator that a vulnerable commitment exists—a judgment, I discovered, that was erroneous more often than not. These cases also suggested the hypothesis that faulty judgment was related to policy makers' needs to act. When policy makers became convinced of the necessity to achieve specific foreign policy objectives, they became predisposed to see these objectives as attainable.

The study documented this assertion in the July 1914, Korea (1950), and Sino-Indian (1962) crises. In all three cases, political leaders in the initiator states felt compelled to pursue aggressive foreign policies in response to strategic and domestic political imperatives. They convinced themselves that they could achieve their respective policy objectives without provoking war with their adversaries. Because they knew the extent to which they were powerless to back down, they expected that their adversaries would have to. Some of these leaders also took comfort in the false hope that they would emerge victorious at relatively little cost to themselves if the crisis got out of hand and led to war.

German, U.S., and Indian policy makers maintained their illusory expectations despite the accumulation of considerable evidence to the contrary both before and during the crisis. They resorted to elaborate personal and institutional defenses to avoid having to come to terms with this information. The most prevalent defense mechanism was denial. The Kaiser and those around him used it to discredit reports that Britain would intervene in a continental war. Acheson and Nehru and their advisors resorted to it to discount the possibility that U.S. or Indian policies would provoke a military response by China. On an institutional level, denial took the form of structuring feedback channels to filter out dissonant information and to reinforce the preconceived notions of political leaders. In such a closed decision-making environment, events during the crisis did little to disabuse policy makers of their unrealistic expectations. These case histories suggest the pessimistic hypothesis that those policy makers with the greatest need to learn from external reality appear the least likely to do so.

These empirical findings raise serious questions about the utility of deterrence. If policy makers rationalize the conditions for the success of a foreign policy to the extent they feel compelled to pursue it, efforts to impart credibility to commitments may have only a marginal impact on an adversary's behavior. Even the most elaborate efforts to demonstrate prowess and resolve may prove insufficient to discourage a challenge when policy makers are attracted to a policy of brinkmanship as a necessary means of preserving vital strategic and domestic political interests. The Fashoda, July 1914, Korean (1950), Sino-Indian, and Cuban crises all attest to the seriousness of this problem.

These cases and others point to the importance of motivation as the key to brinkmanship challenges. To the extent that leaders perceive the need to act, they become insensitive to the interests and commitments of others that stand in the way of the success of their policy. The converse may also hold true. In the absence of compelling domestic and strategic needs, most leaders may be reluctant or unwilling to pursue confrontational foreign policies even when they hold out a reasonable prospect of success. Hitler was the only policy maker in the sample whose foreign policy challenges could not be traced to such needs.

If my analysis of the origins of brinkmanship is correct, it not only indicates that deterrence is a less than satisfactory strategy of conflict avoidance but points to two reasons why this is so. The first reason has been already noted; when policy makers feel compelled to act, they may employ denial, selective attention, or other psychological sleights of hand to dismiss indications of an adversary's resolve. In such circumstances, the complex and ambiguous nature of the international environment does not encourage restraint but rather encourages irrational confidence. The second and more important reason is that aggression may be less a function of opportunity and more of perceived need. I found reasonable opportunity for aggression (that is, a vulnerable commitment) in only one-third of the cases but discovered strong needs to pursue an aggressive foreign policy in almost every instance. This indicates that policy makers, at least in brinkmanship crises, are more responsive to internal imperatives than they are to external opportunities.

If need is an equal or even more important source of aggression than opportunity, it calls for a corresponding shift in the focus of efforts to prevent aggression. Too much attention in theory and practice is probably devoted to the credibility of commitments and not nearly enough to trying to understand what might prompt an adversary to challenge a commitment. The more realistic goal of conflict avoidance may not be in denying an adversary the *opportunity* to act but rather in minimizing its perceived *need* to do so. To what extent is this a feasible policy objective? What strategies are most appropriate to this end? What light do the cases shed on these questions?

Manipulating Incentives for Aggression

Four of the five incentives for brinkmanship noted in the preceding description are domestic; they pertain to internal weaknesses of a would-be aggressor. Unfortunately, while these incentives seem to be important sources of aggressive foreign policies, they do not on the whole seem subject to external amelioration.

Intra-elite competition is difficult to influence principally because it is so often hidden from view. To try to understand, let alone influence, policy outcomes in terms of their internal dynamics, it is necessary to identify individuals and groups who actually play a key role in shaping foreign policy, to decipher their interests, and to chart the means by which they acquire and exert influence. Outsiders are rarely privy to this sort of information even when dealing with relatively open societies. In the case of authoritarian regimes, informal policy making processes are more important and less visible because such governments often go to considerable extremes to keep their deliberations secret. In the absence of any real knowledge about the internal dynamics of an adversary, it is impossible to know where and when to apply leverage even when the means of such influence are at hand.

The Korea crisis (1903–1904) and the Fashoda crisis (1898) illustrate the difficulties involved in dealing with a foreign policy challenge prompted primarily by an intra-elite struggle for power. In the Korean case, the Japanese were unaware of the efforts of Alexander Bezobrazov and his supporters within the Russian government to expand Russian influence in Korea principally as a means of undermining the position of Sergei Witte, the foreign minister. Tokyo negotiated with the Witte faction and reached an understanding, the Rosen-Nissi Convention, that it expected to reduce the friction between the two countries. When that agreement was repudiated by Moscow, a reflection of Bezobrazov's political ascendancy, Japanese leaders not unreasonably concluded that the Russians had been insincere and double-dealing all along. Understandable ignorance of Russian court intrigue encouraged the Japanese to draw a more extreme picture of the Russian threat than might have otherwise been the case. This sense of threat underlay Tokyo's decision to go to war in February 1904.[2]

Fashoda highlights the second difficulty in coping with intra-elite competition: the problem of finding any means of influencing the outcome of such a struggle. Unlike the Japanese, the British were aware from the beginning of the extent to which the French challenge of Britain's position on the Nile was tied up in and even largely motivated by domestic political concerns. They were also quite well informed as to the details of the conflict and in particular about which individuals and groups sought to profit from a confrontation over the Sudan. This insight did not help London, because it lacked the means to influence the outcome of the struggle before it propelled France into a crisis with Britain. British policy makers were in effect frustrated spectators.[3]

The two crises have disheartening implications. When intra-elite conflict concerns the parochial interests of the actors, it is likely to remain poorly understood or even invisible to outsiders. But when it is more open and comprehensible, it is likely to reflect a wider and deeper struggle within the society beyond the power of outsiders to affect in a significant or predictable way. This was certainly true in France, where the struggle for control over foreign policy between the colonial and the foreign ministries was symptomatic of their differing views not only as to the nature of France's foreign interests but also toward Dreyfus, the Church, the Republic, and the very destiny of France.

The *political weakness* of leaders is a second domestic source of foreign policy aggression. It probably played a role in ten of the brinkmanship crises studied. Its importance as a catalyst of confrontation varied considerably from case to case, and only in the Arab-Israeli crisis of 1967 could it be considered the principal cause of conflict. Efforts to alleviate the pressures upon vulnerable leaders to pursue aggressive foreign policies are accordingly likely to succeed only if they are coupled with an attempt to address other important sources of conflict. This caveat aside, such efforts can easily encounter difficulties of their own. Concessions that enhance an adversary leader's domestic standing may not be in one's own national interest to grant. Even when this is not a problem, they may make the leaders responsible for them vulnerable to criticism from their own political opponents and public opinion. Efforts to strengthen the political base of an adversary leader also risk being misunderstood by the leader they are designed to assist, with consequences that could be more damaging than the effects of having done nothing at all.

Sub rosa South African support of President Kenneth Kaunda of Zambia probably constitutes the best contemporary example of a sustained and on the whole successful attempt to enhance the domestic standing of an adversary leader. Despite Kaunda's active support of efforts to end white domination in Southern Africa, Pretoria has for years quietly supplied his government with cooking oil and other essential items in very short supply in Zambia in order to help him to retain power by keeping a lid on domestic unrest. The South Africans apparently reason that their assistance to some extent moderates Kaunda's policies and, even more importantly, keeps at bay the more extreme Zambian politicians who would almost certainly replace him. From time to time, the Soviet Union attempted to reward some Western European leaders for essentially similar reasons. Most recently, Helmut Schmidt was so blessed, in the opinion of some foreign policy analysts, as part of an unsuccessful campaign to help him retain power in the Federal Republic of Germany.

The weakness of a state's political system has also been identified as a particularly important incentive to pursue an aggressive foreign policy. Once again, there are definite limits on the ability of other powers to ease the pressure on leaders to pursue confrontational policies that such weakness often generates. All of the difficulties attendant upon efforts to enhance the domestic standing of adversary leaders apply to adversary regimes as well. If anything, the kinds of problems that sap a regime's legitimacy are even more intractable and less amenable to outside influence. Among the most important of these, the cases suggest, are nationality conflicts, acute class tensions, and economic malaise.

The Arab-Israeli conflict gives testimony to the foreign policy problems internal instability can create. Throughout much of the Arab Middle East, traditional authority was swept away in coups organized by officers committed to nationalism and economic modernization. These new leaders and their successors aroused expectations that for the most part they were unable to fulfill. The Arabs remain as divided as ever; Israel continues to exist; and prosperity for most Arab states appears as distant a goal as it did twenty years ago. For Nasser's Egypt, Syria, and Iraq, hostility to Israel became an important source of internal legitimacy. The very existence of a Jewish state in their midst was offered as an explanation for whatever ills these countries suffered from. Even conservative Arab states like Jordan and Saudi Arabia were drawn into the conflict because their leaders, fearful for their own survival, dared not antagonize nationalist opinion at home, aroused and supported by their more radical Arab neighbors.

Israel, for its part, could do nothing to defuse the hostility of its enemies without sacrificing its own security. In the case of Nasser's Egypt and Syria even this would probably not have succeeded in easing tensions. For to paraphrase Metternich, if Israel did not exist, the radical Arab states would have had to invent it—or find a substitute, as Iraq recently has—as a convenient foil and scapegoat for their internal disarray. Egypt under Sadat, the only one of Israel's neighbors that has been able to extricate itself from this destructive conflict, succeeded in doing so because of the initial success of Egyptian arms in the October War. This regained Egyptian honor and, with it, her leader's freedom of action. But as the isolation and subsequent assassination of Sadat reveal, the freedom of any Egyptian leader to ignore wider Arab opinion remains circumscribed.

Domestic problems can be so severe as to arouse concern for *the frangibility of the state* itself. This most frequently happens when serious economic or political problems are superimposed upon preexisting nationality or communal conflicts. Structural problems such as these rarely lend themselves to peaceful internal resolution; they are even less amenable to outside stabilization.

To return once again to the cases, it is unclear with regard to Austria-Hungary what the other powers could have done to alleviate her nationality problem and increase her sense of security. If asked, Vienna would almost certainly have indicated support in opposing southern Slav aspirations to statehood. Even if such a policy had been politically feasible for the other powers—and for Russia certainly it was not—it would only have succeeded in postponing the ultimate day of reckoning. If a solution to the empire's nationality problem was to be found, it had to be an internal one. However, this was precluded by German and Hungarian opposition to any reforms that threatened their political and economic privileges. Imperial Russia, that other empire in difficulty, faced a similar dilemma. Plehve's apparent belief in the domestic political utility of "a short victorious war" was a dangerous fantasy. Like its Habsburg rival, Russia had internal problems that could have been dealt with in the long run only by meaningful structural reforms, a course of action that was anathema to those in power.

If there was little the other powers could do to dampen Austria-Hungary's perceived need to act aggressively, there was much they could do to make it more pronounced. This was because Vienna's effort to alleviate her nationality problem through territorial expansion ultimately assumed a significance out of proportion to its original intent. The empire's success or lack of it in imposing her political will on the southern Balkans became the template others used to judge her capability and, even more, her will. Once Vienna had defined the destruction of Serbia as an essential condition of her security, her apparent hesitation to act decisively toward this end led the Germans at least to question her political spine. Growing Austrian fears that Germany would dismiss her as *bündnisunfähig* (unworthy of alliance) and that Russia would pursue a more aggressive policy in the Balkans because she too doubted Austrian resolve, led the empire's frightened leaders to seize upon the assassination of Archduke Franz Ferdinand as a pretext for war with Serbia.

Viewed from St. Petersburg, passive acceptance of Austria's destruction of Serbia was out of the question because of the czarist regime's own dependence on nationalist and pan-Slavic opinion, almost its sole remaining base of political support. Opposition to Austria was doubly important to Russian leaders because of their earlier, still smarting humiliation at Austria's hand in the Bosnian annexation crisis of 1909. This event, coming four years after Russia's military defeat by Japan, had led many to question or even discount her ability to play a significant role in shaping the course of events in Europe. For these reasons, St. Petersburg perceived it just as essential as did Vienna to pursue an uncompromising policy in the Balkans. It was this clash of irreconcilable domestic imperatives *and* their impact upon the perceived external status of the two powers that more than anything else brought about World War I.

The observation to be drawn from the preceding case discussion is that serious domestic problems can create two kinds of incentives to pursue aggressive foreign policies. The first are a function of the problems themselves. If these initiatives are frustrated, they can generate, or be perceived to generate, doubts about that state's capability or resolve in the minds of third parties. Concern for a state's international reputation in the context of unresolved domestic problems further intensifies its perceived need to act "tough." The most dangerous situation of all is when two powers or blocs feel the need, for these reasons, to display resolve in the same arena. This was true of Austria-Hungary and Russia prior to World War I.

The principal external incentive for brinkmanship is *the perceived need to forestall or compensate for a dramatic adverse shift in the political-strategic balance of power.* Perhaps the most important finding here is the extent to which perceptions of threat are frequently exaggerated. The two crises we have previously cited as motivated by such perceptions are both cases in point.

The Morocco crisis of 1904–1905 was brought on by German fears of encirclement. German leaders erroneously perceived the Entente as being specifically directed against them and greatly exaggerated the extent of the Anglo-French military conception mandated by the agreement. In point of fact, the Entente was at first the most tenuous of agreements; it was viewed suspiciously or even disapprovingly by many influential British and French alike who had not forgotten the traditional enmity between their two countries. Only German bullying of France in the hope of destroying the fragile Entente brought about the very collaboration German leaders had feared. France and Britain drew closer together and initiated plans for joint military action. "It is essential to bear in mind," Sir Eyre Crowe observed, "that this new feature of the Entente was the direct effect produced by Germany's effort to break it up."[4]

Cuba too could be called an overreaction, albeit a more understandable one. The Kennedy administration had decided to put the Russians on notice that it was aware of the full extent of their strategic vulnerability. The reason for doing this was avowedly defensive: to encourage Khrushchev to moderate his challenge of the Western position in Berlin. Moscow may well have perceived the message differently. When placed within the broader context of Soviet-U.S. hostility and the Kennedy administration's pronounced and costly effort to achieve strategic superiority, it could have appeared to Soviet leaders as the opening salvo of a U.S. strategic-political offensive. If so, putting missiles into Cuba in an attempt to reduce the U.S. strategic advantage, even if it entailed considerable risk, could have been seen as preferable to passivity in the face of a grave threat. Jerome Kahan and Anne Long go so far as to suggest that the crisis was actually caused by U.S. insensitivity to the Soviet's strategic dilemma. "The Kennedy Administration's early emphasis on superiority can be said to have helped cause the Cuban crisis by tilting the nuclear balance so far against the Soviets that they were forced to emplace missiles in Cuba in order to rectify the strategic relationship. Had the U.S. become more sensitive to the Soviet need—both political and military—for equality, it might not have pressed its advantage as far as it did, and avoided the risks of the Cuban confrontation."[5]

Agadir (1911) is a third example of a crisis that was triggered by an exaggerated notion of threat. By 1911, Britain and Germany had become so deeply suspicious of each other that their leaders read hostile intent into almost every foreign initiative of the other. In the case of Agadir, the British reaction to a German *démarche* to France, all out of proportion to the degree of threat intended, transformed a colonial dispute into a grave international confrontation. From the German perspective, the British reaction to their *démarche* seemed not a reaction at all but a deliberate attempt to exploit the incident as a pretext for a full-fledged diplomatic assault on Germany. Both powers emerged from the confrontation all the more convinced of the other's hostile intentions.[6]

These several examples suggest two disturbing conclusions about adversarial relations. The first is the apparent difficulty adversaries have in predicting the effect of their actions upon each other. Robert Jervis has pointed to one reason for this: a general tendency among policy makers to exaggerate the likelihood that others will interpret one's behavior as it is intended.[7] When policy makers believe their country's motives to be benign they expect others to interpret them accordingly. If other states protest, policy makers are more likely to impugn their motives for doing so than seek reasons why others might interpret their actions differently. John Kennedy and his advisors, secure in their knowledge that they sought to ameliorate, not aggravate, Soviet-U.S. relations, appear to have had no inkling that Moscow would interpret their signal as a grave threat to Soviet security. German policy makers in 1911 were similarly surprised by London's reaction to their bid for colonial compensation from France. A third example is U.S. insensitivity in 1950 to the consequences for Peking of Korean unification under U.S. auspices.[8]

Even when policy makers are sensitive to the ways in which their actions are perceived by others, they may be unable to alter or correct those impressions if they are misleading. The British effort to reassure Germany about the Entente is a case in point. After the agreement was concluded, London undertook to explain its content and purpose to German leaders. With this end in mind, Edward VII was sent to Kiel Week, the yearly German naval regatta in June 1904 and personally briefed both Bülow and the Kaiser about it. The king's assurances did not succeed in dispelling German suspicions and may actually have intensified them. Edward reported: "The agreements that we have negotiated apart from him without his permission and without his help, have stupefied him; they have produced in him a sense of isolation, hence his agitation and ill-humor."[9]

Edward's failure seems due to the fact that his assurances ran counter to the cognitive predispositions of German leaders. Bülow, the Kaiser, and their advisors were terrified by the prospect of Germany's encirclement. They took for granted France's enmity and viewed Britain as a jealous rival out to thwart German's natural ascendancy as a world power. The Entente, if interpreted as the harbinger of an anti-German alliance, confirmed German expectations of French and British behavior. Edward's assurances, on the other hand, flew in the face of them. The only interpretation of Edward's behavior consistent with German expectations was that it was part of a clever ruse designed to blind Germany to the dangers in store for her. Such an interpretation had the effect of magnifying German perceptions of the threat conveyed by the Entente.

More recent examples of this phenomenon could be drawn from Soviet-U.S. or Arab-Israeli relations. The general conclusion they point toward is that efforts by one adversary to reassure another about its intentions are least likely to succeed in the situations where they are needed most. Success may well depend upon a prior improvement in relations, some kind of détente, or lessening in tensions, that establishes the cognitive preconditions for leaders to perceive such initiatives as possibly being well intentioned. Of course, acute crises are far less likely to develop in such a climate. In the absence of at least some receptivity to signals of reassurance or cooperation, it may require truly dramatic gestures to break through the other side's cognitive wall of distrust. Here, an analogy to the Middle East conflict might be helpful.

For four decades, relations between Egypt and Israel were characterized by acute hostility that erupted into four major wars. The antagonism between these two countries was in every way as extreme and deeply rooted as—probably more so than—that which exists between the Soviet Union and the United States. Yet, a peace treaty, something most contemporary observers dismissed as inconceivable at the time, was made possible by Anwar el-Sadat's unexpected and stunning offer to go to Israel and address the parliament. The same man who several years earlier had unleashed an initially devastating assault upon Israel now held out the olive branch and asked Israelis to trust him. His gesture achieved credibility principally because the very act of making it made the Egyptian president vulnerable. He opened himself up to strident criticism and possibly isolation at home and in the Arab world, and even more so if he returned home from Jerusalem empty-handed. Building upon this breakthrough, Sadat and Begin, knowing that both their peoples favored peace, were able to reach an agreement to normalize relations and return the Sinai to Egypt. What Sadat could not achieve by a surprise attack he gained through a surprise peace offensive.

In the absence of some mutual receptivity to signals of reassurance or cooperation, a truly dramatic gesture like Sadat's may be necessary to break down adversarial distrust. When viewed in the context of Soviet-U.S. relations, there are probably many possible strategic equivalents to Sadat's offer to come to Israel to address the *Knesset*. Perhaps a significant step toward unilateral nuclear disarmament by one of the superpowers would have the same effect, provided it was not accompanied by an obvious and strident propaganda campaign designed to embarrass the other superpower.

The cases discussed in this chapter suggest some disheartening conclusions about the ability of outside actors to alleviate in any significant way the kinds of internal and external pressures upon states to pursue confrontational foreign policies. This finding points to a disturbing paradox. Deterrence, which, relatively speaking, is easy to implement, may nevertheless not be a very effective strategy of conflict management, because it does not address the most important sources of aggression. On the other hand, efforts to alleviate the kinds of insecurities that actually encourage or even compel leaders to pursue aggressive foreign policies do not seem very likely to succeed.

No striking example of successful reassurance comes readily to mind. One of the reasons this is so may be simply that such an approach to conflict management has rarely been employed. Another reason may be methodological; it is extremely difficult to recognize the success as opposed to the failure of such a policy. Failure is manifest in crisis or war, events that readily impinge upon historical consciousness. Success, which results in greater tranquillity than would otherwise be the case, can easily go unnoticed, for it may produce no observable change in the level of tension. Even if relations improve, it is impossible to determine just how much this could be attributed to reassurance as distinct from other causes.

These observations aside, the difficulty of pursuing a policy of reassurance must be recognized. The implementation of reassurance in a consistent and meaningful way requires a degree of freedom from domestic, political, and bureaucratic constraints that is extremely difficult to achieve and maintain. Even if these conditions are met, it is by no means certain that a policy of reassurance will succeed, for all of the reasons that have been elaborated. This does not mean that such a policy ought not be tried. As there is no easy road to conflict resolution, any strategy that offers some hope of ameliorating conflict is worthy of serious consideration.

There is another, more telling point in favor of reassurance. A sophisticated approach to conflict management would make use of both strategies. It would seek to discourage confrontation by attempting to reduce both the need *and* the opportunity to carry it out. It would aim never to allow one's own state to be perceived as so weak or irresolute as to invite a challenge but at the same time to avoid encouraging an adversary to feel so weak or threatened that it has the need to do so.

There are some obvious but by no means insuperable obstacles in the way of pursuing such an approach to conflict. To begin with, it is necessary to confront the trade-offs between deterrence and reassurance. The two strategies are not mutually exclusive, but many of the actions designed to enhance deterrence may also have the effect of intensifying an adversary's perceptions of threat and with it its need to display greater resolve. A precondition to applying a combined strategy of deterrence and reassurance is therefore the identification of the range of trade-offs that must be made between them and the elaboration of some criteria for doing this. This is an intellectually demanding task and one that runs counter to the tendency and perhaps also to the need of political leaders to simplify, not complicate, their conceptualization of problems.

The difficulty of first recognizing and then making trade-offs points to the importance of political leadership. Any sophisticated strategy of conflict management demands equally sophisticated leaders to carry it out. It also requires leaders who possess adequate political backing for their policy and the skill and fortitude to impose their will on the foreign policy and defense bureaucracies whose parochial interests almost inevitably stand in the way of the execution of any rational and coordinated policy. Such a policy-making environment is only infrequently achieved and is more often the result of fortuitous circumstances than it is of conscious planning.

Managing Soviet-U.S. Relations

U.S. policy toward the Soviet Union ultimately depends on assumptions made about Soviet motives. If Moscow really seeks world domination and is willing to use force to achieve it, as the traditional Cold War view contends, then deterrence is an appropriate, indeed essential, strategy for the West. If, on the other hand, Moscow is motivated principally by a concern for its own security and has sought to strengthen its position, militarily and politically, to protect itself against the West, as many revisionists argue, then a policy of reassurance is a more appropriate response. Few students of international affairs find either description of Soviet motives satisfactory, for each represents a one-sided characterization of Soviet policy. Most describe Soviet foreign policy as both offensive and defensive, although there is no consensus among Kremlinologists as to the nature of this mix. To the extent that Soviet policy is in fact motivated by a mix of offensive and defensive goals, then some combination of deterrence and reassurance is required to cope with it.

A detailed elaboration of a strategy that successfully melds deterrence and reassurance must be the subject of another study. Here, I will merely identify some of the more important trade-offs between the two approaches to conflict that must be confronted by policy makers.

The first trade-off to be considered concerns the appropriate response to an adversary's domestic problems. For the West, this dilemma has already arisen in connection with the Soviet economy. Nixon and Kissinger sought to moderate Soviet policy by increasing Moscow's dependence upon the West, a goal they hoped to achieve at least in part through expanded trade and technology transfer. The Reagan administration, by contrast, has sought to exacerbate Soviet economic vulnerability by denying Moscow access to Western technology and by forcing it to spend even more for armaments in order to keep pace with the United States. On the face of it, neither policy seems to have been very effective. The Reagan approach has also had the drawback of antagonizing not only the Soviets but also the Western Europeans, committed as they are to maintaining broad economic and political contacts with the East.

The most serious domestic problem the Soviet Union is likely to face in the long term is the growing disaffection of non-Russian nationalities. The Soviet Union is the last of the great empires. The Russians, who constitute a bare majority of the population, monopolize political and economic power and have assiduously pursued, without noticeable success, a policy of Russification toward the other nationalities.

Moscow already confronts national problems in Eastern Europe, where the combination of economic stagnation and nationalism has led to a revolution in Poland. For the time being this threat has been contained by the imposition of a military dictatorship, but Poland's new leaders appear as incapable as their predecessors of coping with the root causes of unrest. The conditions that led to the emergence of Solidarity in Poland can be found in varying degrees elsewhere in Europe and must constitute a serious cause of concern for Moscow.[10]

Soviet military intervention in East Germany, Hungary, Czechoslovakia, and by proxy in Poland, makes it apparent that Moscow views its primacy in Eastern Europe as an essential precondition of its security. One reason for this is the permeability of the Soviet Union to events in Eastern Europe, an ironic outcome of almost four decades of Soviet efforts to orient the political, economic, and cultural lives of these countries toward the east. At the time of the Czechoslovakian invasion, Brezhnev himself is reported to have told Wladyslaw Gomulka that all Warsaw Pact nations must contribute forces for the operation because, in the absence of East bloc solidarity, the unrest might spill over into the Ukraine.[11]

Moscow appears to subscribe to a domino theory of its own. The fall of a communist government anywhere in Eastern Europe would threaten Soviet domination everywhere in Eastern Europe. Loss of influence in Eastern Europe would encourage separatist sentiment within the Soviet Union and possibly end up threatening the viability of that multiethnic state. This challenge, still remote, might become more a reality in the years ahead if the economy continues to stagnate and if the post-Brezhnev leadership responds to this and other problems with pronounced bureaucratic rigidity.[12]

The frangibility of the Soviet empire would present a serious problem not only to Moscow but also to Washington, which would have to confront a series of difficult and altogether awkward choices. Put crudely, is it in the interest of the United States to encourage "cracks" in the Soviet monolith with the aim of sapping Soviet strength, or should Washington assist in shoring up the Soviet empire in the hope of avoiding the risk of confrontation that the threat of fragmentation is likely to create? Ought we to try to undermine the Soviet capability to challenge the West or their perceived need to do so?

Arguments, political, economic, and moral, can be made in support of both positions and already have been in connection with the Western response to Poland's default on her hard currency debt. The controversy over Poland and, before it, that which surrounded the question of a grain embargo, took place *in vacuo*, unconnected for the most part with any conception of how the decisions made were likely to affect the long-term security interests of the United States and Western Europe. These controversies also revealed the range of domestic political, economic, and bureaucratic tugs and constraints that affect policy decisions of this kind and will continue to do so in the future. This latter problem is unavoidable, but its effects might be minimized by the commitment of this or a subsequent administration to a more coherent and carefully articulated approach to the problem. The first step toward this goal is a thorough analysis of the benefits and costs of both strategies and the trade-offs that must be made between them. Studies of this kind are a pressing political as well as intellectual need.

The second source of weakness that may influence foreign policy in the coming decade is external. Both superpowers are particularly sensitive to the other's strengths and their own weaknesses. For this reason they are both likely to perceive themselves to be increasingly on the defensive in the years ahead. From the vantage point of Moscow, these weaknesses derive from a frustrating war in Afghanistan, a continuing conflict with China, and the declining political reliability of the Warsaw Pact. None of these problems can possibly be offset by the prospect of greater influence in the Third World.

From the perspective of Washington the world outlook is likely to be equally bleak and threatening. The United States' position of leadership in the West will almost certainly continue to decline for both economic and political reasons. This will result in a further deterioration of NATO's cohesion. In the Third World, U.S. influence will also wane, especially in Latin America where Washington may confront even more serious politico-military challenges than the ones it currently faces in El Salvador and Guatemala. A revolution in South Korea or the Philippines that took on strong anti-American overtones or another shock in the Middle East, say the overthrow of the Saudi monarchy and the resulting demise of the Western position in the Persian Gulf, would further aggravate the United States' sense of vulnerability.

By the mid-1980s, the world may witness the bizarre and frightening phenomenon of two awesomely powerful but painfully vulnerable superpowers each acutely sensitive about its own sources of weakness and deeply fearful of the other's efforts to exploit them. If this portrayal of the superpowers seems far-fetched, the reader is reminded of the historical precedent of Wilhelminian Germany, awesomely powerful for its day but so insecure in its power that it acted in ways that made it the principal menace to the peace of Europe.

The paranoia of the powerful can constitute—and has constituted—a profound source of international instability. Policy makers in such circumstances tend to exhibit an exaggerated concern for their credibility, convinced that any sign of weakness will only encourage further challenges from their adversaries. In the case of

Germany it led to a series of aggressive foreign policy ventures that brought about the very situation of encirclement she feared and ultimately led to war.

If anything is more disturbing than a great power acting in this manner it is the prospect of *two* superpower adversaries doing so. Both already display tendencies in this direction. The United States has a remarkable, some call it pathological, concern for its credibility. Democratic and Republican policy makers alike have also exaggerated the extent to which Soviet or Soviet-Cuban machinations lay behind every threatening Third World upheaval. The Shaba invasion, Nicaragua and, most recently, El Salvador are cases in point. All of this has prompted U.S. leaders to cast about for cheap and dramatic ways of displaying resolve. They have succumbed to what could be called the *Mayaguez* mentality, after the first attempt to do this in the immediate aftermath of the Indochina disaster. Not surprisingly, such displays of force, of which there have been several, have most often had the opposite result of what was intended.

Soviet policy makers also appear to exaggerate greatly the malevolent influence their adversary is capable of exercising. Soviet spokesmen have repeatedly charged the United States with responsibility for the turmoil it confronts in both Afghanistan and Poland. Many of these charges are propaganda, but there is no reason to doubt that some of them actually reflect the real views of Soviet officials, as sincerely held if equally far-fetched as some of the anti-Soviet charges made by their U.S. counterparts. This may be particularly true with regard to the Polish situation, which must pose a serious cognitive dilemma for Soviet leaders. To recognize it for what it is, a real workers' revolution against a bureaucratic dictatorship, imposed and maintained by Moscow, would entail calling into question the most fundamental myths of Soviet-style Marxism. The men of the Kremlin have therefore every psychological and political incentive to explain away Polish developments by any means they can. The long arm of U.S. imperialism can play a useful role in this regard just as the Soviet communist conspiracy was invoked by Americans a generation earlier to explain their "loss" of China. Unfortunately, such illusions, while comforting, also tend to have damaging long-term foreign policy consequences.

The acute sensitivities of the superpowers, especially with respect to the arenas in which they feel the most vulnerable, must significantly affect any evaluation of the trade-offs between deterrence and reassurance. To me this state of affairs suggests an even greater need for a policy of reassurance. It also calls for some degree of foreign policy restraint on the assumption that the strategic gain of one-upping one's superpower rival in any important arena is likely to be more than offset by the cost of the heightened perception of threat it generates among its leaders.

The opposing argument must also be considered. Efforts to reassure adversaries, particularly those whose hostility is long-standing and intense, hold out only a limited prospect for success. They are also ill advised if they risk being misinterpreted as signs of weakness, as spokesmen for the Reagan administration allege. Administration strategists accordingly advocate an intensified military build-up as both a matter of prudence and a means of strengthening deterrence.

Both strategies entail considerable risk. Reassurance, if directed toward an adversary whose policy is truly motivated by aggressive goals, is akin to appeasement and will succeed only in whetting its appetite for further encroachments. Deterrence, on the other hand, when it takes the form of a massive military build-up and search for military alliances abroad, will evoke similar behavior from an adversary and lead to a rapid escalation of international tensions. It may end up by making mutual fears of war self-fulfilling. The resulting tragedy would be greater still if the adversary in question, like its would-be deterrer, was motivated not by aspirations for world conquest but rather by concern for its own security.

The third area in which trade-offs must be made between deterrence and reassurance is that of strategic weaponry. Unfortunately, the current strategic debate has tended to gloss over this requirement. Advocates of the two principal schools of U.S. strategic thought often even deny the necessity of making any trade-offs. Most "finite deterrence" theorists insist that war prevention is the only proper concern of nuclear strategy. They advocate something similar to a strategy of reassurance in that they favor strategic systems that enhance the second-strike capability of the United States without at the same time threatening the capability of the Soviet Union to mount a retaliatory strike. Finite deterrence theorists generally reject the notion that nuclear war between the superpowers could have a victor; instead, they think it likely to result in the destruction of both protagonists. "War-fighting" theorists evade the issue of trade-offs by a neat cognitive sleight of hand; they assert that the capability to fight a nuclear war is also the best way to deter one.

Neither argument is convincing. Deterrence may well fail despite general Soviet and U.S. recognition of the destructiveness of nuclear war. The refusal of many finite deterrence advocates to recognize this unpleasant possibility will not diminish and may actually enhance the chance of a nuclear war. For their part, most war-fighting theorists err by denying the equally disturbing truth that efforts to improve the U.S. capability to fight a nuclear war are in many ways detrimental to deterrence. The development of a time-urgent counterforce capability, an essential requirement of any war-fighting strategy, is a case in point. As has often been pointed out, by threatening the survivability of the Soviet Union's second-strike capability, over 70 percent of which resides in its stationary land-based missile force, such capability enhances Moscow's incentive to preempt in a crisis if war appears likely.

Perhaps the most disturbing tendency of the current strategic debate is the extent to which doctrine and force structure are so often analyzed independently of the political context in which they exist. When the broader political setting is considered, it puts the respective risks of the two strategies in a sharper light. U.S. doctrine and force structure have shifted toward a war-fighting posture at the same time as political relations between the superpowers have deteriorated. This can only have the effect of making such a shift more threatening in Soviet eyes. For the same reason, Soviet efforts to upgrade their strategic arsenal, and with it their ability to conduct a nuclear war, appear much more provocative to the United States than they would otherwise. The intensification of superpower hostility therefore makes the trade-offs between war prevention and war fighting all the more stark and the corresponding need for Washington and Moscow to face them all the more imperative. Tragically, the intensification of the Cold War is likely to push both powers further in the direction of developing their war-fighting capabilities.

Conclusion

The principal policy finding of the research described in this chapter is that policy makers may be able to do very little to alleviate the kinds of pressures that encourage their adversaries to act aggressively. At the same time, they may have it in their power to do quite a bit to intensify these pressures. This points to the need for both superpowers to exercise caution in their words and deeds.

Words are actions in their own right and significantly affect a state's perception of the nature and intensity of the threat it faces. Careless or ill-considered remarks, even those directed at an altogether different audience, can easily and dramatically exacerbate international tensions. Nikita Khrushchev's famous boast—"We will bury you"—caused an instant sensation in the West, where it was interpreted by many as an admission of Soviet willingness to resort to nuclear war to spread communism. Khrushchev himself insisted that this was not at all what he had said—translated properly it would have come out: "We will attend your funeral." His explanation did little to dispel the tension that his unfortunate remark had created.

Sino-U.S. hostility was similarly aggravated in the 1960s by Peking's brash and stridently reiterated assertions that the United States was a "paper tiger," that China would emerge victorious from a nuclear war with the West, and that Third World peoples constituted an "international proletariat" that, led by Peking, would rise up against U.S. imperialism. Lin Piao's article calling for such a world revolution against the United States, first published in 1965, was widely circulated in the West.[13] We know today that most of these diatribes were actually directed at Moscow and other communist parties and can be understood only in the context of the Sino-Soviet split. At the time, however, they were taken as proof by many Americans that Peking was committed to advancing the cause of communism though brush-fire and guerrilla wars.

Soviet and Chinese rhetoric in the early 1960s significantly affected U.S. perceptions of events in Indochina. It encouraged U.S. intervention in Vietnam, as it was seen by Washington as the very kind of challenge Moscow and Peking had long been boasting about inciting. President Kennedy, in particular, took Soviet and Chinese pronouncements offering support of "wars of national liberation" very seriously. In the aftermath of one of Khrushchev's more bellicose speeches in this regard, Kennedy told the American Newspaper Association: "[We] are opposed around the world by a monolithic and ruthless conspiracy that relies primarily on covert means for expanding its sphere of influence." The struggle, Kennedy went on to say, had been switched from Europe to Asia, Africa, and Latin America, from nuclear and conventional weapons to irregular warfare, insurrection, and subversion. If those methods were successful in countries like Laos and South Vietnam, Kennedy told reporters, then "the gates will be opened wide."[14] For much the same reason, the Johnson administration continued Kennedy's commitment in Indochina, with results that are well known.

These examples illustrate how propaganda, even propaganda that may have been aimed at a domestic or an altogether different foreign audience, can easily achieve unanticipated salience in the eyes of an adversary and be taken as confirmation of its worst fears or expectations. The spate of ill-considered statements on the feasibility of limited nuclear war emanating from the Reagan White House seems to have done just this and may be analogous in effect to Khrushchev's bellicose utterings in the early 1960s.

In this connection, it is noteworthy that Soviet officials have repeatedly remarked, publicly and privately, that their concern about U.S. intentions has been aroused not only by the recent emphasis on limited nuclear war in U.S. doctrine, which after all was noticeable in the Ford and Carter administrations as well, but by the fact that it has been accompanied by provocative statements from the Reagan White House. The combination of Reagan's words and actions, like Khrushchev's before him, imparts an acute sense of threat to foreign audiences. Georgi Arbatov, director of the Institute of the United States and Canada, recently declared: "Right now, because of the Reagan administration's rhetoric—and maybe more than just rhetoric—some of our military people and even some members of the Central Committee believe America is preparing for nuclear war."[15]

Perhaps the most extreme Soviet reaction to these developments was the public demand by Marshal Nikolai Ogarkov, then Soviet chief of staff, for a series of measures to meet the U.S. military threat that would have the effect of putting the Soviet Union on a war footing. In a book published by the Ministry of Defense, Ogarkov acknowledged that the United States has always planned to destroy the Soviet Union in the case of nuclear war but argues that "this course has become particularly dangerous in connection with the Reagan administration's confrontational strategy and its direct and all-embracing preparations for war."[16]

Certainly, the temptation exists to dismiss some of Moscow's indignant reaction to Reagan rhetoric as self-serving propaganda of its own. However, the threatening portrait many U.S. strategic analysts draw of the Soviet Union is to a great extent attributable to that country's effort to develop a war-fighting capability and its periodic assertions that it would emerge the victor in a nuclear war. There is every reason to believe the Soviet thinking has been similarly influenced by recent developments in U.S. doctrine and force structure. The writings of Henry Trofimenko and Georgi Arabatov might be cited in evidence; they provide an object lesson of how readily the most alarming implications can be drawn about an adversary's intentions from his capability and propaganda.[17]

Given the current political climate, the administration should take care not to exacerbate any further the existing tensions by its pronouncements. No doubt, some of the more extreme utterances of Reagan and Weinberger are motivated by a perceived need to look "tough" in the eyes of the Russians and conservative European opinion in order to compensate for Soviet strategic and Euro-strategic potency. The Administration would do well to remember that tough talk in the absence of power has a hollow ring to it. When backed by ample power, as no doubt the Russians perceive it is, it is simply threatening. Either way it is self-defeating.

9

■

CONCLUSIONS

Richard Ned Lebow

■ The unifying theme of this volume is disenchantment with deterrence both as a theory of state behavior and as a strategy of conflict management.[1] There is a consensus among the authors that deterrence is inadequate as an explanatory theory of international relations because the growing body of empirical evidence—some of it presented here for the first time—indicates that neither leaders contemplating challenges nor leaders seeking to prevent them necessarily act as the theory predicts.[2] Several of the authors are equally critical of deterrence as a prescriptive strategy; they contend that it can provoke the very behavior it seeks to prevent. If valid, these charges call into question the conceptual foundations of much of post–World War II U.S. foreign policy.

The major strengths and weaknesses of deterrence can both be said to derive from the theory's most fundamental characteristic: it is a system of abstract logic all of whose principal postulates have been derived deductively. This contributed to the theory's appeal because it facilitated the development of coherent, elegant, and seemingly powerful explanations for important aspects of interstate behavior. For statesmen and scholars alike, deterrence theory held out the promise of a pathway through the forbiddingly complex and increasingly dangerous maze of international relations, a pathway that began with one's own national interest and led in the end to enhanced security. This was particularly attractive in a world of nuclear weapons because it encouraged statesmen to believe that efforts on their part to reduce uncertainties surrounding a state's willingness to defend its commitments could prevent miscalculation by an adversary and forestall the kinds of challenges that had so often led to war in the past. For this reason, deterrence remains the principle intellectual and policy bulwark against nuclear holocaust.

Despite the obvious appeal of deterrence theory, its sometimes sophisticated but always abstract rationality fails to provide an adequate description of how states actually behave. Case studies indicate that states are both more cautious and more prone to risk taking than the theory predicts.[3] They also suggest that judgments of the credibility of another state's commitment may have little to do with its bargaining reputation. In addition, there is some evidence that the timing of foreign policy challenges may be independent of the relative military balance between the parties involved. The several chapters in this volume and related work by their authors document these assertions. The most telling criticism of deterrence they make is that it fails to address the most serious causes of resort to force by states. They also identify a number of important barriers to effective communication among states that also constitute serious impediments to deterrence.

Barriers to Signaling

A pictorial map of the world drawn by a deterrence theorist would highlight commitments. These might be portrayed by heavily drawn lines in front of which were posted "No Trespassing" signs erected by states to put others on notice that they were prepared to defend these interests by force if necessary. The most important commitments might even be shown surrounded by chain link fences and posted with prominently displayed "Beware of Dog" notices, all part of elaborate efforts by states to convince others of the seriousness of their intent to defend their commitments.

The deterrence theorist would assume that a state would trespass against another's commitment only if its leaders were looking for a fight or for some reason doubted the willingness of the state in question to defend its commitment. A would-be trespasser state might be tempted to intrude if it saw, for example, that the other's fence was rusted or incomplete or that, despite the sign advertising a fierce guard dog, there was in reality no such beast but only a lazy old retriever that rolled over on its back and wagged its tail whenever someone approached.

Because deterrence places so much emphasis on the credibility of commitments, it assumes that statesmen engage in an ongoing effort to maintain the credibility of their own commitments and to monitor and periodically update and review their assessments of the commitments of others. This process might be represented on our map by a series of watchtowers erected by states at the confines of their own territory. These would be manned by diplomats and generals who peered through binoculars to observe activities in and around the commitments of their neighbors, friend and foe alike. Adversaries would be particularly attentive in this regard, as they would be ever on the lookout for an opportunity to take advantage of each other's weaknesses.

The success of deterrence as a strategy of conflict avoidance depends not only upon the capability and resolve of the defender of a commitment but just as much upon its ability to communicate that capability and resolve to adversaries. Deterrence theorists attribute whatever difficulties arise in this regard to structural causes, among them the military weakness, internal political division, or poor reputation for resolve of the state in question. When deterrence is predicated upon nuclear reprisal, they also stress the difficulty of making this threat credible when it would entail war with another nuclear power.

Deterrence theorists tend to ignore difficulties that might be associated with the actual signaling process.[4] They generally assume that adversaries, who usually speak different languages, nevertheless share common symbols that facilitate effective communication. Everyone is thought to understand, so to speak, the meaning of fierce guard dogs, barbed wire and "No Trespassing" signs. In practice, however, this may not be so. Statesmen, moreover, frequently adopt complex and finely calibrated strategies of coercion that make quite unrealistic demands on their adversaries' interpretative abilities. In chapter 1 Jervis observes that the adoption of such strategies is consistent with deterrence theory and thus perhaps a partial confirmation of it. However, the frequent failure of these strategies, most often attributable to the other side's inability to understand the signals, certainly is not. Nor does deterrence theory offer any explanation for the striking fact that statesmen continue to rely upon subtle signals despite their poor record of success.

Carefully calibrated signals most often fail to make the desired impression because they are based on distinctions that seem obvious to the sender but to which the receiver is oblivious. A striking example of this was the U.S. decision in 1965 to send ashore a "light" marine division instead of a "heavy" army division in order to signal to Hanoi Washington's limited objectives. The intended significance of the type of unit deployed was undoubtedly lost to the North Vietnamese, for whom the salient fact was that of the deployment itself.[5] Bombing pauses were used later in the war as another means of signaling to Hanoi. There short duration, fine graduations in targets, and the complex messages they were meant to convey presupposed the existence of a common bargaining framework. This simply was not the case.

The examples highlight a generic problem of signaling: that it often occurs in the context of far more dramatic events with which such a signal must compete for attention. However, the absence of dramatic surrounding events by no means guarantees better reception of subtle signals. Policy makers may be correspondingly less attentive to events or to relatively straightforward signals emanating from what they have previously decided to be a quiet or unthreatening arena. Berlin in 1948 is a case in point. W. Phillip Davison found that because the attention of the Truman administration was focused elsewhere, on matters that appeared to be more urgent at the time, the president, the secretary of state, and their immediate advisers were remarkably insensitive to the series of Soviet probes that preceded the imposition of a full blockade around the Western sectors of Berlin.[6] The Soviets, for their part, may have misinterpreted the U.S. failure to respond as a signal that they could get away with even more serious challenges of the Western position in Berlin. Gregg Herken suggested that Washington may have been insensitive because General Lucius Clay, the commander on the scene, had cried wolf so often in the past that his warnings were discounted.[7] Either way, Washington failed to understand and respond in time to Soviet probes that were in effect tests of U.S. resolve.

A second and probably equally common cause of insensitivity to signals arises from the failure to understand the context in which they are made and in terms of which they take on meaning. A signal can easily be missed if it is not recognized as a significant deviation from the norm. Allen Whiting describes several such occurrences preceding China's entry into the Korean War in November 1950. Peking increased both the frequency of newspaper articles on Korea and the strength of the language used to indicate Chinese interests on that peninsula. There is no evidence that the Americans picked this up or, if they did, were in any way aware of the manner in which the foreign language press especially was being used to signal intensified Chinese concern with developments in Korea.[8]

Signals can also be misunderstood if they are interpreted in an inappropriate context. In this connection Jervis cites Ernest May's description of Spain's failure to understand the threat conveyed by President McKinley's quasi ultimatum of 1898. Because the Americans and the Spanish had little knowledge of each other's domestic concerns and constraints, inferences that were perfectly clear to the author of a communication went unnoticed by the recipient. What McKinley conceived of as the bluntest of messages was actually interpreted by the Spanish as reassuring.[9]

The history of international relations abounds with examples of such distortion. In 1961 Chinese soldiers surrounded Indian outposts that had been set up in contested areas of Ladakh. Having demonstrated their ability to cut off several of these outposts, the Chinese subsequently withdrew, leaving the Indian pickets unharmed. Peking intended the action as a demonstration of resolve, but one that would allow Indian leaders to back down without loss of face because violence had been avoided. However, government officials in New Delhi interpreted the Chinese withdrawal as a sign of timidity. They reasoned that Chinese forces had failed to press their tactical advantage because Peking feared the consequences of a wider conflict with India. As a result, Indian leaders became even bolder in their efforts to occupy as much of the disputed territory, east and west, as was possible.[10]

The reason why the Chinese signal failed to have its intended effect was the belief on the part of Nehru, Menon, and their military advisers that Peking was loath to start a war with India because it feared defeat. They were also convinced that China wished to avoid being branded as the aggressor by the nonaligned bloc. As later events demonstrated, these Indian assessments were based on serious misjudgments about both the political and military consequences of a Sino-Indian conflict. The Chinese, who were unaware of the nature and extent of India's illusions, behaved in a way damaging to deterrence by reinforcing in Indian minds the very expectations about themselves they sought to forestall.[11]

The Falklands conflict provides a more recent and even more dramatic example of the importance of the underlying context as it is understood by the adversary state in assessing its resolve. There were many causes of miscalculation in both capitals, but one important one surely was the fact that Buenos Aires and London conceived of the conflict in quite different terms. From the Argentine perspective the Malvinas were national territory that had been occupied by a colonial power since 1833. British sovereignty over the islands was an atavism in a world that had witnessed numerous wars of national liberation that had all but brought the age of colonialism to an end. Viewed in this light, it seemed a far-fetched notion indeed that a colonial power in the year 1982 would try to reimpose its rule, let alone succeed in doing so, on a "liberated colony" by force of arms. World opinion, international morality, and, most importantly of all, the constellation of international political forces, all seemed to militate against it. The analogies that sprang into Argentine minds were Goa and Suez—an early invasion scenario concocted by the navy was actually called Plan Goa. The original Goa operation resulted in the colonial power, Portugal, accommodating itself to the loss of its colonial enclave on the Indian subcontinent when it was overrun by India. Suez, of course, remains the best example of how an attempt to reimpose colonial domination failed for all of the reasons mentioned above.

The British conceived of the Falklands controversy in an altogether different light. Politicians, the press, and public opinion for the most part dismissed the colonial metaphor as inappropriate because the population of the islands was of British stock and wished to remain under the protection of the Crown. Majority opinion did not see the Argentine invasion as an example of national liberation but rather as an act of naked aggression carried out by a brutal dictatorship against a democratic and peaceful people. For the British, the relevant historical analogy was Hitler and the origins of World War II. Newspapers made frequent references to the events and lessons of that period. Chief among the lessons was the need to stand up to aggression lest failure to do so whet the appetites of would-be aggressors everywhere. The Thatcher government pursued this line of reasoning: it justified the need to retake the Falklands with the twin arguments that "aggression must not be allowed to succeed" and that "freedom must be protected against dictatorship."

If it was inconceivable for Argentina that Britain would go to war to regain the Falklands, it was equally inconceivable to most Britons that they would not if it proved the only way to effect an Argentine withdrawal. The different cognitive contexts of the two sets of leaders led not only to contrasting visions of justice but also to quite different imperatives for action. Unfortunately, policy makers in both London and Buenos Aires, while not altogether ignorant of the others' conceptualization of the conflict, seemed unable to grasp its implications for that country's behavior.

The three cases discussed above illustrate three quite different kinds of contextual problems. McKinley's difficulty in communicating with Spain was due in the first instance to cultural differences; Americans and Spaniards read the same message in contrasting ways because of the different associations they brought to the words in question. There may also have been some motivated perceptual bias on the Spanish side. Officials in Madrid focused on that part of McKinley's message that conveyed what they so badly wanted to hear while they apparently ignored other passages that indicated that Spain and the United States were on a collision course.

The Sino-Indian misunderstanding was the result of different estimates of the relative political and military strengths of the two sides. As Chinese leaders considered themselves very definitely the stronger party in any military confrontation, they believed that restraint on their part might encourage compromise by India. But because the Indians saw themselves as militarily superior, they interpreted Chinese restraint as lack of resolve and became more intransigent in their position. Nehru and Menon's flawed assessment of the military balance can be traced to a series of self-serving and entirely unrealistic intelligence reports from a highly politicized military bureaucracy. The Chinese, who formulated their military assessment on the basis of more thorough and objective analysis of the capabilities of the two sides, had no way of knowing the extent to which the Indian leadership was misinformed.

Chinese awareness of the unrealistic nature of Indian estimates of the military balance would have required an intimate and detailed knowledge of privileged communications of the Indian government, something not normally at the disposal of other states, especially adversaries. For this reason, the problem posed to effective communication by asymmetrical assessment seems to be all but insurmountable in cases in which such assessments cannot be inferred from diplomatic discussions, public statements or actual policies. Even analysts sensitive to this problem would no doubt face great difficulties in convincing their own governments that adversarial assessments of the military or political balance were completely at variance with their own. Take the case of Pearl Harbor. The Japanese attack was predicated upon the erroneous assumption that the U.S. reaction to destruction of its Pacific fleet would be to withdraw from the Western Pacific. As Japanese leaders wanted to avoid an all out war against the United States, a struggle they knew they could never win, their attack made sense only if the resulting war could indeed be kept limited. Imagine, if you will, the difficulties that a U.S. intelligence analyst who had succeeded in second-guessing this scenario would have had in trying to convince his superiors of Japanese intentions. The premise upon which the attack rested, that the United States would accommodate itself to loss of its fleet instead of fighting back, would have struck U.S. officials as so absurd that they would likely have dismissed out of hand any warning flowing from this assumption.

The Falklands intelligence failure is only a little less disheartening in its implications. Had the British and Argentines read each other's press with an open mind they would readily have become aware of the dramatically different political contexts in which they envisaged their dispute over the Falklands. Possibly, they could have fathomed what this meant for the policies of both countries. They failed to do so, one suspects, for a combination of reasons. For a start, neither side may have been alert to the need to understand the other's political referent as a means of comprehending and predicting its behavior. In addition, politicians and diplomats on both sides were so convinced of the validity of their respective frameworks for conceptualizing the dispute that they found it difficult to take their adversary's very different conceptualization of the problem seriously, let alone comprehend the policy imperatives that resulted from it. Instead, they tended to dismiss it as propaganda put forward primarily for domestic consumption. There may also have been a strong bias against empathy because it would have called into question the justice and probability of success of the policies to which both sides were already committed.

Statesmen could be educated to the importance of trying to conceptualize conflicts as they are experienced by their adversaries. This does not mean they would necessarily succeed in doing so. The obstacles that stand in their way are both self-imposed, consisting of all the personal, political, and cultural constraints to the development of empathy, and structural, a function of differing conceptual contexts and asymmetries in assessment. There is already quite a literature in psychology on empathy and techniques of encouraging it. Some of it has been useful in sensitizing people to the manifestations and effects of prejudice, thereby easing racial tensions in various institutional settings. In theory, policy makers could also be taught empathy. In practice, this is unlikely to happen because most policy makers will have neither the time nor the inclination for such training.

The external impediments that hinder proper interpretation of an adversary's signals are probably even more difficult to overcome. This may require an intimate familiarity with the political culture in question. However, leaders of countries themselves rarely possess any special area expertise. U.S. presidents are even unlikely to have very much foreign experience. But this does not mean that they lack firm opinions on such subjects, especially when it concerns the motives of their country's principal adversary. They also tend to surround themselves with advisers who hold similar views. However, leaders may be no better informed when they rely on the advice of the "experts." Familiarity with a country or culture is in itself no guarantee of accurate insight or prescience. It can even be a hindrance to the extent that the "old Russia hand" or Arabist is the prisoner of deeply held but not necessarily accurate opinions about what goals motivate that country's policy makers or what factors they weigh when they make decisions. For all of these reasons, misunderstandings and incomprehension will always be rife. Given this unpleasant fact of international political life, a theory based upon the premise that clear, unambiguous signaling is readily attainable seems quite unrealistic.

The Causes of Aggression

In the Hobbesian world of deterrence theory, the very existence of a questionable commitment becomes an incentive for challenge independently of other considerations. To forgo an opportunity to take advantage of an adversary can be expected to convey an image of weakness or at least irresolution. A state must exploit an adversary's vulnerability if only to discourage challenges of its own commitments.

Case studies of actual conflicts contradict this depiction of international relations in important ways. They suggest that the existence of a vulnerable commitment is neither a necessary nor a sufficient condition for a challenge. Vulnerable commitments may never be challenged, while credible ones may be. This phenomenon points to the existence of serious misperceptions on the part of challengers and/or the presence of different, or at least additional, causes of aggression.

My own study of brinkmanship, described briefly in the text, analyzed a class of acute international crisis whose defining characteristic was the expectation on the part of the initiating state that its adversary would back down when challenged.[12] I found that, much more often than not, brinkmanship challenges were initiated in the absence of good evidence that the adversary lacked either the capability or resolve to defend this commitment. In most instances, the evidence available at the time pointed to the opposite conclusion because the commitments in question appeared to meet the four necessary conditions of deterrence: they were clearly defined, repeatedly publicized, and defensible, and the committed state gave every indication of its intention to defend them by force if necessary. Not surprisingly, most of these challenges resulted in setbacks for the initiators, who were themselves compelled to back down or go to war.

Faulty judgment on the part of initiators was most often the result of motivated bias. This arose from their perceived need to carry out a brinkmanship challenge in response to pressing foreign and domestic threats. The policy makers involved believed that these threats could be overcome only by means of a successful challenge of an adversary's commitment. Brinkmanship was conceived of as a necessary and forceful response to danger, as a means of preserving national strategic or domestic political interests before time ran out.

When policy makers believed in the necessity of challenging commitments of their adversaries, they became predisposed to see their objectives as attainable. They convinced themselves that they would succeed without provoking war. Because they knew the extent to which they were powerless to back down, they expected that their adversaries would accommodate them by doing so. Some of the policy makers involved also took comfort in the illusion that their country would emerge victorious at little cost to itself if the crisis got out of hand and led to war.

To the extent that there is a strong tendency for policy makers to rationalize the conditions for the success of a foreign policy once they become committed to it, efforts by defenders to impart credibility to their commitments will have only a marginal impact on their adversaries' behavior. Even the most elaborate efforts to demonstrate prowess and resolve may prove insufficient to discourage a challenge when policy makers are attracted to brinkmanship as a necessary means of preserving vital strategic and political interests. Policy makers in several of the cases I examined were able to maintain illusory expectations about adversarial behavior despite the accumulation of clear evidence to the contrary both before and during the crisis.

My brinkmanship study indicates that would-be challengers are to a great extent inner-directed and inwardly focused. This is also a central theme of Janice Gross Stein's first contribution to this volume, an analysis of the five occasions between 1969 and 1973 when Egyptian leaders seriously contemplated the use of force against Israel. Stein argues that decision making in all of these instances departed significantly from the postulates of deterrence theory. All five decisions revealed a consistent and almost exclusive concentration by Egyptian leaders on their own purposes, political needs, and constraints. They spoke in almost apocalyptic terms of Egypt's need to liberate the Sinai, to uphold the rights of Palestinians, and, above all, to wipe out the humiliation of 1967 by waging a successful military campaign. By contrast, Israel's interests, and the imperatives for action that could be expected to flow from them, were not at all salient for Egyptian leaders.

The Egyptian failure to consider the relative interests of both sides resulted in a flawed estimate not of Israel's credibility but rather of the scope of Israel's military response. In 1969 Egyptian leaders attached a very low probability to the possibility that Israel would carry the war of attrition onto Egyptian territory in order to maintain her position in the Sinai, a miscalculation of major proportions given the magnitude of the punishment Israel in fact inflicted upon Egypt. In 1973 the Egyptians similarly failed to consider the possibility that Israel would invade Egypt proper as a means of reasserting its authority along the canal.

Egypt's inability to understand that Israel's leaders believed that defense of the Sinai was important both for its own sake and as an indicator of resolve was merely one cause of its miscalculation in 1969. Stein demonstrates that Egyptian leaders overestimated their own capacity to determine the course of a war of attrition and underestimated that of Israel. They also developed a strategy to fight the war, to culminate in a crossing of the canal, that was predicated on a fatal inconsistency: the belief that Egypt could inflict numerous casualties on Israel in the course of a war of attrition but that Israel would refrain from escalating that conflict in order to reduce her casualities.

Stein considers these flawed assessments and the toleration of logical contradictions by the Egyptians in their expectations as evidence of pervasive wishful thinking. She believes that this was a response to the strategic dilemma faced by Egyptian planners in 1969. Egypt could neither accept the status quo nor sustain the kind of military effort that would have been necessary to alter it. Instead, Egypt embarked upon a poorly conceived limited military action. The wishful thinking and biased estimates associated with it were a form of bolstering, the means by which Egyptian leaders convinced themselves that their strategy would succeed. Once again Israel's deterrent failed, not because of any lack of capability or resolve, but because Egypt's calculations, in the words of Stein, "were so flawed that they defeated deterrence."

Egyptian decision making in 1969 provides one more example of the phenomenon that my study of brinkmanship identified as the most frequent cause of serious miscalculation in international crisis: the inability of leaders to find a satisfactory way to reconcile two clashing kinds of threats. The psychological stress that arises from this decisional dilemma is usually received by the adoption of defensive avoidance as a coping strategy. Leaders commit themselves to a course of action and deny information that indicates that their policy might not succeed. As was true in most of my cases, the Egyptian decisional dilemma that prompted defensive avoidance was the result of incompatibility between domestic imperatives and foreign realities. The domestic threat, the political and economic losses, was the overriding consideration for Egyptian policy makers, as it was for the Argentines.

The primacy of domestic political concerns may not be entirely attributable to the political self-interest of the policy makers involved, although this factor should not be discounted. It may also be related to their ability to foresee and visualize domestic disasters more vividly than foreign ones. The domestic costs of passivity in these cases probably appeared greater and more probable than a more detached assessment might have indicated and certainly also more difficult to deny. Foreign catastrophe, by contrast, depended upon the behavior of adversaries whose political systems were less well understood than one's own and whose policies were accordingly more difficult to predict. It was simply much easier for policy makers to delude themselves that somehow their foreign ventures would succeed than it was for them to convince themselves that the domestic price of restraint would be less than horrendous. Not surprisingly, they chose to avoid what appeared to be certain loss in favor of a policy that held out the prospect of at least lower costs in the Egyptian case and some prospect of substantial gain in the case of Argentina.

If deterrence theory describes one's own vulnerability as the catalyst for aggression, it prescribes credible, defensive commitments as the most important means of discouraging it. The empirical evidence marshaled in this study once again challenges the validity of the theory's assumptions. This is most apparent with respect to the role of military capability, and adversarial restraint is both more uncertain and more complex than deterrence theory allows.

Stein found that Egypt went to war in 1973 in spite of its leaders' adverse estimate of the military balance. The same domestic political considerations that compelled Egyptian leaders to challenge Israel also provided the incentives for Egyptian military planners to devise a strategy that compensated for their military weakness. Human ingenuity and careful organization succeeded in exploiting the flexibility of multipurpose conventional weaponry to circumvent many of the constraints of military inferiority. The Egyptians achieved defensive superiority in what they planned to keep a limited battle zone.

According to Stein, two other considerations were crucial catalysts for the Egyptian decision to challenge Israel in 1973. These were the twin assumptions made by Sadat and his advisors that there was no chance of regaining the Sinai by diplomacy and that, the longer they postponed war, the more the military balance would favor Israel. Both assumptions helped to create a mood of desperation in Cairo, so much so that Sadat repeatedly purged the Egyptian military command until he found generals who were optimistic of finding a way around Israel's awesome air and armored capability.

The Japanese decision to attack the United States in December 1941 seems analogous in almost every important respect to the Egyptian decision of 1973. Like the Egyptians, the Japanese fully recognized the military superiority of their adversary, in this instance founded on greater naval power and a vastly superior economic base. The Japanese nevertheless felt compelled to attack the United States in the forlorn hope that a limited victory would facilitate a favorable settlement of their festering and costly conflict with China. As the Egyptians were to do more than thirty years later, the Japanese military devised an ingenious and daring strategy to compensate for their adversary's advantages; they relied on air power and surprise to neutralize U.S. naval power in the Pacific in one sharp blow. They, too, deluded themselves into believing that their foe would come to accept the political consequences of a disastrous initial defeat instead of fighting to regain the initiative, a miscalculation with a monumental price. The Japanese strategy was also an act of desperation. Japan's leaders opted for war only after it became clear that they could not attain their objectives by diplomacy. They were also convinced that the military balance between themselves and their adversaries would never again be so favorable as it was in 1941.[13]

These two cases suggest that the military balance, even when correctly assessed, is only one of several considerations taken into account by policy makers contemplating war. They are also influenced by domestic and foreign political pressures that push them to act, frustration with the low probability of achieving their goals by peaceful means, and their judgments about future trends in the military balance. As we have just seen, these considerations may even prove decisive.

If there is any single example that drives home the point that challenges may be unrelated to the military balance, it is the recent war in the Falkland Islands. The Argentine decision to invade in March 1982, analyzed in chapter 5, was found to be the result in the first instance of the faltering legitimacy of the military *junta* and its increasingly desperate need to do something to shore up its public support. Like the Japanese and the Egyptians, the Argentines had also lost all faith in the prospect of achieving their goal, sovereignty over the islands, by diplomacy. Disenchantment with negotiations was all the more a catalyst for military action because peaceful resolution of the dispute had appeared a very real possibility until the failure of the so-called lease-back proposal in the late fall of 1981. A transfer of sovereignty had seemed so likely that the *junta*, both as a bargaining tactic and as a means of drumming up domestic support for itself, had actively encouraged public expectations to this effect. The Argentine military now became the prisoner of the passions it had helped to arouse.

Had a military appraisal of the situation dominated Argentine deliberations, the *junta* would almost certainly have waited another year before launching its invasion of the Falklands. It was public knowledge that in the interim, *Invincible* would have gone to the Australian navy, *Hermes* would have been paid off, and *Intrepid* and *Fearless*, the two amphibious assault ships, would have been scrapped, together with some of the supporting frigates. Britain, which possessed barely sufficient naval assets to retake the Falklands in 1982, would almost certainly have been unable to do so in the absence of these vessels. However, the *junta*, composed of generals and admirals, no less, deemed political considerations more important than calculations of relative military balance, with results that were nothing short of disastrous.

Most of the twenty-odd cases examined by Lebow and Stein in their most recent studies support the conclusion that policy makers who risk or actually start wars pay more attention to their own strategic and domestic political interests than they do to the interests and military capabilities of their adversaries. Their strategic and political needs appear to constitute the principal motivation for a resort to force. When these needs are pronounced, policy makers are prone to disregard the ways in which the same kinds of strategic and political needs might compel adversaries to stand firm in defense of their commitments. They may discount an adversary's resolve even when the state in question has gone to considerable lengths to demonstrate that resolve and to develop the military capabilities needed to defend its commitment.

Deterrence theory can be accused of standing reality on its head. It assumes a constant level of hostility between adversaries and expects that a challenger will seek an external opportunity to act. Our cases point to just the opposite causation: that the principal incentive for a resort to force is probably a state's own perceived vulnerabilities, which lead its policy makers to challenge an adversary even when external opportunity to act, a vulnerable commitment, is absent. A challenger's needs and the perceptual distortions they engender may actually constitute the greatest threat to the peace. This conclusion has obvious and important policy implications.

Deterrence dictates that the defending state attempts to manipulate its adversary's calculus of cost and gain so as to reduce its incentive to attack or to challenge an important commitment. The research described in this volume suggests that one important reason why deterrence often fails is that defenders attempt to manipulate attributes of the situation, especially adversarial perceptions of resolve and relative military capability that may be critical to the calculations of the would-be aggressor. Efforts to influence the adversary state may require attention to *its* strategic dilemmas, domestic political costs of inaction, and assessment of achieving at least some of its objectives by nonviolent means. All of these parameters must be considered by defenders as proper and productive targets for manipulation.

Does Deterrence Deter?

The preceding sections have discussed some of the ways in which state behavior is at variance with deterrence theory. This section examines the record of deterrence as a strategy of conflict management; it looks at what deterrence policies accomplish in practice. It argues that, while deterrence may sometimes succeed in discouraging the use of force, it may also be instrumental in provoking it. Deterrence can at times encourage a resort to force both by the state that practices it and by its target.

William W. Kaufmann's *Requirements of Deterrence*, published in 1954, remains the classic formulation of deterrence as a strategy of conflict management. Kaufmann stressed the need to surround a commitment with "an air of credibility." He identified three components to this task: capability, cost, and intentions. Capability he defined as the operational ability to inflict a burdensome cost upon an adversary. That cost had to be great enough to exceed whatever gain the adversary expected to attain by a challenge. The adversary also had to believe that punishment was certain. Kaufmann argued that an intelligent adversary would carefully evaluate its opponent's resolve to carry out its threats by looking at its past performance, current pronouncements, and the support the commitment had among its public opinion. Kaufmann believed that evidence of widespread public support for a commitment was an absolutely essential component of credibility.[14]

Subsequent attempts to describe the conditions for successful deterrence have continued to emphasize the importance of credibility and of a state's reputation for honoring past commitments as the principal factor influencing an adversary's assessment of the credibility of a current commitment. This theme lies at the core of Thomas Schelling's argument in *Arms and Influence*, one of the most influential works on deterrence. Schelling describes commitments as interdependent; failure to defend any one of them will make willingness to defend any of the others questionable in the eyes of an adversary. "We tell the Soviets that we have to react here because, if we did not, they would not believe us when we say that we will react there."[15]

The U.S. intervention in Vietnam was of course the most far-reaching expression of this logic. As is well known, the consensus among policy makers in the 1960s was that failure to hold the line against communism in Southeast Asia would lead Moscow to doubt U.S. resolve with regard to commitments elsewhere in the world. Lyndon Johnson told the American people in April 1965, "To leave Vietnam to its fate would shake . . . confidence . . . in the value of an American commitment and in the value of America's word."[16] Secretary of State Dean Rusk warned that "the communist world would draw conclusions that would lead to our ruin and almost certainly to a catastrophic war."[17] Although Vietnam ended in disaster, belief in the United States in the interdependence of commitments appears undiminished and unquestionably continues to influence policy makers. In 1974–75 it prompted the Ford administration to provide covert aid to two of the contending factions in the Angolan civil war. When Congress compelled the Administration to terminate this support, an irate Henry Kissinger predicted that this "would lead to further Soviet and Cuban pressures on the mistaken assumption that America has lost the will to counter adventurism or even to help others to do so."[18] The Carter administration employed similar arguments to justify its commitment to defend the Persian Gulf. More recently, President Reagan has argued that the Soviet Union would grow even more emboldened in its aggressive forays in the Third World if the United States fails to help Central American governments combat left-wing military challenges.

Critics of deterrence charge that this approach to foreign policy is distinctly apolitical. They argue that commitments are or ought to be expressions of national interests. When a commitment does not reflect major interests, it will be difficult to persuade others to take it seriously regardless of how elaborate an effort is made to do so. As George and Smoke have put it, in the quest for credibility is no substitute for underlying national interests.[19] Conversely, some interests may be so intrinsically important that other governments will not question a state's willingness to defend them whether or not it has even voiced its intention to do so. U.S. defense of Europe from Soviet attack might be an example. It is what Jervis has called an "intrinsic interest," one that is so vital that a commitment to go to war on its behalf is all but taken for granted. This is distinct from strategic interests or commitments, where judgments about credibility may turn more on what efforts a state makes to convey its resolve.[20]

The degree to which commitments are interdependent depends upon the relative importance of a state's bargaining reputation, as opposed to its interests, as the criterion of credibility in the eyes of a would-be challenger. Yet, as Morgan observes, there has been very little effort until quite recently to determine empirically just what influences the decisions of challengers. This is quite remarkable given the ongoing debate about interdependence and its policy implications. In chapter 6 Morgan addresses this phenomenon: why post–World War II U.S. foreign policy has always acted on the assumption that commitments are in fact interdependent and that a state's bargaining reputation is therefore all-important.

Morgan speculates that the well-documented U.S. fixation on resolve derives from what he calls the "paradox of credibility." Leaders of nuclear powers are uncertain as to how they would respond to a major challenge by another nuclear power because of the suicidal nature of nuclear war. As a result, they become more disposed to uphold lesser commitments because these are the only ones that are safe to defend. By doing so they seek a reputation for resolve in the hope that it will discourage challenges of more important commitments. A concern for reputation, Morgan argues, may be less a rational extension of the art of commitment and more an effort by policy makers to hide their insecurity over what to do if their most vital interests are challenged.

According to Morgan, defenders may describe commitments as interdependent not because they really believe that they are but rather in the hope that adversaries will see them that way. But to convince their opponents that commitments are a "seamless web," policy makers must act as if they were. They must attempt to foster a reputation for resolve, a quest that has no natural bounds. The effort to build such a reputation can prompt policy makers to intervene in situations that cannot by any reasonable stretch of the imagination be described as challenges. A case can be made that the United States has behaved this way; the U.S. policy-making elite's pursuit of a reputation for resolve has frequently resulted in policies devoid of perspective and judgment.

Morgan is quick to point out that this kind of behavior is not an inevitable consequence of the possession of nuclear weapons. Neither Britain nor France has displayed the same preoccupation with credibility as has the United States. There was no grave concern in Europe that Western credibility was at stake in the 1973 Middle East war nor in the aftermath of either the fall of the Shah in Iran or the Soviet invasion of Afghanistan. The Soviet Union also seems much less concerned than the United States with fostering a reputation for resolve. Moscow has accepted the necessity of retreat in a series of crises and, unlike Washington, has chosen not to react to provocations in the Middle East and Southeast Asia involving the death of Soviet servicemen. There is nothing, moreover, in the Soviet foreign policy literature that stresses the interdependence of commitments. Instead, Soviet commentators place emphasis on military strength and feasible plans for its use as the essential components in discouraging aggression.

Morgan suggests that deterrence, in theory and practice, is largely an expression of the political culture in the United States. He traces its development to insecurities that arose in the early post–World War II years and have persisted to the present time. These were attributable in the first instance to fears on the part of the U.S. foreign-policy-making elite that the public would not sustain a resolute, responsible posture in world affairs. Policy makers worried about a return to isolationism and, later, about a political backlash on the right, triggered by communist gains in Asia. The U.S. deterrence posture was formulated with a domestic as well as a foreign audience in mind; a reputation for resolve was sought abroad in order to reassure Americans at home. According to Morgan, another contributing factor to the appeal of deterrence was the equally pronounced concern that any sign of weakness or irresolution would encourage allies and neutrals to seek an accommodation with the Soviet Union. This concern was a principal motivation behind NSC-68 and finds its current expression in the often voiced assumption that any significant erosion of U.S. capability or resolve would lead to the "Finlandization" of Western Europe.

Finally, Morgan argues, there are the memories of the failures of the 1930s and the "lessons" of Munich. When Stalin's Russia became the linear descendent of Hitler's Germany in American minds, so too was it expected that World War III would begin the same way as World War II. Since appeasement had abetted Hitler's aggression, policy makers believed that it was essential that Stalin and his successors be confronted with resolve. The extent to which the lessons of Munich have influenced U.S. foreign policy has usually been ascribed to cognitive bias; having observed the disastrous consequences of appeasement, policy makers became predisposed to respond to all threats with displays of resolve.[21] Morgan theorizes that the Munich analogy might be more an effect than a cause of U.S. foreign policy. It offers a plausible rationalization for policies that really derive from unspoken doubts about the use of nuclear weapons in defense of vital interests.

Morgan's analysis of U.S. policy is, by his own admission, highly speculative. The phenomenon he describes, the U.S. fixation with credibility, is nevertheless observable and well documented. It reflects, as Morgan and others have pointed out, the peculiar, perhaps unique nature of the U.S. approach to security. To base a universal theory of international relations upon such a singular experience seems foolish in the extreme. The fact that this has happened raises a second intriguing and probably unanswerable question: Has deterrence theory helped to shape U.S. security policy, or is it an expression and justification of it? If it is the former, an effective intellectual challenge of the theory could have profound policy implications. But if the theory, as Morgan argues, is largely a rationalization for policies pursued for other reasons, then even the most persuasive critique of deterrence will be greeted by policy makers rather the way die-hard cigarette smokers have responded to studies linking tobacco with cancer. The insignificant impact of studies critical of deterrence upon the way in which both policy makers and academic defense analysts think about the subject might be adduced as evidence in support of Morgan's position.[22]

It was noted earlier that deterrence policies can encourage aggressive behavior on the part of defender and challenger alike. In the case of the defender, this is attributable to the need to develop and maintain a reputation for resolve, which may entail the threat or actual use of force in a whole range of situations that involve no obvious substantive interests. From the perspective of the would-be challenger, a more assertive and confrontational foreign policy ironically may be a response to policies designed to deter it from aggression. The Japanese decision to attack the United States in December 1941 is a well-documented case in point.

The United States and other Western powers imposed first an asset freeze and then an oil embargo upon Japan in July-August

1941 in the hope of moderating Tokyo's policies. In practice, however, these actions were catalysts for the Japanese decision to go to war. Japan's leaders feared that the embargo would deprive them of the means of continuing their struggle against China and would ultimately put them at the mercy of their adversaries. It accordingly fostered a mood of desperation in Tokyo, an essential precondition for the attack on Pearl Harbor that followed.

The orgins of the Spanish-American War of 1898–99 offer a second example of this phenomenon. The festering insurrection in Cuba brought Spain into conflict with the United States. U.S. investments on the island were endangered and American public opinion aroused when the yellow fever epidemic, caused by a deterioration in sanitary conditions due to the fighting, spread to the southeastern part of the United States. Popular support among Americans for the rebels also resulted in a series of "filibustering" expeditions—private attempts to supply the rebels with arms—that proved embarrassing to both governments. Mounting congressional demands to get Spain out of Cuba led President Cleveland and then President McKinley to explore a variety of diplomatic solutions. None of them proved acceptable to successive Spanish governments, all of which were under increasing domestic pressure to make no concessions to the rebels. U.S. demands on Spain in the aftermath of the destruction of USS *Maine* inflamed Spanish opinion further, restricting the government's freedom of action with regard to Cuba. Washington nevertheless expected that continued U.S. pressure would bring Madrid to its senses. Instead, it provoked war.

Policy makers in these two cases felt cornered; the Japanese saw themselves as victims of foreign circumstances, the Spanish thought of themselves as hostages to public opinion. In both instances, U.S. deterrent policies backfired because they intensified the pressures on leaders in the target states to act in even more extreme ways. Ironically, Spanish leaders ultimately welcomed a forceful U.S. posture because it offered an escape from their policy dilemma: how to cede Cuba without provoking a miliary-led coup at home. If the United States declared war, they reasoned, they could go to war in defense of Spain's honor, the principal concern of the army and conservative opinion. But it they lost the war, and the Spanish politicians had no illusions in this regard, they would be compelled to withdraw their forces from Cuba and renounce sovereignty over the island. What Spanish leaders failed to anticipate was that the United States would attack not only Cuba but Spain's naval and ground forces in Puerto Rico and the Philippines. Crushing military defeats and loss of these colonies triggered a popular revolution in Spain, the very outcome the government had gone to war to avoid.

The Spanish and Japanese experiences illustrate that there is no simple relationship between demonstrations of resolve on the part of the defending states and moderation on the part of would-be challengers. The efficacy of deterrence or any strategy of conflict management depends very much upon the adversary's intentions, the degree and kinds of constraints that affect its leaders, and the political context in which that strategy is pursued. Appeasement of a Hitler only elicits more demands. But the same policy applied to a state with limited aims may resolve important outstanding differences, as did British appeasement of the United States in the second half of the nineteenth century, in the Oregon and Venezuela crises.[23] It was a necessary first step toward transforming a long-standing hostile relationship into an enduring and remarkably close alliance. Resolve, when applied to leaders who do not feel compelled to respond to domestic or strategic imperatives, may also succeed in this objective. But, as we have seen, it may have the opposite effect when directed against leaders who feel cornered, do not believe that they have the freedom to back down, or see the loss associated with passivity as greater than that attributed to action.

If deterrence is not a universally applicable strategy, it is imperative for its proponents to reformulate the theory so that it specifies the kinds of conflicts or situations in which it is germane. Herein lies the primary contribution of the Snyder paper. It offers a typology of conflicts and shows some of the reasons why deterrence as it is normally practiced can be counterproductive.

International relations literature distinguishes between deterrence and spiral models of conflict.[24] The former stresses the role of credible threats in deterring aggression, while the latter emphasizes the need for concessions to assuage mutual security fears. According to Snyder, this dichotomy ignores a third generic kind of conflict, what he calls a "security dilemma." This occurs when each adversary believes that its security requires the other's insecurity. When this happens, neither unyielding deterrent policies nor concessions will succeed in moderating, let alone resolving, conflict.

Snyder attributes the outbreak of war in Europe in 1914 to the existence of a security dilemma. He argues that because a strategic balance was unattainable, deterrence policies failed to induce caution. Instead, they intensified adversarial perceptions of the zero-sum nature of strategic competition and the resulting dangers of inferiority. Deterrence policies also spawned the widespread belief that war was all but inevitable. Both developments heightened the resolve of the inferior party to redress the strategic balance. But efforts to do this encouraged the superior party to strike before its advantage disappeared.

If threats could not resolve this security dilemma, neither could concessions. The major powers were able to negotiate a series of compromises on minor issues, most of them pertaining to colonial competition. However, these agreements could do little to address the fundamental cause of insecurity; this arose from nearly universal feelings of acute vulnerability to attack from neighboring states. Agreements or concessions could not resolve this problem because a neighbor's security fears could be alleviated only at the cost of aggravating one's own. The security dilemma was a spiral process in that one adversary's fear, hostility, and military preparations prompted the same response on the part of the other. However, it was not a spiral that could be unwound by the kinds of concessionary policies that spiral theorists usually advocate.

For Snyder, the distinguishing characteristic of a security dilmma is that behavior perceived by adversaries as aggressive is in fact initiated as a defensive response to strategic circumstances. This is why such policies are immune to both threats and concessions. To moderate them it is necessary to change the objective circumstances that give rise to them or the adversary's understanding of these circumstances. In this connection, Snyder identifies four kinds of perverse incentives that can strain entrapped states. They produce four kinds of security dilemmas: the structural security dilemma, the perceptual security dilemma, the imperialist's dilemma, and deadlock.

The structural security dilemma assumes that each state formulates its defense strategy in response to incentives and constraints created by military technology, geography, and the relative power of other states. A security dilemma develops when a military offense becomes easier than defense and/or when the relative power of adversaries is changing, and one of them concludes as a result that attacking now is better than defending later. A perceptual security dilemma differs only in the fact that strategic assessments and the policies based upon them are the result of perceptual biases. In effect, policy makers overrate the advantages of the offensive, the magnitude of power shifts, and the hostility of others.

The imperialist's dilemma requires that at least one state desires to expand but that no state pursues this goal *à outrance*. The problem the expansionist state faces is how to overturn the status quo without provoking a major war. To do this, expansionist states usually develop offensive military capability and start arms races in order to shift the balance of military power in their favor. They then threaten war to extract concessions. The kind of competition this behavior sets off may create or intensify a security dilemma by forcing one of the states to choose between war and unilateral vulnerability.

Finally, there is a deadlock, a situation that prevails when the nonsecurity interests of states are totally incompatible. As a result, there is no compromise that both sides would prefer to war. In this circumstance, Snyder suggests, war may occur in a manner reminiscent of a security dilemma. It can be triggered by the expectation of a major shift in the relative power of adversaries. This could serve as a catalyst for war, although not as its underlying cause. Even in the absence of a dilemma, war can be expected to occur at some point.

Snyder argues that 1914 embodied elements of several of these security dilemmas. It was structural in the sense that German security in the east required the vulnerability of Russian forces in Poland, whereas Russian security required the elimination of this weakness. In the west, French and German security requirements were similarly contradictory, especially with regard to the status of Belgium.

Nineteen fourteen was also a perceptual security dilemma since perceptual bias significantly intensified the sense of threat conveyed by the strategic situation. The German military overrated both the hostility of its neighbors and the inevitability of war and was accordingly attracted to a preventive war-fighting as opposed to defensive deterrent strategy. Once committed to the Schlieffen plan, the very embodiment of a war-fighting offensive strategy, the German government became extremely sensitive to any military measure on the part of the other powers that would threaten the plan's success. Convinced that their advantage was soon to disappear, they exploited a window of opportunity in 1914 to start a war. German leaders could have extricated Germany from its security dilemma by shifting to a defensive military strategy based on deterrence through denial. That they consistently ignored this option, Snyder asserts, had more to do with their perceptions than with the structure of their dilemma.

Snyder also considers the possibility that 1914 was in part the result of an imperialist's dilemma. German diplomacy in the decades prior to 1914, often explained in terms of the expansive requirements of the Schlieffen plan, nevertheless proved counterproductive in security terms. Snyder believes that it might therefore better be explained as an expression of nonsecurity interest in expansion, interests that derived from domestic pressures and contradictions.[25] This interpretation has of course also been put forward by many German historians. The effect of such policies,

Snyder argues, was to touch off an international competition that followed the characteristic pattern of the imperialist's dilemma: recurrent crises, competitive armament, tightening alliances, windows, and war. As a result, Germany's dilemma in 1914 may indeed have become one of "world power or decline."

Snyder's analysis indicates several kinds of conflict in which deterrence is counterproductive. Even when deterrence is an appropriate strategy, as in the imperialist's dilemma, it is not without risk. An expansionist state will attempt to overturn the status quo by coercive diplomacy based on superior military capability. Deterrence theory assumes that this threat is best met by matching the adversary's military capability and yielding no ground politically. However, in the imperialist's dilemma such a response, which almost inevitably provokes arms competition and risk taking, can create strong incentives for preventive or preemptive war.

To avoid war, a status quo power must pursue two distinct and not easily reconcilable objectives. It must maintain its own power and credibility while at the same time working to forestall the development of the kind of unstable conditions that lead to a security dilemma. As Snyder puts it, the status quo power "must worry about everyone's security, not just its own." The best way to accomplish this, he indicates, is to deploy defensive forces that create no obvious first-strike advantage and thus avoid bringing about a situation of strategic instability. Policy makers should also shun commitments and alliances that can be defended only by forces and strategies that pose a threat to the adversary's ability to provide for its own defense and those of its clients.

Snyder's policy recommendations resemble my own. My contribution to this volume also makes the point that deterrence policies are counterproductive when they intensify an adversary's fears for its own security. But in contrast to Snyder, my cases also point to the importance of the domestic impact of deterrence policies in this regard. To the extent that they aggravate a state's frangibility or the political insecurity of its regime or individual leaders, they can also increase the willingness of its leadership to take foreign policy risks.

If domestic and strategic vulnerabilities are an equal or even more important source of confrontational policies than the existence of an opportunity to take advantage of an adversary because it has a vulnerable commitment, then a corresponding shift in the focus of efforts to prevent the use of force is required. Too much attention is devoted in theory and practice to making commitments credible and not nearly enough to trying to understand what might prompt an adversary to challenge these commitments. A more sophisticated approach to conflict management would make use of both deterrence and reassurance. Leaders must seek to discourage challenges by attempting to reduce both the opportunity and the perceived need to carry them out. They must aim never to allow their own state to be perceived as so weak or irresolute as to invite challenge, but at the same time to avoid making an adversary state feel so weak or threatened that it has the need to do so.

Like Snyder, I urge a mixed strategy that incorporates elements of deterrence but attempts to moderate its ill effects. Both of us want to arrive at a procedure that will reduce tensions without at the same time making the state militarily vulnerable. We do, however, place a different emphasis on the relative importance of the military and political components of such a strategy.

For Snyder, success or failure depends upon the structural requirements of security and how they are perceived by adversaries. If each side believes that its security can be met only through the insecurity of the other, then little can be done to alleviate tensions; political agreements in other arenas will not resolve or even mitigate the effects of this fundamental dilemma. It can be alleviated, or better yet, prevented from developing in the first place, only by one or both adversaries renouncing offensive military strategies, which Snyder identifies as the root cause of assymetrical security requirements. Unfortunately, a state's choice of strategy does not seem particularly amenable to outside influence; Snyder attributes this choice to historical and organizational traditions. The pattern of Soviet-U.S. relations nevertheless suggests that the security policies of one adversary can intensify the perceived need for an offensive strategy on the part of the other. Certain kinds of arms control agreements or a decline in adversarial tensions might also conceivably minimize this need. Snyder might usefully proceed to explore the nature and relative weight of the domestic and foreign influences that encourage the adoption of offensive strategies and the possible ways, if any, of minimizing their appeal.

Snyder's analysis of structural and perceptual security dilemmas places little emphasis on political as opposed to military sources of conflict. But it seems evident that even pre-1914 German strategy was not formulated entirely in response to technical military requirements. German perceptions of the hostile intentions of their neighbors, based on their political behavior as well as their military preparations, provided incentives for an offensive military strategy. Success in alleviating some of these tensions might have weakened the bonds of the opposing alliance and have eased the Germans' perception of their military dilemma sufficiently for them to believe that war against one or possibly both of their continental adversaries was less likely or even avoidable.

There are nevertheless imposing obstacles in the way of any political strategy aimed at easing perceptions of hostility. In democracies, the most important of these is probably domestic and consists of the political and bureaucratic constraints that often prevent leaders from pursuing sophisticated and innovative foreign policies. Beyond this, there is the problem of mutual cognitive rigidity. Years or even decades of hostile relations can result in a situation where leaders on both sides take for granted the aggressive intentions of the other. They put the most threatening interpretation on actions even when this is unwarranted by the evidence. Leaders in either country who want to improve relations with their adversary must recognize the gravity of this challenge and devise a strategy for coping with the problem. For any measure, no matter how well conceived, will usually do little to diffuse tensions unless it is somehow perceived as sincerely motivated by the other side. Finding a way of breaking through this wall of mistrust may be a necessary step in escaping from the spiral of fear and insecurity that is currently pushing both superpowers closer to war.

In this connection the Sadat peace initiative of 1975 could usefully be studied with the objective of deriving some general lessons. Egyptian-Israeli relations were certainly characterized by extreme hostility at the time; the two states had fought a war just four years before. Yet Sadat's dramatic statement of his willingness to go to Jerusalem to address the Israeli parliament set in motion a chain of events that led to a peace treaty two years later. Most observers agree that the fundamental reason for Sadat's success was that his initiative helped to dissipate some of the hostility and mistrust that dominated Israeli and Egyptian perceptions of each other. Stein and I are currently engaged in a study of how Sadat, who had masterminded the surprise attack against Israel on Yom Kippur 1973, nevertheless managed to convince Israeli leaders and public opinion that he was seriously interested in peace. Our preliminary findings emphasize the irreversible nature of the initiative, the great political cost to Sadat of breaking the long-standing Arab policy of not treating directly with Israel—something that helped to establish his *bona fides* in Jerusalem—the fact that his action required no immediate political or military concessions from Israel, and the belief on both sides that renewed fighting would not serve either of their interests. Could analogues of the Sadat initiative be developed in other long-standing conflicts, including the Soviet-U.S. relationship?[26]

*   *   *

The demonstrable insensitivity of adversaries to each other's signals and interests and the clashing perceptions they so often have of each other's intentions and motivations point to what is perhaps the central failing of deterrence theory. This is the assumption, on which everything else depends, that adversaries relate to each other in terms of a common frame of reference. Deterrence purports to describe an *interactive* process between the defender of a commitment and a would-be challenger. The defending state is expected to define and publicize its commitment and do its best to make that commitment credible in the eyes of its adversary. Would-be challengers are expected to update frequently their assessment with regard to their capability and resolve. The repetitive cycle of test and challenge is expected to provide both sides with an increasingly sophisticated understanding of each other's interests, propensity for risk taking, threshold of provocation, and style of foreign policy behavior.

There is some evidence that such a process does sometimes occur. Jan Kalicki attempted to document it in the case of Sino-U.S. relations. He attributes their confrontation in Korea to faulty communication, which left Peking and Washington insensitive to each other's needs and signals. The experience of Korea and succeeding Sino-U.S. crises in the 1950s, Kalicki argues, brought increased empathy and sensitivity in signaling. This facilitated crisis resolution as "crisis interactions became more bilateral and responsive, each crisis phase—escalation, declension, and de-escalation—was experienced by the U.S. and the PRC simultaneously: and messages and signals, threats and warnings, were exchanged with less exaggerated responses, at least in operational terms."[27]

Several of the cases analyzed or referred to in this study cast doubts upon the expectation that repetitive interaction between adversaries contributes to a better understanding of their respective intentions and *modi operandi.* From the perspective of the challenger, one reason for this may be the inner-directed focus of policy makers. Leaders contemplating challenges of other states' commitments were remarkably insensitive to external realities. The Americans in Korea in the fall of 1950, Sadat in 1973, the Argentine *junta* in 1982, to mention but three examples, initiated challenges primarily in response to their domestic political needs. These internal imperatives, not their external opportunities to act, were decisive to their decisions to proceed. Only in the case of Korea can such an opportunity even be said to have existed. In the Egyptian and Argentine cases, domestic political pressures determined the timing of the challenge as well. In the Egyptian decision, the putative resolve and capability of the adversary did not figure prominently in the policy debate. When external military and political realities were considered, as in the Korean and Falklands decisions, they were on the whole subordinated to political needs; the information available was distorted or processed selectively in order to make a challenge appear feasible. Policy makers in these several cases can hardly be said to have based their challenges on their judgments of the credibility of their adversaries' commitments. Their process of risk assessment differed markedly from that described by deterrence theory.

From the perspective of the defender, the picture appears much the same. Examples spring readily to mind of conflicts in which repeated clashes failed to lead to a better understanding of adversarial motivations of foreign policy style. Anglo-German relations on the eve of World War I are a case in point. By 1914, most British policy makers had come to view their adversary as willing to risk a European war in pursuit of its far-reaching aggressive ambitions. Their understanding of Germany was based on the lessons they had drawn from recent German foreign policy.

The Agadir crisis of 1911 was an important episode in this regard. In retrospect, however, what historians have found so striking about it was the extent to which both Britain and Germany misjudged and misinterpreted the other's intentions and signals. British and German policy makers had become so convinced of their rival's hostility that they attributed the worst possible motivation to its foreign policy initiatives. In this instance, the British overreaction to a colonial *démarche* transformed a colonial dispute into a grave confrontation that threatened the peace of Europe. British and German leaders for the most part came away from the crisis even more convinced of the other's hostility and its willingness to provoke a continental war if the situation seemed favorable.[28]

Soviet-U.S. relations can be cited as another example of this phenomenon. The "lessons" U.S. policy makers have drawn from the series of Cold War confrontations can only in the loosest sense be said to derive from the behavior of their adversary, the Soviet Union. They seem more the result of a subjective unilateral process whereby U.S. policy makers tended to interpret Soviet behavior in terms of their preexisting notions of the motivations behind Soviet foreign policy. I have tried to document elsewhere how the Cuban missile crisis provides a striking illustration of the way in which assumptions about adversaries can be confirmed tautologically.[29] This only enhances their grip over the minds of the policy makers who approach international affairs using these assumptions. In retrospect, it seems apparent that the president projected his concern for his and U.S. credibility onto Khrushchev and interpreted his behavior in terms of this concern. Persuasive and articulate as he was, President Kennedy managed to convince journalists close to him of the validity of his fears. Their subsequent descriptions of the crisis, as well as those of the Kennedy inner circle, have confirmed in the minds of Americans what has now become one of the most deeply entrenched shibboleths of the Cold War: the belief that caution and hesitation invite challenge, while a reputation for resolve deters it.

Our analysis of adversarial relationships in this study indicates that the expectations that the two sides have of each other may bear little relationship to reality. Challengers, as has been demonstrated, tend to focus on their own needs and do not seriously consider, or often distort if they do, the needs, interests, and capabilities of their adversaries. Defenders, in turn, may interpret the motives or objectives of a challenger in a manner consistent with their expectations whether or not those expectations are in any way warranted. Both sides, moreover, may also prove insensitive to each other's signals for a variety of political, cultural, or other reasons. In such circumstances, recurrent deterrence episodes may not facilitate greater mutual understanding. Experience may actually hinder real learning to the extent that it encourages tautological confirmation of misleading or inappropriate lessons.

This chapter began by describing a pictorial map of international relations as it might be drawn by a deterrence theorist. The most prominent landmarks on this map were "No Trespassing" signs, signifying important commitments, and watchtowers from which statesmen observed each other's commitments. Their principal concerns were assumed to be safeguarding the credibility of their own commitments and discovering vulnerabilities in those of their adversaries.

Our findings indicate that this map, appealing in its metaphorical simplicity, is nevertheless a grossly inaccurate representation of international reality. This may be only partially so from the perspective of the defender; its leaders do evidence varying degrees of concern for the definition, communication, and credibility of their commitments, although few states seem to manifest the same kind of obsession in this regard as does the United States.

For would-be challengers the most prominent features on the

map are probably their own vulnerabilities, foreign and domestic, which induce anxiety for their national security, internal cohesion, or the personal political well-being of the leaders. These vulnerabilities and the pressures they generate may be the most important incentives for foreign policy challenges. When the policy makers of a would-be challenger ascend the watchtowers, they are just as likely as not to be looking inward at their own society, the source of so many of the threats they face.

The inner-directedness of policy makers points to one of the ironies of international life: much of the effort made by defenders to impart the appearance of credibility to their commitments is probably wasted because challengers may not pay much attention to them. Even when they do, they may distort or simply not understand the signals being directed their way. Cultural, contextual, and organizational barriers to interpretation abound, not to speak of motivated biases on the part of policy makers already committed to proceeding with a challenge.

Efforts to deter challenges by making visible preparations to defend against them may also have the reverse effect. They may appear as harbingers of aggressive intentions in the eyes of the target state and prompt it to expand or improve its own military capability. The resulting arms race, search for allies, and competition in risk taking may bring about the very conflict that deterrent policies set out to avoid. Deterrence may also be self-defeating in situations where geographic or strategic considerations permit the security of one adversary only at the expense of the other. Here, efforts by one side to look after its defense may succeed only in increasing the security anxieties of both.

The reality of international relations is less ordered, less comprehensible, more contradictory, and more unpredictable than deterrence theory admits. A more realistic attempt to describe the causes of international conflict and to offer guidance to statesmen for coping with their manifestations must take all these disturbing realities into account. To do so, it must sacrifice the elegance of abstract theory in favor of a more elaborate array of hypotheses based on careful empirical research.

■
NOTES

1. Introduction: Approach and Assumptions

1. Glenn Snyder, *Deterrence and Defense* (Princeton: Princeton University Press, 1961); Robert Jervis, *The Illogic of American Nuclear Strategy* (Ithaca, N.Y.: Cornell University Press, 1984).

2. Good examples are Ernest May, *The World War and American Isolation, 1914–1917* (Cambridge, Mass.: Harvard University Press, 1959); Roger Dingman, *Power in the Pacific* (Chicago: University of Chicago Press, 1976); and Chihiro Hosoya, "Miscalculations in Deterrence Policy: Japanese-U.S. Relations, 1938–41," *Journal of Peace Research* no. 2 (1968): 79–115. A general framework for viewing interactions in this way has been developed by Ole Holsti, Robert North, and Richard Brody, "Perception and Action in the 1914 Case," in *Quantitative International Politics,* ed. J. David Singer (New York: Free Press, 1968), 123–58.

3. Alexander George and Richard Smoke, *Deterrence in American Foreign Policy: Theory and Practice* (New York: Columbia University Press, 1974).

4. Richard Ned Lebow, *Between Peace and War: The Nature of International Crisis* (Baltimore: Johns Hopkins University Press, 1981).

5. For further discussion of this point, see Robert Jervis, "Deterrence Theory Revisited," *World Politics* 31, no. 2 (1979): 303ff; Jervis, *Illogic of American Nuclear Strategy,* 165–68; and Jack L. Snyder, "Perceptions of the Security Dilemma in 1914," below, chap. 7.

6. By contrast, some visual illusions can be traced to the learning patterns produced by the physical environments of modern society. See Marshall Segall, Donald Campbell, and Melville Herskovits, *The Influence of Culture on Visual Perception* (Indianapolis: Bobbs-Merrill, 1966), and the marvelous example in Colin Turnbull, *The Forest People* (New York: Simon & Schuster, 1961), 252ff.

7. M. Brewster Smith, Jerome Bruner, and Robert White, *Opinions and Personality* (New York: Wiley, 1956), frame their analysis around the question, Of what use to a man are his opinions?

8. But in some instances, the failure to see the obstacles that confront a person can be analyzed in terms of Albert Hirschman's ingenious concept of the "hiding hand." If the person had been clear-sighted, he would have seen obstacles so large as to deter him from adopting a policy. But once committed to it, he has no choice but to find ways over, around, or through the obstacles when he finally gets close enough to recognize them. Such paths can often be found, and so the hiding hand has been a necessary part of the policy's success. Unfortunately, little research has developed this important idea, and we therefore do not know much about the conditions under which the hiding hand operates or the circumstances in which it contributes to success or failure. Hirschman's discussion is in his *Development Project Observed* (Washington, D.C.: Brookings Institution, 1967), 9–34. Similar functions can be served by ego defenses that buy time for the person to consider his situation and alternative courses of action without succumbing to fear and desperation.

9. An exception is Ralph K. White, *Fearful Warriors* (New York: Free Press, 1984).

10. See, for example, Philip Green, *Deadly Logic* (Columbus: Ohio State University Press, 1966); Charles Osgood, *An Alternative to War or Surrender* (Urbana: University of Illinois Press, 1962); Ralph K. White, *Nobody Wanted War* (Garden City, N.Y.: Doubleday, 1968); and Jerome Frank, *Sanity and Survival: Psychological Aspects of War and Peace* (New York: Random House, 1967).

11. Robert Ableson and Ira Rosen, "Love Appeals and Anger Appeals in Political Persuasion," in *Political Cognition,* ed. Richard Lau and David Sears (Hillsdale, N.J.: Erlbaum, forthcoming).

12. Michael Ross and Fiore Sicoly, "Egocentric Biases in Availability and Attribution," *Journal of Personality and Social Psychology,* 37, no. 3 (1979): 334. Also see Matthew Erdelyi, "A New Look at the New Look: Perceptual Defense and Vigilance," *Psychological Review* 81, no. 1 (1974): 1–25; Matthew Erdelyi and B. Goldberg, "Let's Not Sweep Repression under the Rug: Towards a Cognitive Psychology of Repression," in *Functional Disorders of Memory,* ed. John Kihlstrom and Frederick Evans (New York: Halsted Press, 1979); William McGuire, "The Yin and the Yang of Progress in Social Psychology: Steven Koan," *Journal of Personality and Social Psychology,* 26, no. 3 (1973): 446–56; and Philip Tetlock and Ariel Levi, "Attribution Bias: On the Inconclusiveness of the Cognition-Motivation Debate," *Journal of Experimental Social Psychology* 18, no. 1 (1982): 68–88.

13. Milton Friedman, "The Methodology of Positive Economics," in Friedman, *Essays in Positive Economics* (Chicago: University of Chicago Press, 1957), 3–43; Kenneth Waltz, *Theory of International Politics* (Reading, Mass.: Addison-Wesley, 1979). For an attempt to refute theorizing based on the assumption of "economic man" by showing that people in fact do not maximize their welfare, see George Katona, "Rational Behavior and Economic Behavior," *Psychological Review,* 60, no. 5 (1953): 307–18. A recent statement of this position with many interesting arguments from psychology is Shlomo Maital, *Minds, Money, and Markets: Psychological Foundations of*

Economic Behavior (New York: Basic Books, 1982.) The most interesting of the critiques of orthodox economics as being too narrow is Richard Nelson and Sidney Winter, *An Evolutionary Theory of Economic Change* (Cambridge, Mass.: Harvard University Press, 1982).

14. Oran Young, *The Politics of Force* (Princeton: Princeton University Press, 1968), 217–20; Jervis, "Deterrence Theory Revisited," 303–5; Richard Ned Lebow, "Windows of Opportunity: Do States Jump through Them?" *International Security* 9 (Summer 1984): 147–86.

15. Lebow, *Between War and Peace;* Lebow, "Conclusions," below, chap. 9.

16. Jack Snyder, "Perceptions of the Security Dilemma in 1914"; Jack Snyder, *The Ideology of the Offensive: Military Decision Making and the Disasters of 1914* (Ithaca, N.Y.: Cornell University Press, 1984).

17. Richard K. Betts, *Surprise Attack* (Washington, D.C.: Brookings Institution, 1982), 16–24; also see George and Smoke, *Deterrence in American Foreign Policy,* for a similar argument.

18. Wallace Theis, *When Governments Collide* (Berkeley and Los Angeles: University of California Press, 1980).

19. John Mueller, "The Search for the Single 'Breaking Point' in Vietnam: The Statistics of a Deadly Quarrel," *International Studies Quarterly,* 24 (December 1980): 497–519.

20. George and Smoke, *Deterrence in American Foreign Policy,* note that both analysts and decision makers have often made the mistake of assuming that deterrence is a substitute for an adequate foreign policy.

21. For discussions of this problem, see Alexander George, David Hall, and William Simons, *The Limits of Coercive Diplomacy* (Boston: Little, Brown, 1971), 100–103; Glenn Snyder and Paul Diesing, *Conflict among Nations* (Princeton: Princeton University Press, 1977), 489–93; Jervis, *Illogic of American Nuclear Strategy,* 165–8; Richard Ned Lebow, "The Deterrence Deadlock: Is There a Way Out?" below, chap. 8; White, *Fearful Warriors;* and Robert Axelrod, *The Evolution of Cooperation* (New York: Basic Books, 1984).

22. Stephen Maxwell, *Rationality in Deterrence,* Adelphi Paper no. 50 (London: Institute of Strategy Studies, 1968); Glenn Snyder, *Deterrence and Defense,* 30–40; Young, *The Politics of Force,* 316, 387, 391; George, Hall, and Simons, *The Limits of Coercive Diplomacy,* 215–28; Jervis, "Deterrence Theory Revisited," 314–22; Snyder and Diesing, *Conflict among Nations,* 496–97; Paul Huth and Bruce Russett, "What Makes Deterrence Work? Cases from 1900 to 1980," *World Politics* 36 (July 1984): 517.

23. Patrick M. Morgan, "Saving Face for the Sake of Deterrence," below, chap. 6.

24. In some cases, statesmen do pay more attention to others' pledges than a logical analysis would lead one to expect. See Robert Jervis, *The Logic of Images in International Relations* (Princeton: Princeton University Press, 1970), 96–102.

25. This was noted by Bernard Brodie, in a letter to the editor, *New York Times,* 13 Nov. 1962. See also the reply by Fred Warner Neal, ibid., 3 Dec. 1962.

26. Even in the relations among firms in cartels, an area that more closely resembles international politics and in which the relevant theories are quite weak, it is rare that one or two events would be of overriding importance.

2. Perceiving and Coping with Threat

1. For good studies see Raymond Cohen, "Threat Perceptions in International Crisis," *Political Science Quarterly* 93 (Spring 1978): 93–107; Cohen, *Threat Perception in International Crisis* (Madison: University of Wisconsin Press, 1979); and Klaus Knorr, "Threat Perception," in *Historical Dimensions of National Security Problems*, ed. Knorr (Lawrence: University Press of Kansas, 1976). A marvelous brief case study is George Kennan, *The Decline of Bismark's European Order* (Princeton: Princeton University Press, 1979). 11–21.

2. Matthew Evangelista, "Stalin's Post-War Army Reappraised," *International Security*, 7 (Winter 1982–83): 110–38.

3. I know of only one good study in this area: Anthony D'Amato, "Psychological Constructs in Foreign Policy Prediction," *Journal of Conflict Resolution* 11, no. 3 (1967): 294–311. It does seem apparent, however, that decision makers generally neglect the importance of domestic and bureaucratic politics within the other side. See Robert Jervis, *Perception and Misperception in International Politics* (Princeton: Princeton University Press, 1976), 319–42.

4. The discussion here presents a somewhat idiosyncratic interpretation of attribution theory. The main lines of the theory have been applied to international relations in Jervis, *Perception and Misperception*. The recent psychological literature in this area is summarized in Harold Kelley and John Michela, "Attribution Theory and Research," *Annual Review of Psychology* 31 (1980): 457–501. A good critical discussion of attribution theory is Mansur Lalljee and Robert Abelson, "The Organization of Explanations," in *Attribution Theory: Social Function Extensions*, ed. M. Hewstone (Oxford: Basil Blackwell, 1983).

5. Cohen, *Threat Perception in International Crisis*. See also Richard Ned Lebow, *Between Peace and War: The Nature of International Crisis* (Baltimore: Johns Hopkins University Press, 1981), 316.

6. Eyre Crowe, "Memorandum on the Present State of British Relations with France and Germany," in *British Documents on the Origins of the War, 1898–1914*, 11 vols., ed. G.P. Gooch and Harold Temperly (London: His Majesty's Stationery Office, 1926–1932), 3: 397–431.

7. Charles Harding, in ibid., 4:206.

8. Quoted in Peter Padfield, *The Great Naval Race: The Anglo-German Naval Rivalry: 1900–1914* (New York: McKay, 1974).

9. John Gaddis, *The United States and the Origins of the Cold War* (New York: Columbia University Press, 1972), 175.

10. Bernard Bailyn, *The Ideological Origins of the American Revolution* (Cambridge, Mass.: Harvard University Press, 1967), 101.

11. Quoted in Gaddis, *The United States and the Origins of the Cold War*, 329.

12. Harry S. Truman, *Memoirs* (Garden City, N.Y.: Doubleday, 1955), vol. 1, *Year of Decisions*, 412.

13. For a further definition and discussion, see Jervis, "Introduction: Approach and Assumptions," above, chap. 1.

14. Jervis, *Perception and Misperception*, 143–202; Jervis, "The Theory-Driven Nature of Cognition," manuscript.

15. See, for example, Robert Putnam, *Beliefs of Politicians* (New Haven: Yale University Press, 1973).

16. Henry Kissinger, *Years of Upheaval* (Boston: Little, Brown, 1982), 488.

17. Janice Gross Stein, "Calculation, Miscalculation, and Conventional Deterrence I: The View from Cairo," below, chap. 3.

18. Kissinger, *Years of Upheaval*, 460, 465.

19. Janice Gross Stein, "Calculation, Miscalculation, and Conventional Deterrence II: The View from Jerusalem," below, chap. 4. It should be noted that this predisposition was both partly derived from and partly contradicted by the belief that the Arabs were too weak to launch an unprovoked attack.

20. Stein, "Calculation, Miscalculation, and Conventional Deterrence II."

21. Nathan Leites's original study, *A Study of Bolshevism* (Glencoe, Ill.: Free Press 1953), grounded the analysis of the operational code in a psychoanalytical approach. But later work has tended to separate these two approaches. For a good critique of the operational code literature see Martha Cottam, "Cognitive Limitations and Foreign Policy Decision-making" (Ph.D. diss., University of California, Los Angeles, 1983), 12–16.

22. Jervis, *Perception and Misperception*, 217–71.

23. Stein, "Calculation, Miscalculation, and Conventional Deterrence II."

24. Amos Tversky and Daniel Kahneman, "Availability: A Heuristic for Judging Frequency and Probability," *Cognitive Psychology*, 5, no. 2 (1973): 207–32; Baruch Fischhoff, Paul Slovic, and Sarah Lichtenstein, "Knowing with Certainty the Appropriateness of Extreme Confidence," *Journal of Experimental Psychology: Human Perception and Performance* 3, no. 4, (1977): 562–63.

25. F. H. Hinsley, E. E. Thomas, C. F. Ransom, and R. C. Knight, *British Intelligence in the Second World War*, 4 vols. (New York: Cambridge University Press, 1979), 1:299.

26. Daniel Kahneman and Amos Tversky, "On the Psychology of Prediction," *Psychological Review* 80, no. 4 (1973): 241.

27. The question of when base rate data are underutilized is explored in Icek Ajzen, "Intuitive Theories of Events and the Effects of Base Rate Data on Prediction," *Journal of Personality and Social Psychology* 35, no. 5 (1977): 303–14; Amost Tversky and Daniel Kahneman, "Causal Schematic in Judgments under Uncertainty," in *Progress in Social Psychology*, ed. Martin Fishbein (Hillsdale, N.J.: Erlbaum, 1977); and Robert Jervis, "The Repre-

sentativeness Heuristic in Foreign Policy Judgments," *Political Psychology*, forthcoming.

28. Of course, a crucial question is what an objective definition of similarity would be and how observers make judgments of similarity. See Amos Tversky, "Features of Similarity," *Psychological Review* 84, no. 4 (1977): 327–52 and Maya Bar-Hillel, "What Features Make Samples Seem Representative?" *Journal of Experimental Psychology: Human Perception and Performance* 6, no. 3 (1980): 578–89, 46.

29. Lebow, *Between Peace and War;* Jack Snyder, *The Ideology of the Offensive: Military Decision Making and the Disasters of 1914* (Ithaca, N.Y.: Cornell University Press, 1984). Much of the theoretical underpinning for this argument comes from Irving Janis and Leon Mann, *Decision Making: A Psychological Analysis of Conflict, Choice, and Commitment* (New York: Free Press, 1977).

30. Paul Schroeder, *Austria, Great Britain, and the Crimean War* (Ithaca, N.Y.: Cornell University Press, 1972).

31. Ernest May, *The Making of the Monroe Doctrine* (Cambridge, Mass.: Harvard University Press, Belknap Press, 1975).

32. Richard Cottam, *Foreign Policy Motivation* (Pittsburgh: University of Pittsburgh Press, 1977).

33. Robert Jervis, "Deterrence and Perception," *International Security* 7 (Winter 1982–83): 3–30.

34. The alarming implications of this bias for deterrence are explored by Lebow in the conclusion, below.

35. See Robert Scalapino, Introduction, to *The Fateful Choice: Japan's Advance into Southeast Asia, 1939–1941*, ed. James Morley (New York: Columbia University Press, 1980), 118–23; and Gordon Prange, *At Dawn We Slept* (New York: McGraw-Hill, 1981), 16, 21. Alternative explanations for these perceptions are hard to rule out. First, unmotivated biases may have played a role. Second, Sagan argues that it was not so unreasonable to believe that the United States would fight a limited war and that it was the attack on Pearl Harbor, in addition to the conquest of the Philippines, that ensured that the conflict would be fought to the bitter end. This decision, Sagan argues, was made by the navy, not by the top decision makers who had called for military action. (Scott Sagan, "The Failure of Deterrence: Pearl Harbor and Nuclear Strategy" [Ph.D. diss., Harvard University, 1982], 136–8, 281–86, 310–12). It should also be noted that if the Japanese indeed preferred an all-out war to meeting U.S. terms, then cognitive and bureaucratic distortions neither determined Japanese behavior nor need be considered to explain it.

36. Jack Snyder, *Ideology of the Offensive.*

37. Stein, "Calculation, Miscalculation, and Conventional Deterrence I." See also Yaacov Bar-Siman-Tov, *The Israeli-Egyptian War of Attrition, 1969–1970* (New York: Columbia University Press, 1980).

38. Ernest May, *Imperial Democracy* (New York: Harcourt, Brace, 1961), 161.

39. For a different view see Sagan, "The Failure of Deterrence," 136–40.

40. Glenn Snyder and Paul Diesing, *Conflict among Nations* (Princeton: Princeton University Press, 1977), 325–32.

41. Jervis, *Perception and Misperception,* 128–43.

42. See Jack Snyder, "Rationality at the Brink," *World Politics* 30 (April 1978): 345–65. To some extent, the pattern can be accounted for by the images of the adversary. The hawks believe that the other side is very hostile; the doves think that the two sides are caught in a spiral of intentions and misperceptions. But this cannot explain why the hawks are more confident than the doves that the adversary will retreat if pressed hard or why the doves downgrade the importance of the immediate issue.

43. Lebow, *Between Peace and War.*

44. Jack Snyder, "Perceptions of the Security Dilemma in 1914," below, chap. 7.

3. Calculation, Miscalculation, and Conventional Deterrence I: The View from Cairo

1. For criticism of the ahistorical and apolitical character of formal prescriptive theory, see Alexander George and Richard Smoke, *Deterrence in American Foreign Policy: Theory and Practice* (New York: Columbia University Press, 1974), and Stephen Maxwell, *Rationality in Deterrence,* Adelphi Paper no. 50 (London: Institute for Strategic Studies, 1968). For a discussion of the competing expectations of the rationality postulate and psychological explanations, see above, chap. 1, by Robert Jervis.

2. Scholars have been reluctant to identify cases of successful deterrence because they fear "mistaken identity." First, an adversary may have no intention of using force, and consequently deterrence is irrelevant rather than successful when force is not used. Because an action does not occur, a spurious inference of success may be drawn. Indeed, a strong philosophical tradition would argue that a nonevent cannot be demonstrated at all, and it is very much this line of reasoning that has led most scholars to abjure the study of successful deterrent strategies. Second, it is possible that a challenger who has considered the use of force chooses to refrain from action not in anticipation of the threatened retaliation but rather for unrelated ideological, diplomatic, or domestic reasons. Here, too, deterrence would be irrelevant rather than successful. Access to evidence of leaders' calculations, however, should largely alleviate these problems. A search of the evidence should indicate whether leaders actively considered an option to use force and whether they were deterred by anticipation of military punishment or denial by the defender. It is not inherently more difficult to assess the factors in a decision not to use force than to explain a choice of military action, yet scholars have studied the failure but not the success of deterrence. And if explanations of the failure of deterrence are to be validated, it can be done only through assessment of the impact of critical factors both when deterrence fails and when it succeeds.

3. Senior military officers in Egypt have published detailed accounts of specific decisions, and civilian leaders and advisers have written memoirs and narrative histories. See in particular Anwar el-Sadat, *In Search of Identity* (New York: Harper & Row, 1977); Mohamed Heikal (editor of *Al-Ahram*), *Nasser, The Cairo Documents* (London: New English Library, 1972); Heikal, *The Road to Ramadan* (New York: Quadrangle Books, 1975); Heikal, *The Sphinx and the Commissar: The Rise and Fall of Soviet Influence in the Middle East* (New York: Harper & Row, 1978); and Hassan el-Badri, Taha el-Magdoub, and Mohammed Dia el-Din Zhody, *The Ramadan War* (Dunn Loring, Va.: T. N. Dupuy Associates, 1978). A particularly scathing attack on the policies of President Sadat, one that challenges Sadat's account of the period preceding the October War in many crucial respects, is Saad el-Shazli, *The Crossing of the Suez* (San Francisco: American Mideast Research, 1980).

4. See Baruch Fischhoff and R. Beyth, "I Knew It Would Happen: Remembered Probabilities of Once-Future Things," *Journal of Organizational Behavior and Human Performance* 13, no. 4 (1975): 1–16.

5. See Stephen Maxwell, *Rationality in Deterrence,* and Robert Jervis, "Deterrence Theory Revisited," *World Politics* 31, no. 2 (1979): 289–324.

6. One exception is Daniel Ellsberg's "Crude Analysis of Strategic Choices," *American Economic Review* 51 (1961): 472–78.

7. George and Smoke, *Deterrence in American Foreign Policy,* 526.

8. Glenn Snyder and Paul Diesing, *Conflict among Nations* (Princeton: Princeton University Press, 1977), 187–88; Richard Ned Lebow, "Miscalculation in the South Atlantic: The Origins of the Falklands War," below, chap. 5.

9. Mohamed Heikal, *Al-Ahram,* 7 Mar. 1969.

10. John Mearsheimer, *The Theory and Practice of Conventional Deterrence* (Ithaca, N.Y.: Cornell University Press, 1983), makes this point.

11. See el-Badri, el-Magdoub, and Zhody, *Ramadan War,* and Ahmed Ismail Ali, *Al-Hawadess,* 16 Aug. 1974.

12. Richard Ned Lebow, *Between Peace and War: The Nature of International Crisis* (Baltimore: Johns Hopkins University Press, 1981).

13. Mohamed Heikal, "Soviet Aims and Egypt," *Al-Ahram,* 30 June 1972, reprinted in *Survival,* Sept.-Oct. 1972, 231–35.

14. George Quester, *Offense and Defense in the International System* (New York: Wiley, 1977), 3,7; Robert Art, "To What Ends Military Power?" *International Security* 4, no. 4 (1980): 3–35. For a critical analysis of the ambiguities inherent in the concept of the offensive-defensive balance, see Jack S. Levy, "The Offensive-Defensive Balance of Military Technology: A Theoretical and Historical Analysis," *International Studies Quarterly* 28, no. 2 (June 1984): 219–38.

15. Mearsheimer, *Conventional Deterrence;* George and Smoke, *Deterrence in American Foreign Policy.*

16. See Amos Tversky and Daniel Kahneman, "Judgment under Uncertainty: Heuristics and Biases," *Science,* 27 Sept. 1974, 1124–31, and Tversky and Kahneman, "Availability: A Heuristic for Judging Frequency and Probability," *Cognitive Psychology* 5, no. 1 (1973): 207–32.

17. Heikal, *Al-Ahram*, 7 Mar. 1969; Gamel Abdul Nasser, speech to Arab Socialist Union, 27 Mar. 1969, *Daily Report*, 29 Mar. 1969.

18. Heikal, *Al-Ahram*, 7 Mar. 1969.

19. El-Sadat, *In Search of Identity*, 219–21.

20. Ibid., 234–37; el-Shazli, *Crossing of the Suez*, 173–75.

21. See the *Agranat Report, A Partial Report by the Commission of Inquiry to the Government of Israel* (Jerusalem: Government Press Office, Press Bulletin, 2 Apr. 1974).

22. George and Smoke, *Deterrence in American Foreign Policy*, 531.

23. Nasser, speech, 27 March 1969.

24. Anwar el-Sadat, speech to the People's Assembly, Cairo, 4 Feb. 1971, *In Search of Identity*, 279–80.

25. See Heikal, *Road to Ramadan*, 118–33.

26. Anwar el-Sadat, speech to the Arab Socialist Union, Cairo, 4 Dec. 1972, Radio Cairo.

27. Henry Kissinger, *The White House Years* (Boston: Little, Brown, 1979), 1293; el-Sadat, *In Search of Identity*, 232–33.

28. Anwar el-Sadat, May Day speech, Cairo, 1 May 1973, Middle East News Agency, 3 May 1973.

29. It is beyond the scope of this paper to consider Egypt's—and Israel's—definition of the bargaining range in detail. In 1971, however, negotiations for an interim agreement in the canal zone failed not because of miscalculation by the two sides but rather because of an unwillingness to make the incremental concessions necessary to reach agreement. Nineteen seventy-one was a year of missed opportunities, opportunities forgone not because each side misread the intentions of the other but because each side was unwilling to bear the costs of conciliation. In the light of the war that followed, Egypt's and Israel's evaluations seem unreasonable, but this is an assessment that draws on information leaders themselves did not have. Given the minimum thresholds of both sides in 1971, agreement was impossible. These thresholds were not substantially modified during the course of the negotiations.

30. A criterion of efficiency is not the only possible standard of rationality that can be used to evaluate decisions. There is little agreement on appropriate standards of evaluation: some examine the openness and complexity of the decision-making process while others look to the logical quality of the conceptual schema that organizes subsequent decisional tasks. Yet, no matter how problematic the enterprise, evaluation of the rationality of leaders is essential, since all formal theories of deterrence assume rational choice by the parties to the relationship. For an extended discussion of the multiple standards of rationality, see Janice Gross Stein and Raymond Tanter, *Rational Decision Making: Israel's Security Choices, 1967* (Columbus: Ohio State University Press, 1980), 3–22, and Robert Jervis, *Perception and Misperception in International Politics* (Princeton: Princeton University Press, 1976), 117–202. Cognizant of a cumulative body of evidence documenting motivated and unmotivated biases in processes of choice, some analysts of deterrence posit a concept of rationality that differs substantially from that

of efficiency. Schelling and Morgan, for example, both suggest that rationality is acknowledgment of uncertainty, an acknowledgment that translates into prudent and cautious behavior. A rational leader, recognizing uncertainty, abjures precise calculation of the inherently unknowable, incalculable, and uncontrollable and, in so doing, avoids the fallacy of misplaced concreteness. Indeed, in *Deterrence in American Foreign Policy* George and Smoke argue that rational leaders may consider the risks of military action incalculable but expect to monitor and control these risks after action has been initiated. Acknowledgment of uncertainty is a considerably less demanding criterion for rational decision making but, simultaneously, a far less robust basis for an explanation of the outcome of deterrence. Most "rational" leaders recognize uncertainties in an ambiguous world but choose at times to act and at other times to refrain from challenge. We need to know why. An explanation of conventional deterrence must do more than specify the recognition of uncertainty; it must establish the threshold probabilities that distinguish successful deterrence from failure. How uncertain must leaders be to renounce the use of military force in pursuit of their interests? See Thomas Schelling, *The Strategy of Conflict* (Cambridge, Mass.: Harvard University Press, 1960), and Patrick M. Morgan, *Deterrence: A Conceptual Analysis* (Beverly Hills: Sage Library of Social Science, 1977). Empirical investigation of processes of national security decision making provide some convergent and some conflicting evidence on the impact of uncertainty. George and Smoke find that recognition that the consequences of the use of force are incalculable and/or uncontrollable is a sufficient condition of the success of deterrence. Snyder and Diesing suggest, however, that leaders tend to "gamble" when they are uncertain. Although the impact of gambling on deterrence is not made explicit, the implication is that gambling promotes a choice of military action. See George and Smoke, *Deterrence in American Foreign Policy*, 527–30, and Snyder and Diesing, *Conflict among Nations*, 502–3.

31. Richard Rosecrance, "Deterrence and Vulnerability in the Pre-Nuclear Era," *Adelphi Paper* no. 160 (London: Institute for Strategic Studies, 1980) 14-30, 25.

32. See, for example, Snyder and Diesing, *Conflict among Nations*, and Stein and Tanter, *Rational Decision Making*, for evidence of partial approximation to rational norms. For countervailing evidence, see Jervis, *Perception and Misperception;* Irving Janis and Leon Mann, *Decision Making: A Psychological Analysis of Conflict, Choice, and Commitment* (New York: Free Press, 1977); John Steinbruner, *The Cybernetic Theory of Decision* (Princeton: Princeton University Press, 1974); and George and Smoke, *Deterrence in American Foreign Policy*.

33. See, for example, Paul Slovic and Sarah Lichtenstein, "Relative Importance of Probabilities and Payoffs in Risk Taking," *Journal of Experimental Psychology*, Monograph 78, 3 (1968), 1:1–18, and Daniel Kahneman and Amos Tversky, "On the Psychology of Prediction," *Psychological Review* 80, no. 4 (1973): 237–51.

34. Problems of evidence are particularly acute when one tries to assess decision making by political and military leaders. When they make their choices they do not describe their procedures in any detail, and recollection after the fact is notoriously invalid. In Egypt, moreover, good documentary evidence of military and civilian deliberations is thin. I draw on official statements, interviews, and autobiographies, but the assessment is tentative at best.

35. Heikal, *Al-Ahram*, 7 Mar. 1969; Gamel Abdul Nasser, speech, 27 Mar. 1969.

36. El-Sadat, *In Search of Identity*, 218–27; Mohamed Heikal, editorial, *Al-Ahram*, 17 Dec. 1971.

37. El-Sadat, *In Search of Identity*, 237.

38. Ibid.

39. El-Badri, el-Magdoub, and Zhody, *Ramadan War*, 15.

40. El-Sadat, speech, Cairo, 1 May 1973.

41. Anwar el-Sadat, interview, *Ahbar al Yom*, 3 Aug. 1974; el-Sadat speech, Cairo, Middle East News Agency, 22 Sept. 1974; el-Sadat, interview, Middle East News Agency, 8 Oct. 1974.

42. Anwar el-Sadat, *In Search of Identity*, 249.

43. Ibid, 214.

44. Lebow's comparative investigation of the calculations of challengers supports this conclusion. He, too, finds that leaders acted frequently to avoid the perceived consequences of inaction. They often defined loss in terms of domestic political costs as well as strategic costs abroad and were far more sensitive to the certainty and magnitude of these costs than they were to the losses that might arise from action. See Lebow, *Between Peace and War*.

45. George and Smoke are an exception. In their study they emphasized the need to shift the focus to the initiator and to develop explanatory propositions about the behavior of the challenger as part of an explanatory theory of deterrence outcomes.

4. Calculation, Miscalculation, and Conventional Deterrence II: The View from Jerusalem

1. See Alexander George and Richard Smoke, *Deterrence in American Foreign Policy: Theory and Practice* (New York: Columbia University Press, 1974); Richard Ned Lebow, *Between Peace and War: The Nature of International Crisis* (Baltimore: Johns Hopkins University Press, 1981); and Janice Gross Stein and Raymond Tanter, *Rational Decision Making: Israel's Security Choices, 1967*, (Columbus: Ohio State University Press, 1980).

2. See George and Smoke, *Deterrence in American Foreign Policy;* Robert Jervis, "Deterrence Theory Revisited," *World Politics* 31, no. 2 (1979): 289–324; and Charles Lockhart, "Flexibility and Commitment in International Conflicts," *International Studies Quarterly* 22, no. 4 (1978): 545–58.

3. See Robert Jervis, "Cooperation under the Security Dilemma," *World Politics* 30, no. 2 (1978): 167–214, and Jack L. Snyder, "Perceptions of the Security Dilemma in 1914," below, chap. 7, which examines the impact of four different kinds of dilemmas.

4. See Robert Jervis, "Deterrence, the Spiral Model, and Intentions of the Adversary," in Jervis, *Perception and Misperception in International Politics* (Princeton: Princeton University Press, 1976), 58–113, for a discussion of the competing assumptions of deterrence and the spiral model.

5. It is conceivable as well that the Kaiser especially engaged in wishful thinking and saw a short war as a solution to many of Germany's problems. This historical interpretation is consistent with motivated rather than unmotivated bias.

6. The analogue is to basic statistical reasoning, where the probability of a Type I error is inversely related to the probability of a Type II error.

7. See the analysis by Ezer Weizmann, a former commander of the Israel Air Force and a member of the cabinet during the War of Attrition, in which he argues that Israel lost the war. Weizmann, *On Eagles' Wings* (Jerusalem: Steimatzky's Agency, 1976).

8. See Moshe Dayan, "Between War and Peace," *Jerusalem Post,* 10 Aug. 1973.

9. See Stein, "Calculation, Miscalculation, and Conventional Deterrence I: The View from Cairo," above, chap. 3. See also Ahmed Ismail Ali, *Al-Hawadess,* 16 Aug. 1974.

10. See *Agranat Report, A Partial Report by the Commission of Inquiry to the Government of Israel* (Jerusalem: Government Press Office, Press Bulletin, 2 Apr. 1974), English translation, p. 7. This is the authoritative report of an independent commission of inquiry appointed by the government to investigate the causes of the intelligence failure.

11. General Ze'ira, in a lecture in September 1973, reportedly expected that by 1975 Arab armies would have the capability to launch an effective attack. See Zeev Schiff, *October Earthquake, Yom Kippur 1973* (Tel Aviv: University Publishing, 1974).

12. Elihu Ze'ira, interview, "All the Inefficiencies of any Intelligence Service," *Armed Forces Journal International* 3, no. 2 (1973): 47.

13. Abba Eban, press conference, 26 Apr. 1973 (Jerusalem: Government Press Office, Press Bulletin).

14. Moshe Dayan, *Mapa Hadasha, Yehasim Aherim* (A new map, new relations) (Tel Aviv: Shikmona, 1969), based on an address to students, Haifa, 3 Mar. 1968. There is considerable debate in the intelligence community about the relative advantages of weighting strategic assumptions vs. tactical indications.

15. Anwar el-Sadat, speech to Egyptian soldiers, 21 Nov. 1971, BBC Summary of World Broadcasts/Middle East/3845/A 6–7, 22 Nov. 1971.

16. Hanoch Bartov, *Dado—Arbaim Ve'Shmoneh Shanim V'Esraim Yom* (Dado—48 years and 20 days), 2 vols. (Tel Aviv: Ma'ariv Book Guild, 1978), 1:192. Bartov's prize-winning biography of General David Elazar draws extensively on official documentation and heretofore inaccessible private

papers of the chief of staff to reconstruct the critical deliberations among intelligence officers and military leaders.

17. Ibid., 190.

18. Anwar el-Sadat, interview with Arnaud de Borchgrave, *Newsweek*, 9 Apr. 1973. Sadat told de Borchgrave, "Everything in this country is now being mobilized in earnest for the resumption of battle—which is now inevitable . . . the Russians are providing us now with everything that is possible for them to supply and I am now quite satisfied." On 24 Mar. 1973, Abdal Quddus, editor of *Ahbar al-Yom*, reported that Egypt was "importing arms from the Soviet Union . . . and is no longer concerned with the types of weapons" (Foreign Broadcast Information Service, Middle East, 26 Mar. 1973).

19. See Moshe Dayan, *The Story of My Life* (London: Weidenfeld & Nicolson, 1976), 381, and Bartov, *Dado*, 1:190. Bartov reports the expected date of attack as 15 May.

20. Bartov, *Dado*, 1:192.

21. Ibid., 1:217–18.

22. Ibid., 1:197–98.

23. Ibid., 1:194–95.

24. Ibid., 1:224, 226; member of military intelligence interview with the author, Sept. 1975. The official recalls that only 2 percent of reserve forces were mobilized.

25. Ben-Zvi suggests, for example, that analysts should give priority to tactical indicators rather than strategic assumptions. This is a somewhat oversimplified suggestion, however, since tactical indicators may be deliberately designed to deceive or may be transient. In certain strategic environments, moreover, the slower revision that is characteristic of heavier weighting of strategic assumptions may be more appropriate. See Avi Ben-Zvi, "Hindsight and Foresight: A Conceptual Framework for the Analysis of Surprise Attacks," *World Politics* 28 (April 1976): 381–95.

26. A year after the Six Day War, military intelligence presented to Israel's cabinet an evaluation that suggested that President Nasser had not intended to attack in 1967. Rather, the momentum of troop movements, mobilization, and countermobilization led Egypt's president to provoke a war that neither Israel nor Egypt had intended. Senior officer of military intelligence, interview with the author, Sept. 1975. President Sadat makes a similar argument in his autobiography when he suggests that President Nasser wished initially to deter, but "the situation soon got out of hand." See Anwar el-Sadat, *In Search of Identity* (New York: Harper & Row, 1977), 172. Gen. Bar-Lev offered a different interpretation when he argued that President Nasser did not miscalculate but deliberately provoked a first strike by Israel in 1967. See Chaim Bar-Lev, "Ken Yazanu Le-Milchama" (Thus we went to war), *Ot*, 31 May 1973.

27. See Dayan, *Story of My Life*, 381.

28. Gen. (Res.) Yariv, Ze'ira's predecessor as director of military intelligence, explained, "Israel's preparations were based on the assumption that the 300 tanks located in the forward zone could, together with the air force,

contain the Egyptian thrust long enough to permit the mobilization and deployment of the reserve division." See Aharon Yariv, "The Israeli Army and the War of Atonement," *Moment* 1, no. 4 (1975): 73–75.

29. The chief of staff, David Elazar, listed four operational plans for the defense of the north and three for the south. In the north, operations Current Defense, Ocean Sand, Chalk, and Rock dealt with different contingencies, while in the south the defensive situations considered were Current Defense, Dovecote, and Rock. Although plans existed for several contingencies, they all treated warning and no warning as dichotomous situations. See Bartov, *Dado*, 2:9–47.

30. In a press conference held immediately after the Egyptian and Syrian attack, Dayan explained: "Now and again, they reinforce their forces along the line. . . . If we want to maintain normal life in this country we have to take the risk of not holding the line, especially the Egyptian line, with many forces, because when we say forces that means the young people of Israel, and if we do that with a great number for many years . . . then we cannot have normal life in this country." See Moshe Dayan, press conference, 6 Oct. 1973 (Jerusalem: Government Press Office, Press Bulletin), English translation. Gen. Bar-Lev made a similar point: "The operational concepts of the I.D.F. [include] defense and strategic depth as surrogates for permanent mobilization." See Chaim Bar-Lev, *Likchei Hamilchamah: Torat Hatactica Amda Bamivchan* (The lessons of war: The tactical doctrine withstood the test), *Ma'ariv*, 9 Nov. 1973.

31. Bartov, *Dado*, 1:243.

32. Dayan, *Story of My Life*, 395.

33. *Agranat Report*, 9.

34. Cited by Shlomo Nakdimon, *Yediot Aharonot*, 12 July 1974.

35. *Agranat Report*, 19.

36. One possible explanation of a Soviet-Syrian rift was the failure of the Soviet Union to come to the assistance of Syria during the 13 Sept. air battle with Israel, but intelligence discounted this explanation since the air battle took place outside the range of SAM missiles then in place (Member of military intelligence, interview with the author, Sept. 1975). However, no prominent Soviet leader had attended a ceremony inaugurating the Euphrates Dam, Moscow's principal development project in Syria. Unlike the situation in 1972, however, there had been no slowdown of Soviet arms shipments nor reduction of effort in the strengthening of Syria's air defense system.

37. Damascus Radio had charged that Israel was about to initiate a major military action. The Syrian newspaper *Al-Thawra* also alleged that Israel was preparing for military adventure and insisted that a comparison of the declarations of Israel's leaders issued in early October and before the June 1967 war demonstrated the similarity of Israel's tactics in preparing for aggression. See *Al-Thawra*, 4 Oct. 1973.

38. The error can best be explained by psychological rather than logical processes. Cognitive psychologists suggest that, when people are confronted with evidence inconsistent with their beliefs, they at first seek to

deny or downgrade the quality of the evidence. When they can no longer do so, they acknowledge their inability to explain the inconsistency but still do not change their beliefs.

39. *Agranat Report*, 7. Military intelligence, it appears, gave less weight to evidence from agents in the field than to official documents obtained secretly. This may have been because the agent who was expected to deliver confirmatory intelligence on Egyptian intent had been wrong in forecasting an attack in Dec. 1972 and in May 1973.

40. Shlomo Nakdimon, *Yediot Aharonot*, 19 July 1974.

41. Ibid.

42. Prime Minister Meir stated explicitly that an option of mobilization received no consideration that morning: "I have gone into considerable detail to explain with whom I had meetings and what evaluations of Intelligence I heard and read regarding the possibility of an outbreak of war. These included evaluations given to me by the Minister of Defense, the Chief-of-Staff, a former Chief-of-Staff, the head of Military Intelligence, and the head of Military Intelligence Research. Neither in this group—nor at a later meeting which included the nine Cabinet ministers who were in Tel Aviv on that Friday—did anyone suggest that the reserves be called up." See Golda Meir, letter to the editor, *Jerusalem Post Weekly*, 30 Sept. 1975.

43. David Elazar, "Memorandum to the Prime Minister on the Reports of the Agranat Committee on the Yom Kippur War," published by Shlomo Nakdimon, *Yediot Aharonot*, 14 Sept. 1975.

44. Ibid.

45. Cited by Shlomo Nakdimon, *Yediot Aharonot*, 26 July 1974. In an interview with the author, (Tel Aviv, Mar. 1974) Elazar elaborated on the dynamic of escalation. "If the Syrians retaliate, and we respond even more strongly, the Egyptians might then open fire."

46. *Agranat Report*, 20.

47. For a report of the content of the warning, see Dayan, *Story of My Life*, 375. Such a conditional warning is not unprecedented or inappropriate. If the defender anticipates the challenge in time and responds effectively, the challenger can cancel the planned offensive. The Japanese strike force en route to Pearl Harbor, for example, was under orders to reverse course should it become apparent that the United States had anticipated the attack. More generally, "hedging" or even division among an adversary's leaders, makes estimation extraordinarily difficult for a defender.

48. Bar-Lev, for example, argued that 1800 hours was an incomprehensible starting time for an attack; it would not provide sufficient daylight hours. The commander of the air force, Binyamin Peled, also found it illogical that Egypt and Syria would attack without allowing time for at least two initial air strikes, which would require a few hours of daylight. See Chaim Herzog, *The War of Atonement* (Jerusalem: Steimatzky's Agency, 1975), 54, 255.

49. Elazar said: "Saturday, at 0400 hours, the telephone rang and told me that Egypt and Syria will attack at 1800 hours. This had happened several times. We were given a precise hour of attack, but the attack did not

occur" (Elazar interview, Mar. 1974). The prime minister was even more explicit. "No one in this country realizes how many times during the past year we received information from the same source that war would break out on this or that day, without war breaking out." See Golda Meir, interview, *Jerusalem Post Weekly,* 11 Dec. 1973. Dayan confirmed the receipt of several such warnings in the past. "We had received similar messages in the past, and later, when no attack followed, came the explanation that President Sadat had changed his mind at the last moment." See Dayan, *Story of My Life,* 375. Though military intelligence did not know it, the "reliable source" was in fact correct: President Sadat had changed his mind at the last moment at least once before.

50. *Agranat Report,* 7. However, a few pages later, the commission concluded, "Early on Saturday morning, the further information was received which raised the opening of total war by the enemy to a degree of near-certainty." Ibid. 10.

51. See Golda Meir, *My Life* (Jerusalem: Steimatzky's Agency, 1976), 358; for Dayan, see Shlomo Nakdimon, *Yediot Aharonot,* 26 July 1974.

52. *Agranat Report,* 24.

53. Meir, *My Life,* 358.

54. Dayan, *Story of My Life,* 377–78.

55. See my "Calculation, Miscalculation, and Conventional Deterrence I," above, chap. 3 for evidence of Egyptian calculations.

56. See Robert Jervis "Introduction: Approach and Assumptions," above, chap. 1 for a discussion of the impact of the availability heuristic on information processing.

57. Lebow, *Between Peace and War;* Lebow, "The Deterrence Deadlock? Is There a Way Out?" below, chap. 8. See also Jack S. Levy, "Misperception and the Causes of War: Theoretical Linkages and Analytical Problems," *World Politics* 36, no. 1 (1983): 76–99.

58. See Stein and Tanter, *Rational Decision-Making,* 326–29.

59. Schelling defines *autonomous risk* as the likelihood that the parties will lose control of events. This may happen because of the logic of military planning and technology, cessation of rational calculation due to stress, or as a consequence of a diplomatic process of commitment that is itself unpredictable. See Thomas Schelling, *Arms and Influence* (New Haven: Yale University Press, 1966).

60. Mohamed Heikal, *The Road to Ramadan* (New York: Quadrangle Books, 1975), 17; official in the Office of the President of Egypt, interview with the author, Cairo, May 1980.

61. Whaley finds that 79 percent of the cases of successful deception exploited the preconceptions of the defender. See Barton Whaley, *Stratagem, Deception, and Surprise in War* (Cambridge, Mass.: MIT Center for International Studies, 1969).

62. Richard K. Betts, *Surprise Attack* (Washington, D.C.: Brookings Institution, 1982).

63. Richards C. Heuer, Jr., "Improving Intelligence Analysis: Some Insights on Data, Concepts, and Management in the Intelligence Community," *Bureaucrat* 8, no. 4 (1979–80), 1–11.

64. See Lebow, *Between Peace and War,* and Glenn Snyder and Paul Diesing, *Conflict among Nations* (Princeton: Princeton University Press, 1977), 254–56. See also Alexander George, David K. Hall, and William E. Simons, *The Limits of Coercive Diplomacy* (Boston: Little, Brown, 1971); Robert Jervis, "Deterrence Theory Revisited"; and Ralph K. White, *Fearful Warriors* (New York: Free Press, 1984).

65. Snyder and Diesing, *Conflict among Nations,* 187–88.

66. See Stein, "The Alchemy of Peacemaking: The Prerequisites and Co-requisites of Progress in the Arab-Israeli Conflict," *International Journal* 38, no. 4 (1983), 531–55.

5. Miscalculation in the South Atlantic: The Origins of the Falklands War

1. This analysis was written in July 1982. The subsequent evidence that has come to light, most notably in connection with the Franks Report, has been entirely consistent with my thesis. The Franks Report, the official British investigation of the origins of the war (published in January 1983), must be criticized as a whitewash of the Thatcher government.

2. *Economist,* 19 June 1982, 49.

3. Both the OSUS satellites and the Central Intelligence Agency's KH 11 photo-reconnaissance satellites are reported to be capable of monitoring the Falklands at latitude 52° south. Their range is said to extend as far south as 70°. The U.S. Navy also operates the South Surveillance System (SOSUS), which consists of 22 systems of underwater microphones placed in strategic waterways around the world. It seems unlikely that this system was in place in the waters between Argentina and the Falklands. "How We Spy on Argentina," *New Statesman,* 30 Apr. 1982, 5.

4. *Chicago Tribune,* 1 May 1982; *New Statesman,* 30 Apr. 1982, 5.

5. *Chicago Tribune,* 1 May 1982; *Los Angeles Times,* 4 May 1982; *Economist,* 10 Apr. 1982, 27.

6. *Times,* 5 Apr. 1982; 6 Apr. 1982.

7. *Times,* 5 Apr. 1982.

8. Robert Jervis, *Perception and Misperception in International Politics* (Princeton: Princeton University Press, 1976), 194.

9. Janice Gross Stein, "Calculation, Miscalculation, and Conventional Deterrence II: The View from Jerusalem," above, chap. 4; see also Michael Handel, *Perception, Deception and Surprise: The Case of the Yom Kippur War,* Jerusalem Papers on Peace Problems, no. 19 (Jerusalem, 1976), and Avraham Shlaim, "Failures in National Intelligence Estimates: The Case of the Yom Kippur War," *World Politics* (April 1976): 348–80.

10. *Agranat Report, A Partial Report by the Commission of Inquiry to the Government of Israel* (Jerusalem: Government Press Office, 2 Apr. 1974).

11. This was reported to the *Times,* 6 Apr. 1982, by John Cheek, a member of the Falkland Islands Council and of the British delegation to the New York talks. Lord Carrington alluded to the same scenario on the BBC's "Panorama" program, 5 Apr. 1982.

12. Stein, "Calculation, Miscalculation, and Conventional Deterrence II."

13. For the background to the conflict see Peter J. Beck, "Cooperative Confrontation in the Falkland Islands Dispute," *Journal of Interamerican Studies and World Affairs* 24 (Autumn 1982): 31–50; Maroldo Foulkes, *Las Malvinas: Una Causa Nacional* (Buenos Aires: Corregidor, 1978); José Enrique Greno Velasco, "El 'Informe Shackleton' Sobre las Islas Malvinas," *Revista de Politica International (Madrid)* 153 (September-October, 1977): 31–57; Juan E. Gugliamelli, "Las Negociaciones por las Malvinas en una Nueva Etapa?" *Estrategia* (Buenos Aires) 43–44 (November-December 1976, January-February 1977): 6–19; John Hickey, "Keep the Falklands British? The Principle of Self-Determination of Dependent Territories," *Inter-American Economic Affairs* 31 (Summer 1977): 77–78; Eduardo van der Kooy, "Malvinas. Despúes de la Visita de Nicholas Ridley se Hace Más dificil la negociación por la dovolución del Archipiélago," *Estrategia* 59 (July-August 1979): 37–42; J. Metford, "Falklands or Malvinas? The Background to the Dispute." *International Affairs* 44 (July 1968): 463–81; Ezequiel Federico, *Las Islas Malvinas—Soverania Argentina, Antecedentes, Gestiones Diplomáticas* (Buenos Aires: Ediciones Culturales Argentinas, 1969); Lidia Rogrigues, "Malvinas: Su Estructura Socioecoñomica," *Revista Argentina de Relaciones Internacionales* 2 (May-August 1976): 17–36; Camilo Hugo Rodriguez Berrutti, *Malvinas: Ultima Frontera del Colonialismo* (Buenos Aires: Ediciones Universitaria, 1975); J. Santa-Pinter, "Islas Malvinas or Falkland Islands?" *Horizontes* (Ponce) 21 (Spring 1977): 37–52; Edward Arthur Shackleton, "Prospects of the Falkland Islands," *Geographical Journal* 143 (March 1977): 1–13; and Hermann Weber, *"Falkland Islands" oder "Malvinas"? Der Status der Falklandinseln im Streit zwischen Grossbritannien und Argentinien. Eine völkerrechtliche Fallstudie* (Frankfurt a. M.: Metzner, 1977).

14. *Times,* 3 Dec. 1980.

15. *Economist,* 19 June 1982, 42.

16. On the domestic situation in Argentina see Charles Maechling, Jr., "The Argentina Pariah," *Foreign Policy,* no. 45 (Winter 1981–82), 69–83; Gary W. Wynia, "The Argentine Revolution Falters," *Current History* 81 (February 1982): 74–77, 87–88; and Jorge Louis Bernetti, Joŝe Ricardo Eliaschev, and Mempo Alfaro, "Argentina, Seis Anos Despúes," *Uno Mas Uno* (Mexico City) 23, 24, 26 Mar. 1982.

17. For the 1982 economic figures see *Clarin* (Buenos Aires), 8 and 14 Mar. 1982; and *El Cronista Comercial* (Buenos Aires), 16 Mar. 1982.

18. *Clarin,* 29–30 May 1982; *Latin America Weekly Report,* 2 Apr. 1982; *Times,* 2 Apr. 1982.

19. Manfred Shonfeld, *La Prensa,* 23–27 Mar. 1981; *Buenos Aires Herald,* 25 Mar. 1981.

20. *Economist,* 19 June 1982, 43.

21. On this incident see *Economist,* 3 Apr. 1982, 98, 19 June 1982, 49; *Clarin,* 23 Mar. 1982; and *Times* 20 Mar., 1 Apr. 1982.

22. Stein, "Calculation, Miscalculation, and Conventional Deterrence II."

23. Lord Carrington in the House of Lords, 4 Apr. 1982, reported in the *Times*, 5 Apr. 1982.

24. *Economist*, 19 June 1982, 49.

25. Irving L. Janis and Leon Mann, *Decision-Making: A Psychological Analysis of Conflict, Choice, and Commitment* (New York: Free Press, 1977), 57–58, 74, 197–233. For a discussion of the concept of defensive avoidance and its application to several cases of crisis decision making, see Richard Ned Lebow, *Between Peace and War: The Nature of International Crisis* (Baltimore: Johns Hopkins University Press, 1981).

26. Janis and Mann, *Decision-Making*, 74–95.

27. *Economist*, 19 June 1982, 43.

28. *Times*, 6 Apr. 1982: *Economist*, 19 June 1982, 44.

29. *Times*, 6 Apr. 1982. Air Commodore Frow is quoted as saying: "Last September we warned that we clearly envisaged the crisis that was going to occur around the end of this year. I have been accused of crying wolf and of exaggeration, and when I said a government was likely to fall over the Falkland Islands issue people said don't be silly, it's only 1,800 people."

30. *Economist*, 19 June 1982, 44.

31. *New York Times*, 5 May 1982.

32. The Argentine strategy was not unlike that pursued by the People's Republic of China prior to its intervention in the Korean War. Peking attempted to demonstrate its resolve to the United States by making its military preparations for intervention highly visible. For a discussion of this case see Lebow, *Between Peace and War*, 148–229.

33. Debate in the House of Commons, 3 Apr. 1982, reported in the *Times*, 5 Apr. 1982.

34. Ibid., 7 Apr. 1982, citing British intelligence sources.

35. Ibid., 12 June 1982.

36. Ibid., 22 Apr. 1982.

37. *Guardian*, 29 Apr. 1982.

38. Leopoldo Fortunato Galtieri, interview with Oriana Fallaci, *Times*, 12 June 1982.

39. *Wall Street Journal*, 27 Apr. 1982.

40. *Washington Post*, 4 Apr. 1982.

41. *New York Times*, 7 Apr. 1982.

42. Ibid., 12 May 1982.

43. Walters, together with Thomas O. Enders, assistant secretary of state for Latin American affairs, is reported to have opposed outright support of Britain during the war as well as the severing of relations with Argentina. This was also the position of about a dozen influential congressmen. Within the administration this group was opposed by Lawrence S. Eagleburger, under secretary of state for political affairs, and later by Alexander Haig. *New York Times*, 8 Apr. 1982; *New York News*, 17 May 1982.

44. *New York Times*, 3 and 8 Apr. 1982.

45. Ibid., 19 Apr. 1980.

46. *Times*, 12 June 1982. Haig and his party of mediators were apparently equally disenchanted with Galtieri and the *junta*. One of them de-

scribed the generals to Leslie Gelb of the *New York Times* as "a bunch of thugs who were almost impossible to deal with." *New York Times*, 2 May 1982.

47. Galtieri's response is reminiscent of that of William II upon learning of Britain's entry into the war in 1914. The Kaiser resorted to paranoid projection to justify his illusory but deeply held expectations of British neutrality. Rather than admit his miscalculation, he sought to escape from his own aggressiveness by portraying Germany and himself as unwitting victims of British duplicity. See Lebow, *Between Peace and War*, 139–45, for an analysis of William's behavior.

48. The full text of this speech is reprinted in English in the *Times*, 3 May 1982.

49. With some exceptions, Latin American countries took one of two positions on the Falklands question. The moderate position, taken for example by Brazil, Mexico, Colombia, Ecuador, Paraguay, Nicaragua, Uruguay, and Chile, supported Argentina's claim to the islands but not her invasion. The more radical position, adopted by Bolivia, Grenada, Guatemala, Cuba, Panama, Peru, and Venezuela, supported her military action as well.

50. *La Prensa*, 3 Apr. 1982.

51. Some Labour M.P.s subscribed to the colonial analogy, as did some left-wing journalists. The editors of the *Labour Herald* described the Falkland islanders as "company slaves" and insisted that there was no justification for Britain to cling to its "colonial possession." *Times*, 10 Apr. 1982.

52. The *New Statesman*, 11 Apr. 1982, p. 5, and 28 May 1982, p. 7, provided a good analysis of these differences as well as a description of left-wing opposition to a military reconquest of the Falklands.

53. *Times*, 1 Apr. 1982.

54. Ibid., 8 Apr. 1982.

55. Margaret Thatcher in Parliament, 20 May 1982, reported in the *Times*, 21 May 1982.

56. Ibid., 5 Apr. 1982.

57. The *Economist*, 1 May 1982, p. 14, reported that the latest Market and Opinion Research International (MORI) poll revealed that 76 percent of the public was behind Thatcher's response to the invasion.

58. For the most balanced discussion of this problem, see David S. McLellan, *Dean Acheson: The State Department Years* (New York: Dodd, Mead, 1976), 267–70.

59. *Times*, 5 Apr. 1982.

60. Ibid., 3 Apr. 1982.

61. *Daily Mail*, 6 Apr. 1982.

62. *Times*, 14 Apr. 1982.

63. R. W. Apple, Jr., *New York Times*, 7 Apr. 1982.

64. *Times*, 5 Apr. 1982; for the short-term effect of the Falklands invasion on the Gibraltar negotiations, see the *Times*, 10 Apr. 1982; 24 May 1982; and 31 May 1982.

65. Drew Middleton, *New York Times*, 7 Apr. 1982.

66. *Economist*, 17 Apr. 1982, 27.

67. *Times,* 1 Apr. 1982; 20 May 1982; *Economist,* 1 May 1982, 29.
68. *Times,* 14 June 1982.
69. Lord Shackleton in the House of Lords, 3 Apr. 1982, reported in the *Times,* 5 Apr. 1982; editorial, *Times,* 28 Apr. 1982.
70. *Times,* 12 June 1982.
71. Lebow, *Between Peace and War,* 57ff.
72. *New York Times,* 9 and 25 Apr. 1982.
73. *New York Times,* 19 Apr. 1982.

6. Saving Face for the Sake of Deterrence

1. A very broad classification of attackers, based on the probable presence of nonincrementally inclined leaders, is offered in Morgan, *Deterrence, A Conceptual Analysis* (Beverly Hills: Sage Library of Social Science, 1977), but it falls far short of being a detailed typology.

2. It is interesting to speculate what deterrence theory would look like if the initial assumption was that governments are—in some predictable fashion or pattern—irrational. For instance, one might argue that deterring an adversary is akin to spanking a small child or housebreaking a puppy, all are manipulated because they will not respond to appeals that require rational thought.

3. Alexander George and Richard Smoke, *Deterrence in American Foreign Policy: Theory and Practice* (New York: Columbia University Press, 1974).

4. Richard Ned Lebow, *Between Peace and War: The Nature of International Crisis* (Baltimore: Johns Hopkins University Press, 1981), 274.

5. Ibid, 279.

6. Thomas Schelling, *The Strategy of Conflict* (Cambridge, Mass.: Harvard University Press, 1960); Schelling, *Arms and Influence* (New Haven: Yale University Press, 1966).

7. Morgan, *Deterrence.*

8. See George and Smoke, *Deterrence in American Foreign Policy,* 550–61, and Stephen Maxwell, *Rationality in Deterrence,* Adelphi Paper no. 50 (London: Institute for Strategic Studies, 1968).

9. Schelling, *Arms and Influence,* 52.

10. Robert Jervis, "Deterrence Theory Revisited," *World Politics* 31, no. 2 (1979): 314–20. The distinction first appeared in Glenn Snyder and Paul Diesing, *Conflict among Nations* (Princeton: Princeton University Press, 1977) pp. 183–84.

11. The inherent incredibility of threats to use nuclear weapons is a recurring theme in Lawrence Freedman's history of deterrence thinking, *The Evolution of Nuclear Strategy* (New York: St. Martin's Press, 1981), in particular pp. 200–201, 219–23, 296, 297–98, 315, 320, 396–97. Others who have emphasized this include A. F. K. Organski and Jacek Kugler, *The War Ledger* (Chicago: University of Chicago Press, 1980), 158, 178, and Richard Rosecrance, "Strategic Deterrence Reconsidered," in *Strategic Deterrence in a Changing Environment,* ed. Christoph Bertram (Montclair, N.J.: Gower & Allanheld, Osmun, 1981), 22–27.

12. See the discussion and the listing of numerous relevant works in Lebow, *Between Peace and War,* 276–77.

13. Jervis, "Deterrence Theory Revisited," 1–3.

14. See *Foreign Relations of the United States, 1950,* (Washington, D.C.: Government Printing Office, 1977), 1:22–44.

15. See Snyder and Diesing, *Conflict among Nations,* 310–39.

16. See Lebow, *Between Peace and War,* 270–73.

17. Earl Ravenal, "Counterforce and Alliance: The Ultimate Connection," *International Security* 6, no. 4 (1982): 28.

18. George and Smoke, *Deterrence in American Foreign Policy,* 117.

19. See, for example, the comments by Gordon Arneson on a draft of Kennan's memo disparaging the utility of nuclear weapons to the effect that renouncing nuclear weapons or the H-bomb would have this effect. *Foreign Relations of the United States, 1950,* (Washington, D.C.: Government Printing Office, 1977), 1:4. This was Omar Bradley's main argument (Bradley was chairman of the joint chiefs of staff). See Gregg Herken, *The Winning Weapon* (New York: Vintage Books, 1982), 316–17.

20. Ibid.

21. *Foreign Relations of the United States, 1950,* 1:240.

22. John Gaddis, *Strategies of Containment* (New York: Oxford University Press, 1982), 98.

23. Dean Acheson, *Present at the Creation* (New York: W. W. Norton, 1969), 528.

24. Gaddis, *Strategies of Containment,* 116.

25. Ibid., 116–17.

26. Ibid., 211.

27. George and Smoke, *Deterrence in American Foreign Policy,* 270.

28. See Gaddis, *Strategies of Containment,* 201–6.

29. Ibid., 212; see also p. 233.

30. Quotation taken from Jerome Kahan, *Security in the Nuclear Age* (Washington, D.C.: Brookings Institution, 1975), 80.

31. Gaddis, *Strategies of Containment,* 240.

32. *The Pentagon Papers,* as published by the *New York Times* (New York: Bantam Books, 1971), 432.

33. See Henry Kissinger, "The Viet Nam Negotiations," *Foreign Affairs* 47, no. 2 (1969): 211–34.

34. Cited in Gaddis, *Strategies of Containment,* 288.

35. Ibid., 288.

36. Cited in Amos Jordan and William Taylor, Jr., *American National Security* (Baltimore: Johns Hopkins University Press, 1981), 264.

37. For example, see Department of Defense, *Annual Report, Fiscal Year 1975* (Washington, D.C.: Government Printing Office, 1974), 5–6, 43–4.

38. Kahan, *Security in the Nuclear Age,* 163.

39. Freedman, *Evolution of Nuclear Strategy,* 392.

40. See for example, W. Scott Thompson, ed., *From Weakness to Strength* (San Francisco: Institute for Contemporary Studies, 1980).

41. This conclusion is based on an examination of various volumes in the air force series of translations, especially, U.S. Air Force, *Selected Soviet*

Military Writings, 1970–1975 (Washington, D.C.: Department of Defense, Department of the Air Force, 1976); V. D. Sokolovskiy, *Soviet Military Strategy*, 3d ed. (New York: Crane, Russak, 1984); Derek Leebaert, ed., *Soviet Strategy for the Seventies, from Cold War to Peaceful Coexistence* (Miami: Center for Advanced International Studies, University of Miami, 1973); the several articles on Soviet strategic thinking in *Comparative Strategy* 2, no. 2 (1980); Joseph Douglas, Jr., and Amoretta Hoeber, *Soviet Strategy for Nuclear War* (Stanford, Calif.: Hoover Institution Press, 1979); and Daniel S. Papp, "Nuclear Weapons and the Soviet Worldview," in *Soviet Armed Forces Review Annual*, 11 vols., ed. in David R. Jones (Gulf Breeze, Fla.: Academic International Press, 1980), 4:337–51. I also looked through Stephen Kaplan, *Diplomacy of Power* (Washington, D.C.: Brookings Institution, 1981), to see if numerous Soviet military actions abroad since 1940 were readily ascribable to preoccupations with maintaining the credibility of the Soviet deterrence posture.

42. This idea is developed in somewhat different ways in Ken Booth, *Strategy and Ethnocentrism* (London: Croom, Helm, 1973), and Colin Gray, "National Style in Strategy, The American Example," *International Security* 6, no. 2 (1981): 21–47.

43. See James Payne, *The American Threat* (College Station, Tex.: Lytton, 1981).

44. *Foreign Relations of the United States, 1950*, 1:265.

45. *Foreign Relations of the United States, 1951*, (Washington, D.C.: Government Printing Office, 1979), 1:132.

46. Paul Nitze, "Policy and Strategy from Weakness," in W. Scott Thompson, ed., *From Weakness to Strength*, 452.

47. Ibid., 449

48. Gaddis, *Strategies of Containment*, 242.

49. See Samuel Wells, "Sounding the Tocsin: NSC 68 and the Soviet Threat," *International Security* 4, no. 2 (1979): 127.

50. *Foreign Relations of the United States 1950*, 1:268.

51. Ibid., 314–16, 342–44.

52. George and Smoke, *Deterrence in American Foreign Policy*, 246, 284, 321, 323.

53. Henry Kissinger, *The White House Years* (Boston: Little, Brown, 1979), 228.

54. See Victor Utgoff, "In Defense of Counterforce," *International Security* 6, no. 4 (1982): 53.

55. Freedman, *Evolution of Nuclear Strategy*, 397–98.

56. Ibid., 65–66.

7. Perceptions of the Security Dilemma in 1914

1. Robert Jervis, *Perception and Misperception in International Politics* (Princeton: Princeton University Press, 1976), chap. 3.

2. Ibid., 94, no. 70.

3. The term and concept are from Glenn Snyder and Paul Diesing,

Conflict among Nations (Princeton: Princeton University Press, 1977), 45–48.

4. Kenneth Waltz, *Theory of International Politics* (Reading, Mass.: Addison-Wesley, 1979); Robert Jervis, "Cooperation under the Security Dilemma," *World Politics* 30 no. 2 (1978): 167–214; George Quester, *Offense and Defense in the International System* (New York: Wiley, 1977).

5. Jervis, "Cooperation," 167.

6. Ibid., 186–87.

7. On the consequences of offensive capabilities and strategies, see Jervis, "Cooperation," 188–89; Quester, *Offense and Defense,* especially p. 106; and Stephen Van Evera, "The Causes of War" (Ph.D. diss. University of California, Berkeley, 1984), chap. 5. None of these is as extreme as the above description, perhaps because they do not take the assumption of offensive advantage quite so literally.

8. I am indebted to John Mearsheimer for discussion of this question.

9. Jervis, "Cooperation," 188.

10. Clausewitz argued that since the defense has only a "negative object," no one would ever adopt it unless it were the "stronger form of waging war." Carl von Clausewitz, *On War,* ed. Michael Howard and Peter Paret (Princeton: Princeton University Press, 1976), 359.

11. Jack Snyder, *The Ideology of the Offensive: Military Decision Making and the Disasters of 1914* (Ithaca, N.Y.: Cornell University Press, 1984), 80.

12. On this point, see B. H. Liddell Hart, *The German Generals Talk* (New York: Morrow, 1948). Dupuy attempts to control for the effects of troop quality in World War II by calculating separate offense-defense ratios for German attackers, German defenders, and so forth. T.N. Dupuy, *Numbers, Predictions and War* (New York: Bobbs-Merrill, 1979), chap. 7. For a contemporary discussion of the advantages of the defensive, see John Mearsheimer, "Why the Soviets Can't Win Quickly in Central Europe," *International Security* 7, no. 1 (1982): 3–39. Naval and air engagements often entail a greater first-strike advantage in the tactical sense than do land engagements. Strategically, however, distance and logistical exigencies give the defender a major advantage in naval and aerial warfare as well. Note the "regionalization of seapower" when steam replaced sail, for example. Quester, *Offense and Defense,* chap. 9.

13. Alfred Vagts, *Defense and Diplomacy* (New York: King's Crown, 1956), emphasizes prevention; Thomas Schelling, *The Strategy of Conflict* (London: Oxford University Press, 1960) and *Arms and Influence* (New Haven: Yale University Press, 1966), emphasize preemption. On windows generally, the best discussion is Van Evera, "The Causes of War," chaps. 1 and 2. Van Evera's definition of preemption, following Robert Harvaky, stipulates that both sides have a simultaneous incentive to attack first. With prevention the incentive is one-way.

14. Gerhard Ritter, *The Sword and the Sceptre,* 3 vols. (Coral Gables, Fla.: University of Miami Press, 1972), 1:245.

15. This is Van Evera's concept, also discussed by Kenneth Waltz, *Theory of International Politics,* 126.

16. See Robert Gilpin, *War and Change in World Politics* (Princeton:

Princeton University Press, 1981), on the rising costs of protection; Thucydides on Athen's imperial dilemma; and Ritter, *Sword*, on the dilemmas posed by Bismarck's successful wars.

17. Van Evera gives a full discussion of all these points.

18. Bernard Brodie, *Strategy in the Missile Age* (Princeton: Princeton University Press), 42.

19. In addition to Van Evera, "The Causes of War," see also Barry R. Posen, *The Sources of Military Doctrine: France, Britain, and Germany between the World Wars* (Ithaca, N.Y.: Cornell University Press, 1984), and Jack Snyder, *Ideology of the Offensive*.

20. Quoted by Van Evera from Ferdinand Foch, *Principles of War* (New York: Fly, 1918), 37.

21. Martin Kitchen, *The German Officer Corps, 1880–1914* (Oxford: Clarendon Press 1968), 115ff.

22. Posen, *Sources of Military Doctrine*, 50.

23. Quoted by Bernard Brodie, *War and Politics* (New York: Macmillan, 1973), 11.

24. Posen offers different arguments under the heading of *autonomy*. See *Sources of Military Doctrine*, chap. 2.

25. *Sources of Military Doctrine*, 48.

26. In Russia between 1910 and 1912, regional staffs disliked the general staff's defensive war plan because it left their planning problem too unstructured. Jack Snyder, *Ideology of the Offensive*, 177.

27. Waltz, *Theory of International Politics*, 74–77, 127–28.

28. Van Evera discusses this problem at length. Richard K. Betts, in *Soldiers, Statesmen, and Cold War Crises* (Cambridge, Mass.: Harvard University Press, 1977), shows that the U.S. military has not been more likely to counsel the use of force than have civilian advisers, although the military *has* strongly favored escalation once hostilities occur. Against Betts, Van Evera argues that the attitudes of the military, especially its preference for offense, make war more likely even though its advice does not differ from that of civilians.

29. For these theories, see Jervis, *Perception and Misperception;* Harold Kelley, *Attribution in Social Interaction* (Morristown, N.J.: General Learning Press, 1971); and Richard Nisbett and Lee Ross, *Human Inference* (Englewood Cliffs, N.J.: Prentice-Hall, 1980).

30. See Snyder and Diesing, *Conflict among Nations*, on the evolution of bargaining strategies during international crises.

31. Sidney Fay, *Origins of the World War* (New York: Macmillan, 1928), and more recently, L. C. F. Turner, *Origins of the First World War* (London: Edward Arnold, 1970). Note also the treatments by nonhistorians like Jervis, *Perception and Misperception;* Schelling, *Arms and Influence;* and Herman Kahn, *On Thermonuclear War* (Princeton: Princeton University Press, 1960).

32. Fritz Fischer, *War of Illusions: German Policies from 1911 to 1914*, trans. Marian Jackson (New York: Norton, 1975). Note also Nazli Choukri and Robert North, *Nations in Conflict* (San Francisco: Freeman, 1974).

33. This section is based on Jack Snyder, *Ideology of the Offensive*, chaps. 5, 6, and 7. Most of the evidence can also be found in Gerhard Ritter, *The Schlieffen Plan* (New York: Praeger, 1958), and Ritter, *Sword*, vol. 2. See also Jack Snyder, "Civil-Military Relations and the Cult of the Offensive, 1914 and 1984," *International Security* 9, no. 1 (1984): 108–46.

34. French interest in *revanche* declined by the 1890s, however.

35. It is also possible that they felt that equally favorable conditions would recur.

36. A brief account of the diplomacy of this period can be found in Imanuel Geiss, *German Foreign Policy, 1870–1914* (London: Routledge & Kegan Paul, 1976). The argument of this section is elaborated in Snyder, "Civil-Military Relations," esp. 125–9.

37. Turner, *Origins,* 36ff., and Turner, "The Edge of the Precipice," *Royal Military College Historical Journal* (Canberra) 3 (1974).

38. K. F. Shatsillo, *Russkii imperializm i razvitie flota nakanune pervoi mirovoi voiny (1906–1914gg.)* (Moscow: Nauka, 1968), especially 100–101.

39. Unless otherwise noted, supporting evidence for this section can be found in Jack Snyder, *Ideology of the Offensive*, chaps. 7 and 8.

40. Fischer, *War of Illusions,* especially 377–79, 427.

41. For a fuller discussion of this, see Stephen Van Evera, "The Cult of the Offensive and the Origins of the First World War," *International Security* 9, no. 1 (1984): 58–107, and Jack Snyder, "Civil-Military Relations," 112–15.

42. Ulrich Trumpener, "War Premeditated? German Intelligence Operations in July 1914," *Central European History* 6 (March 1976): 80.

43. Eugenia Nomikos and Robert North, *International Crisis* (Montreal: McGill-Queen's University Press, 1976), 173.

44. Trumpener, "War Premeditated?" especially 77–79. The Germans seem to have been reasonably confident that they would learn of a reserve call-up almost immediately. Shaposhnikov, an officer in Warsaw and later a Soviet chief of staff, argues that Russia gained little practical advantage from the premobilization preparations. B. N. Shaposhnikov, *Vospominaniia, Voennonauchnye trudy* (Moscow: Voenizdat, 1974), 230.

45. Trumpener, "War Premeditated?" 80–83. See also Luigi Albertini, *The Origins of the War of 1914,* 3 vols., trans. and ed. Isabella M. Massey (Oxford: Oxford, University Press, 1952), 3: 24ff.

46. Jack Snyder, *Ideology of the Offensive*, chap. 8.

47. L. C. F. Turner, "The Russian Mobilization in 1914," in *The War Plans of the Great Powers 1880–1914,* ed. Paul M. Kennedy (London: Allen & Unwin, 1979), 265, quoting the Russian Foreign Ministry Diary for 29 July 1914.

8. The Deterrence Deadlock: Is There a Way Out?

1. Richard Ned Lebow, *Between Peace and War: The Nature of International Crisis* (Baltimore: Johns Hopkins University Press, 1981).

2. Ibid., 74–80.

3. Ibid., 71–74.

4. Eyre Crowe, "Memorandum on the Present State of British Relations with France and Germany," in *British Documents on the Origins of the War, 1898–1914,* ed. G. P. Gooch and Harold Temperley, 11 vols. (London: His Majesty's Stationary Office, 1926–1932), appendix A.

5. Jerome H. Kahan and Anne K. Long, "The Cuban Missile Crisis: A Study of Its Strategic Context," *Political Science Quarterly* 87 (December 1972): 564–90.

6. Lebow, *Between Peace and War,* 312–15.

7. Robert Jervis, *Perception and Misperception in International Politics* (Princeton: Princeton University Press, 1976).

8. See Lebow, *Between Peace and War,* for a discussion of the Korean case.

9. Luigi Albertini, *The Origins of the War of 1914,* 3 vols., trans. and ed. Isabella M. Massey (Oxford: Oxford University Press, 1952), 1:145–151.

10. This argument is developed in R. N. Lebow, "The Soviet Reponse to Poland and the Future of the Warsaw Pact," in *The Future of European Alliance Systems: NATO and the Warsaw Pact,* ed. Arlene I. Broadhurst (Boulder, Colo.: Westview Press, 1982), 185–236.

11. *New York Times,* 28 Aug. 1980.

12. Seweryn Bialer, *Stalin's Successors* (Cambridge: Cambridge University Press, 1980).

13. Lin Piao, "Long Live the Victory of the People's War," *Peking Review,* 9 Feb. 1965).

14. John L. Gaddis, *Strategies of Containment* (New York: Oxford University Press, 1982), 208.

15. Georgi Arbatov, interview with Erik Amfitheatrof and Felix Rosenthal, *Time,* 6 Dec. 1982, 16.

16. *International Herald Tribune,* 12 Mar. 1982.

17. H. A. Trofimenko, "The 'Theology' of Strategy," *Orbis* 21 (Fall 1977): 497–515; *International Herald Tribune,* 8 Dec. 1981.

9. Conclusions

1. Here we follow the distinction between deterrence as an explanatory and as a predictive theory as described by Alexander L. George and Richard Smoke in their pioneering study, *Deterrence in American Foreign Policy: Theory and Practice* (New York: Columbia University Press, 1974).

2. Most of this evidence is drawn from prenuclear confrontations or those between non-nuclear powers because there have been only a few serious crises between states with nuclear arsenals. It is a truism that nuclear deterrence differs in many ways from conventional deterrence. We would argue, however, that many of the kinds of problem responsible for serious miscalculations and deterrence failures in conventional conflicts could also occur in nuclear confrontations. See Richard Ned Lebow, *Between Peace and*

War: The Nature of International Crisis (Baltimore: Johns Hopkins University Press, 1981), 15–18, 276–78, for an elaboration of this argument.

3. Only the latter phenomenon will be discussed in this conclusion. For an analysis of some of the reasons why states are often more cautious than deterrence theory would predict, see Richard Ned Lebow, "Windows of Opportunity: Do States Jump through Them?" *International Security* 9 (Summer 1984): 147–80.

4. The term *signal* is used here in the sense described by Robert Jervis, *The Logic of Images in International Relations* (Princeton: Princeton University Press, 1970), 18–40.

5. Stephen Peter Rosen, "Vietnam and the American Theory of Limited War," *International Security* 7 (Fall 1982): 83–113; see also John Gaddis, *Strategies of Containment* (New York: Oxford University Press, 1982), 246–53, for a discussion of the problem of a calibrated strategy in Vietnam.

6. W. Phillip Davison, *The Berlin Blockade: A Study in Cold War Politics* (Princeton: Princeton University Press, 1958), 71–78.

7. Gregg Herken, *The Winning Weapon: The Atomic Bomb in the Cold War, 1945–1950* (New York: Alfred A. Knopf, 1980), 251.

8. Allen S. Whiting, *China Crosses the Yalu: The Decision to Enter the Korean War* (New York: Macmillan, 1960), passim.

9. Ernest R. May, *Imperial Democracy* (New York: Harcourt, Brace, 1961), 161.

10. Neville Maxwell, *India's China War* (Garden City, N.Y.: Doubleday, 1972), 269–304; Allen S. Whiting, *The Chinese Calculus of Deterrence: India and Indochina* (Ann Arbor: University of Michigan Press, 1975), 42–106.

11. For a discussion of this case, see Lebow, *Between Peace and War*, 148–228.

12. Ibid., 57–95.

13. On the Japanese case, see Robert Butow, *Tojo and the Coming of the War* (Stanford, Calif.: Stanford University Press, 1961); Dorothy Borg and Shumpei Okamoto, eds., *Pearl Harbor as History: Japanese-American Relations, 1931–1941* (New York: Columbia University Press, 1973); Saburo Ienaga, *The Pacific War, 1931–1945* (New York: Pantheon, 1978); Nobutaka Ike, *Japan's Decision for War, Records of 1941: Policy Conferences* (Stanford, Calif.: Stanford University Press, 1967); and Bruce Russett, "Pearl Harbor: Deterrence Theory and Decision Theory," *Journal of Peace Research* 4, no. 2 (1967): 89–105.

14. William W. Kaufmann, *The Requirements of Deterrence* (Princeton: Center for International Studies, 1954).

15. Thomas Schelling, *Arms and Influence* (New Haven: Yale University Press, 1966), 374. "Few parts of the world," Schelling wrote, "are intrinsically worth the risk of serious war by themselves, especially when taken slice by slice, but defending them or running risks to protect them may preserve one's commitments to action in other parts of the world and at later times. 'Face' is merely the interdependence of a country's commitments: it is

a country's reputation for action, the expectation other countries have about its behavior" (p. 194).

16. Lyndon Johnson, speech at Johns Hopkins University, 7 Apr. 1965, *Public Papers of the Presidents of the United States: Lyndon B. Johnson, 1965* (Washington, D.C.: Government Printing Office, 1965–69), 395.

17. Dean Rusk, memorandum, 1 July 1965, *The Pentagon Papers: The Defense Department History of United States Decisionmaking on Vietnam*, 4 vols. (Boston: Beacon Press, 1971), 4:23.

18. Henry Kissinger, speech at Dallas, Tex., 22 Mar. 1976, in Henry A. Kissinger, *American Foreign Policy*, 3d ed. (New York: Norton, 1977), 360.

19. George and Smoke, *Deterrence in American Foreign Policy*, 550–61; Stephen Maxwell, *Rationality in Deterrence*, Adelphi Paper no. 50 (London: Institute for Strategic Studies, 1968).

20. Glenn Snyder and Paul Diesing, *Conflict among Nations* (Princeton: Princeton University Press, 1977), 183–84; Robert Jervis, "Deterrence Theory Revisited," *World Politics* 31, no. 2 (1979): 289–324.

21. On this subject, see Ernest R. May, *"Lessons" of the Past: The Use and Misuse of History in American Foreign Policy* (New York: Oxford University Press, 1973); Richard Ned Lebow, "Generational Learning and Foreign Policy: The Lessons of the 'Thirties versus those of the 'Seventies," *International Journal* (Autumn 1985), forthcoming.

22. Three recent policy-oriented books illustrate this phenomenon, two by academics, the third by a policy maker: Harvard Nuclear Study Group, *Living with Nuclear Weapons* (Cambridge, Mass.: Harvard University Press, 1983); Gerald Segal, Edwina Moreton, Lawrence Freedman, and John Baylis, *Nuclear War and Nuclear Peace* (London: Macmillan, 1983); and Harold Brown, *Thinking about National Security* (Boulder, Colo.: Westview Press, 1983). All three accept uncritically the fundamental assumptions of deterrence theory. Their discussions of deterrence studiously ignore any mention of the growing number of studies critical of it, works with which the academic authors are at least presumably conversant.

23. See Frederick Merk, *The Oregon Question: Essays in Anglo-American Diplomacy and Politics* (Cambridge, Mass.: Harvard University Press, 1967); Charles S. Campbell, Jr., *Anglo-American Understanding, 1898–1903* (Baltimore: Johns Hopkins Press, 1957).

24. The security dilemma was first described by Herbert Butterfield, *History and Human Relations* (London: Collins, 1951), 19–20, and by John Herz, "Idealist Internationalism and the Security Dilemma," *World Politics* 2 (January 1950), 158–80; for a more recent treatment, see Robert Jervis, *Perception and Misperception in International Politics* (Princeton: Princeton University Press, 1976), 58–116.

25. It is always hazardous to infer intentions from results. The fact that German policy was counterproductive to German security interests does not necessarily mean that it was motivated by other considerations. It is at least as likely that German policy was poorly conceived and implemented and as a result not conducive to the goals policy makers sought. Con-

siderable historical evidence, moreover, can be marshaled in support of this interpretation.

26. Janice Stein, "The Alchemy of Peacemaking: The Prerequisites and Co-requisites of Progress in the Arab-Israeli Conflict," *International Journal* 38, no. 4 (1983): 531–55, addresses the political conditions that facilitated the Sadat initiative.

27. Jan Kalicki, *The Pattern of Sino-American Crises* (New York: Cambridge University Press, 1975), 211–17.

28. See Luigi Albertini, *The Origins of the War of 1914*, 3 vols., trans. and ed. Isabella M. Massey (Oxford: Oxford University Press, 1952), 1:318–34; Ima C. Barlow, *The Agadir Crisis* (Chapel Hill: University of North Carolina Press, 1940); Fritz Fischer, *War of Illusions: German Policies from 1911 to 1914*, trans. Marian Jackson (New York: Norton, 1975), 71–94; and M. L. Dockrill, "British Policy during the Agadir Crisis of 1911," in *British Foreign Policy under Sir Edward Grey*, ed. F. H. Hinsley (London: Cambridge University Press, 1977), 271–87.

29. Richard Ned Lebow, "The Cuban Missile Crisis: Reading the Lessons Correctly," *Political Science Quarterly* 98 (Fall 1983): 431–58.

INDEX

Acheson, Dean, 138, 150; and use of denial mechanism, 182
Afghanistan, and Soviet Union, 15, 196, 197; and U.S. credibility, 142
Agadir (1911), exaggerated threat, 190
aggression, 183, 211
Agranat Commission, 75, 76, 77, 94, 95
Al-Ahram (newspaper), 38, 43
Alsace-Lorraine, German annexation of, 168
ambiguous evidence, 75
analogies, use of, 115
Anaya, Jorge, 110
anchoring, 45
Angola, civil war in, 140
Anschluss, 115
appeasement: in 1930s, 9; and motivated bias, 26
Arab Socialist Union, 50
Arabatov, Georgi, 201
Argentina: advisors in El Salvador, 113; and Falklands War, viii–ix, 89–124, 207–8; political weakness of, 215–16
arms: competition, spiral logic of, 167; races, dynamics of, 166; races and windows of opportunity, 165–66
Arms and Influence, 218
attribution, 164, and threat perception, 14–18
attrition, 54
attrition warfare. *See* war of attrition, a availability, 22–23, 45, 81

balance of power: shifts in, and brinkmanship, 181; theory of, 13–14
Balkan crisis, 173
Balkan War, First, 173
Banco de Intercambio, 98
bargaining: range of, 58, 241n. 29; space, estimates of, 49–51
Bar-Hillel, Maya, 238n. 28
Baruch Plan, Russian rejection of, 18
base rate data, 23–24
Begin, Menachem, 192
Belgium, 169
Ben-Zvi, Avi, 245n. 25
Berlin: and perception of defender's resolve, 182; Soviet blockade of, 206
Betts, Richard K., 7, 28, 84, 257n. 28
Between Peace and War, 127, 180, 181
Bezobrazov, Alexander, 184
bias, viii. *See also* cognitive bias; motivated bias; unmotivated bias
bipolarity, 137
Bismarck, Otto von, 161, 168, 169
Bittel, Deolindo, 114
blitzkrieg, 42, 44, 48, 159
Bohlen, Charles, 150
bolstering. *See* defensive avoidance
Bosnian annexation (1909), and domestic weakness, 181; and perception of defender's resolve, 182
Brezhnev, Leonid, 195
brinkmanship, 80, 119–20, 175; challenges of, 211; and domestic impera-

The Johns Hopkins University Press

Psychology and Deterrence

This book was composed in Baskerville text
and Eras display type by Brushwood Graphics Studio,
from a design by Cynthia Hotvedt.
It was printed on Sebago Eggshell cream paper
and bound by BookCrafters, Inc.